we

3'S

Vijay Nagaswami is a Chennai-based psychiatrist and has worked closely with relationships for over twenty-five years. Innumerable couples from all over the country have benefitted from his marital intervention and his writing. He has written three books, including the bestselling *The 24 × 7 Marriage* and *The Fifty-50 Marriage*, these two as part of a series called 'The New Indian Marriage'. *3's a Crowd*, the third in this series, deals with infidelity and how to survive it.

He also writes a column for *The Hindu* called 'The Shrinking Universe' and is featured in other national and regional publications too. He regularly conducts workshops for couples and corporates on relationship management.

He draws inspiration for his work from Usha, his wife, and their twenty-two-year-old marriage.

He can be contacted at vijay.nagaswami@gmail.com

3'S A CROWD

UNDERSTANDING AND SURVIVING INFIDELITY

VIJAY NAGASWAMI

westland

westland ltd

Venkat Towers, 165, P.H. Road, Opp. Maduravoyal Municipal Office, Chennai 600 095

No. 38/10 (New No.5), Raghava Nagar, New Timber Yard Layout, Bangalore 560 026

Survey No. A - 9, II Floor, Moula Ali Industrial Area, Moula Ali, Hyderabad 500 040

23/181, Anand Nagar, Nehru Road, Santacruz East, Mumbai 400 055

4322/3, Ansari Road, Daryaganj, New Delhi 110 002

First published by westland ltd 2011

Copyright © Vijay Nagaswami

All rights reserved

10 9 8 7 6 5 4 3 2 1

ISBN: 978-93-81626-27-6

Typeset by Arun Bisht

Printed at Thomson Press (I) Limited

Millions of people all over the world
have struggled with the pain of infidelity,
have survived it and have gone on to find
the inner strength to make their worlds
a better place.
To them this book is dedicated

. . . The best laid schemes o' mice an' men
Gang aft agley,
An' lea'e us nought but grief an' pain
For promis'd joy!

Robert Burns, 1785

Contents

PART II: SURVIVING INFIDELITY

A Note from the Author

It might seem extraordinary to you, but about a third of the couples who come to see me for couples therapy do so because one of them is having an extramarital relationship. Or sometimes because one of them is positive that the other is involved with someone else and has no way of proving this. And every time I work with a couple that is dealing with infidelity and see the emotional pain and distress that both partners struggle with, I marvel at the amazing capacity of human beings to mess up their lives.

For, affairs are not like illnesses. They don't just happen. We make them happen. And what's more, despite knowing the consequences, we actually go out of our way to make them happen.

When people ask me whether marital infidelity is a recent phenomenon, I am hard pressed to give them a clear answer. On the one hand, I know that I don't have any hard data, for this is not the sort of information the Census Board collects (although sometimes I wish they would). However, I do know that when I started psychiatric practice over twenty-seven years ago, people were blithely having affairs even then. The most unlikely of people, really. People who, if you passed them on the street, would give you absolutely no indication of the passion that lurked in their hearts and minds. Your average, conservative, middle-class men and, hold your breath, women, were breaking their marital vows with the same alacrity that their children and perhaps, grandchildren, are doing today.

However, the one key difference is that people used to be much more discreet in those days and many have gone through lifetimes without their dalliances being discovered.

Today, people engage in infidelity much more brazenly, and affairs are more in-your-face than ever before. Technology has contributed its bit, for people can and do conduct extramarital engagements through mobile phones, the Internet and so forth. However, the same technology that abets such relationships also exposes them more readily, for the commonest method of discovery of affairs is a poorly-timed text message (like the one that comes from the paramour when the intended recipient is having a shower and the spouse accidentally reads the text) or an undeleted chat transcript (it's very hard conducting an affair if you're not tech-savvy). In other words, affairs are being detected much more easily than before.

This is probably why the general opinion is that more people are having affairs nowadays. I don't think this is an accurate perception. It's just that since affairs were conducted more surreptitiously in the past, unless you hired a detective—which most people never even considered doing—it was hard to find out if your spouse was having it off with your neighbour. Of course, suspicious spouses have been known to come home unexpectedly and catch their unfaithful partners in flagrante delicto, but it's hard to tell how commonly this happened.

Another thing. There's also a general perception that women today have become more 'licentious' than were women of earlier generations and this whole 'Westernisation' thing is driving them to 'promiscuity'. It is, of course, true that contemporary women have empowered themselves to be more expressive when it comes to the gratification of their need for emotional and sexual intimacy, but women of their parents' generations were also in touch with these needs. They just didn't have the space to express them. There were no glossies that exhorted them to be superwomen, or told them how precisely affairs could be conducted; they had to be content with being referred to (though not necessarily treated) as the goddesses who held the Indian family together, and so on. Whatever needs they experienced had to be either repressed or expressed clandestinely. So let's not put the blame on the West for extramarital relationships. We've obviously been quite busy on that front ourselves, considering how hard that ancient text *Manusmriti*, written by the 'lawgiver' Manu (presumably in the words of the Creator himself), comes down on 'adulterous' women.

So, where does that leave us? We know that many people engage in extramarital relationships. We also know that both partners are traumatised when affairs are discovered. In addition, it's abundantly clear that affairs are easier to discover today. And that many contemporary couples are aggressively seeking to stretch the boundaries of marriage to, perhaps, even include extramarital relationships within its ambit. Does this then mean that infidelity is here to stay and that we should just factor it into our marriages and be blasé about it instead of making such a big deal of it? Should we just provide for the fact that our partners are going to 'stray' and that we should either ignore this or 'stray' ourselves? Or should we just learn to accept infidelity as part of modern life like, say, the Internet, and learn to enjoy it rather than rail against it?

The way I see it, any experience that produces the kind of emotional distress—and indeed devastation—that affairs do in the lives and minds of at least three, if not more, people, can't be treated merely as collateral damage of contemporary married life. Obviously, distress takes place because affairs produce unhappiness. And anything that causes misery needs to be understood and dealt with rather than being accepted as part and parcel of our lives. Which is why I thought of writing this book as the third in Westland's 'New Indian Marriage Series'. My concern in this book is not about the moral aspects of affairs, whether they're right or wrong, for I believe, as will be discussed later, that affairs are not necessarily an issue of morality. Nor is my concern about the legal aspects of affairs. I will stick to my area of experience—the psychodynamics and emotional aspects of affairs.

The hardest part of writing about affairs is the choice of terminology. The general term used to describe the phenomenon is 'infidelity'. Unfortunately, this word has a negative judgement attached to it (even though, mercifully, those engaging in affairs aren't generally referred to as 'infidels'). Words like 'unfaithfulness', 'cheating', 'betrayal', 'duplicity', 'treachery' and the like squarely accuse those engaging in affairs of moral turpitude. The word 'affair' seems to imply a fling (dictionary definition: an intense amorous relationship of short duration) even though many affairs end up in long-term relationships. The term 'dalliance' refers more to light flirtations than anything of a serious nature. The French phrase 'affaire d'amour' refers to any love affair, extramarital or premarital. The term 'extramarital relationship' makes things sound very clinical and prosaic—and is pretty cumbersome on the word processor.

However, I am compelled to choose a term that I can employ in the course of the book. And despite its stated shortcoming, because it's the most popular and easy-to-identify-with term in this context, I'm going with the word 'affair' to refer to an intimate, emotional and/or sexual relationship of whatever duration, that takes place outside the marital space. I will also use the term 'infidelity' to refer to the act of having an affair, again because it's the most popular description of the phenomenon. However, I need to assure my readers that, for reasons that will become clear as you read this book, I pass no judgement on those who have affairs or engage in infidelity.

That leaves one more dilemma: what terms to use to refer to those who engage in an affair and those whose spouses are engaged in affairs? Some people use the terms 'betrayer' and 'betrayed', some use 'perpetrator' and 'victim'. But these terms can only be considered accurate if one views the roles played by the protagonists from the narrow perspective of the affair alone. They tend to vilify one and sanctify the other. And, as we will discover, the 'betrayed' partner may have actually played a role in the genesis of the affair. One can hardly refer to the protagonists as 'infidels' and 'fidels'. And if I use the terms 'cuckold' for the husband whose wife is having an affair and 'cuckquean' for a wife whose husband is having one, I'm going to end up sounding archaic and perhaps slightly supercilious, neither of which I believe myself to be.

I could use clever terms like 'explorer' (for the one who's having the affair) and 'discoverer' (for the one who finds out) and so forth, but I'm going to desist from doing so. I would much rather use the terms 'transgressor' or 'transgressing partner' to refer to the one who's having or had an affair, and 'aggrieved' or 'aggrieved partner' when I speak of the spouse of the transgressor, for regardless of how good or how flawed the person otherwise is, or how good or how flawed the marriage is, an affair does represent the transgression of a marital boundary, and the spouse who's discovered the affair is certainly very aggrieved. Be that as it may, this does not mean that I believe that the aggrieved partner is a 'saint'. I don't, for they often aren't. Nor do I think of all transgressors as 'sinners'. Many aren't. As far as the third point of the triangular relationship is concerned, the term 'paramour' is a handy one, even if clichéd, and I have no hesitation in using it, preferring this to other equally clichéd terms like 'lover' and suchlike.

One more thing. My definition of marriage includes all committed relationships, whether or not preceded by a legal or religious ritual. Even if you're cohabiting with each other in a 'live-in' relationship, I'll still refer to it as marriage, for despite what most people think, the dynamics in both are remarkably similar. I use the terms 'spouse' and 'partner' interchangeably, in order to reflect this. Also, the issues and processes discussed here relate primarily to heterosexual relationships. I have worked with homosexual infidelity as well, but the dynamics in that are a little different, and deserve to be discussed in a separate space.

So, now that we have all that behind us, let's get down to the task of trying to understand why people have affairs, whether an affair is the death-knell of the marriage, and whether and how infidelity can be survived. As I usually do when I write, I have inserted several stories of people who have affairs. While they are all based on fact, they are 'fictionalised composites', by which

I mean I only use the basic kernel of somebody's true story. I then make up the characters so they don't resemble the original protagonists even remotely. This has been done to protect the identities of the people involved.

My hope—not expectation—of you would be that, when you're done with the reading of this book, if you ever were to contemplate an affair, you might think longer and harder about it; if you've recently discovered your partner has had an affair, you might learn how to address the whole issue before making a considered choice of whether to continue with the relationship or not; and if you're already having an affair that your partner doesn't yet know about, you might consider making a decision in favour of one or the other—spouse or paramour—for sooner than later, the decision is going to be forced on you.

Vijay Nagaswami
Chennai

PART I

UNDERSTANDING INFIDELITY

1

'What's Wrong
with Having an Affair?'

When he heard that I was writing a book on affairs, someone I met—let's call him Rakesh—asked me, with considerable belligerence, 'What's so wrong with having an affair that you have to write a book on it?' He told me that he and his wife, Reema, had been married for eighteen years, and that both of them had had several affairs over the years, and that neither of them had felt particularly bothered by them. He claimed that they are still happily married, and are in fact happier for the affairs they'd had. Every time I tried to create an opportunity to find out from Reema what she felt about the whole thing, he assiduously steered me away from her. He went on to grandly proclaim that if monogamy and the institution of marriage had to survive, affairs should be seen as part and parcel of it.

How having multiple relationships constitutes monogamy was something I couldn't quite get my head around. He condescendingly explained to me that for as long as he had only one wife (even if he had several paramours), he was still monogamous. 'After all, it is Reema's bed that I return to every night' was his 'argument-clincher'.

From the dictionary definition, this is of course, true. The term 'monogamy', when applied to humans, refers to being married to only one person at a particular time, and when applied to animals, to having only one mate at any given point of time. The allied terms 'monogyny' and 'monoandry' can describe the social behaviour of monogamous men and women respectively. However, there is nothing in this definition that suggests or legitimises the existence of multiple partners outside of marriage.

Unless you invoke the concepts of sexual monogamy and social monogamy. Social monogamy refers to the phenomenon wherein a species remains, for reasons of protection and security, bonded to one mate for life. Nevertheless, when it comes to sexual activity, the same species may not remain sexually monogamous, but will always return to the original mate. Rakesh was not keen to engage in this discussion. His assertion was that as long as he was not polygamous (having multiple spouses), he remained monogamous. He advised me not be churlish by confining myself to narrow definitional issues but to take a larger perspective on things. In the course of our discussion he advanced several—what he believed were—persuasive arguments relating to the relative merits of having affairs and the demerits of fidelity. Let's begin by exploring them.

Monogamy is not the nature of the beast

'Monogamy is for the birds,' Rakesh said dismissively. I don't know whether he knew the facts when he said this, but there's truth to what he said. About 90 per cent of avian species are indeed socially monogamous (even though they may be sexually polygamous), whereas less than 10 per cent of mammal species are. And as far as the primates are concerned, they are notoriously polygamous. So, the 'nature of the beast' theorists would have it that humankind, having evolved from primates, if you believe, as I do, in Darwinian principles of evolution, are also necessarily polygamous. In fact, some anthropologists too do believe that man is inherently polygamous.

My own questions are simple. Doesn't evolution mean progress? Does it mean that merely because our evolutionary predecessors engaged in a particular form of behaviour, humans should follow the same patterns too? And why only when it comes to sex and relationships? Why not eat only bananas? Why shouldn't men continue to choose their mates by knocking them over their heads (if indeed they ever did this)? And so on.

For a species that prides itself on intellectual and emotional evolution, to argue that we should take as our role models, our evolutionary ancestors, seems at best, specious, and at worst, opportunistic. When the purpose of life is to climb up the evolutionary ladder, any attempt at actively seeking commonalities in patterns with our ancestors amounts, in my eyes, to little more than rationalisation.

I am not for a moment suggesting that monogamy is a higher order on the evolutionary scale of man-woman relationships. I really don't know if it is. Maybe we'll find different patterns and processes as we go on, but to suggest that its opposite number—polygamy—is more desirable, merely because our predecessors practised it, seems to me scientifically unappealing. Needless to say, Rakesh didn't find my explanation convincing.

Marriage is a man-made institution, not a natural one

So, for that matter, is democracy. It is, undoubtedly, an imperfect institution, but, without getting into a political debate, it is by and large true that, in our country, there is little quarrel that democracy is the way to go. And when we are not satisfied with some aspects of it, we try and tweak it around a bit. We don't abandon it because it's not solving all our issues or because some people are more equal than others.

Most social institutions are man-made. None of our ancestors had them, but by virtue of being the most highly socialised species on the planet, we needed to build institutions to ensure our social survival. And we did. Like we did with the joint family that served an excellent purpose up until a few decades ago (it still does in some parts of the country) until it became more of a power base than a facilitating institution.

So today, the joint family is re-inventing itself as clusters of nuclear families in which power-sharing and not power-enforcement is the order of the day. Likewise, the institution of marriage, in our country certainly, existed in the context of patriarchy and for as long as the power of the patriarch (the husband) was not threatened, there were apparently few problems, thereby justifying Engels' belief that marriage was an unjust institution because it oppressed women. However, in the recent era of women's empowerment, marriage is undergoing drastic redefinition, at least in urban India, so that power becomes less of an issue, and *companionable partnership*, a facilitating aspect of the institution, becomes more progressively highlighted.

Over a period of time, by virtue of social development, inequities do get addressed and dealt with. That's the value of man-made institutions. So, to knock an institution because it's man-made makes little sense to me. Nevertheless, it made a lot of sense to Rakesh.

How is it possible to have just one partner throughout your life?

I would imagine that one partner in one's life is strenuous enough. But the underlying tenor of this argument is that variety is the spice of life. It's hard to tell what precisely the Georgian-era poet William Cowper (1731–1800) meant when he wrote the lines, 'Variety's the very spice of life/ That gives it all its flavour.' The Georgian era in Britain was a time of great social change, but the writings of a great novelist of the same era, Jane Austen, say little to suggest that promiscuity was one of the changes in evidence. I can therefore hardly imagine that Cowper was referring to extramarital profligacy when he wrote the words he did.

However, there is some truth to the feeling that having just one partner throughout one's married life may become a trifle boring. As discussed in detail in my earlier book, *The Fifty-50 Marriage: A Return to Intimacy*, boredom is the greatest killer of contemporary marriages, followed only by affairs. One leads to the other. However, it's not as if one doesn't get bored with one's paramour. Just as it is difficult for a spouse to sustain your interest and enthusiasm forever, so too is it with your paramour. Sooner than later, you're likely to become bored with your paramour as well.

So where does that leave you? Some people, to obviate marital boredom, get into a pattern that's come to be called, *serial monogamy*. In other words, you're still committed to monogamy, but you keep dumping partners once you get bored with the current one and find someone else more entertaining. You might divorce and get re-married, or just enter into living-in monogamous relationships. But where does this end? Divorces can be quite expensive and relationship break-ups are hard for all concerned. This notwithstanding, there are many people who choose to live in this manner.

Boredom is inevitable in any long-term monogamous relationship. As you get to know each other well, you will find each other relatively predictable, and even a trifle dull. However, if a couple is committed to growing together and has configured their marriage appropriately, boredom can be dealt with. For, in the final analysis, it's not your partner that you get bored of, it's your life. And merely getting rid of the partner is not going to cure your boredom. You need to re-invent yourself from time to time, and you can do this as well with the same partner, as with another. On the flip side, if both of you are able to re-invent and reclaim your marriage in the manner that's been described in *The Fifty-50 Marriage: A Return to Intimacy*, you can certainly deal with the boredom issue.

My way to look at it is this. If both of you are bored with each other, either reclaim your marriage or visit a therapist. If neither of these work, consider moving on away from each other and do so amicably. Then, you could start looking around for another partner. But having an affair when you're already committed to a partner is not, as I see it, the way to go. However, Rakesh's approach is: why go through all the bother when he can play the field and see whether he finds someone better than Reema? If he does, then he'll dump her and move on.

But if he doesn't, he'll hang on to Reema—the 'bird in hand is worth two in the bush' philosophy. Well, let me tell you this. As long as you take Rakesh's approach, you're less likely to find someone else to relate to, for you're unconsciously using your spouse as a benchmark and are reluctant to take a risk.

Also, you reduce the opportunity to enhance the intimacy in your marriage so it can be appropriately reconfigured for your future. So, like Rakesh, you'll hang around in no-man's land, hitting on all the attractive people you find, likely getting rebuffed more often than not and spouting sexual philosophy to anyone who wants to write a book on Infidelity.

Isn't it possible to love more than one person at a time?

It most certainly is. But the key question is, is it possible to have more than one relationship at a time? As has been extensively discussed in *The Fifty-50 Marriage: A Return to Intimacy*, romantic love is a heady combination of attraction and brain chemistry. When you're attracted to someone very strongly and the feeling is mutual, it is certainly possible to fall in love with that person, even while being in a committed relationship with another. And when you find that the other person has qualities and traits that your partner doesn't have, it seems to strengthen your feelings. And then you get into the 'in-love-vs-love' rationalisation. 'I love my partner, but I'm "in love" with this other person,' you say to yourself, as if this, in some mysterious way, legitimises your extramarital entanglement. You plunge headlong into an affair and start getting into a web of deception, for you certainly don't want your spouse to know of your 'other' relationship.

So you begin to juggle both relationships until romantic loves fades away even from your affair, as it is bound to do, for this is the nature of romantic love. It's fickle and dies out on you when you least expect it. The purpose of romantic love is to get two people with the right chemistry to consummate (both sexually and emotionally) the attraction. Once its job is done, it fades away, to be replaced, if both partners get it right, by intimate love. And even if you and your paramour get into a state of intimate love with each other, this too is a growing entity and will certainly make demands on your time and energy.

And where do you go for these? Obviously you take some from your marriage, where else? So, to stabilise your parallel relationship, you will be compelled to take something *away* from your marriage. Sometime or another, your partner's going to wake up and smell the phenylethylamines (the chemicals associated with romantic love) or the oxytocin (the hormone associated with intimate love), and life is going to become messy. Unless, of course, both of you believe in the virtues of multiple relationships. If you do, you're just going to have a blast. But remember, even in such 'open marriages', jealousy, even though it's not supposed to, can and does surface.

Here's the rub: there's always someone else, maybe even many people, who you'll find physically and/or emotionally attractive during the course of your married life. You can hardly expect to have relationships with each of them, however much you want to, simply because relationships are time-consuming, energy-intensive and if you're committed to a monogamous relationship, the lies and deception that go along with extramarital dalliances can sap your soul. However, if both you and your partner are not particularly monogamously inclined, have fun.

Multiple-partner relationships

In many parts of the world, multiple-partner relationships are not uncommon. These are called '*open relationships*', in which both partners are free to get emotionally and sexually involved with other people without needing the partner's consent every time. In other words, consent is a given. There is also no restriction on the degree of emotional or sexual closeness you can experience with the paramour. It is quite conceivable that you may end up having a committed relationship with the paramour if this is indeed what you want to do, but then, you will have an open relationship with the paramour too, thereby permitting you to still maintain a relationship with your original partner. In other words, the element of exclusivity gets taken out of your relationship, although commitment is part of an open relationship.

This is different from 'swinging' and 'spouse-swapping' in which the focus is more on sexual than emotional intimacy. You're still married to your spouse, but both of you, by mutual consent, engage from time to time in sexual romps with other swinging couples. The idea here seems to be to provide both partners some sexual variety, but in a reasonably controlled situation, so that some degree of exclusivity is retained, and when both partners tire of sexual frolic, they retire to lives of companionable monogamy. Of course, it is not unknown for swingers also to get emotionally attracted to someone they are swinging with, and break away from their avowed partners. Also, some basic sexual anxieties may get heightened if one partner shows greater excitement at the idea of sex with a swinging partner than with the spouse. It is also not uncommon to find swingers who enjoy their swinging a lot, moving on to the open relationship format described earlier.

And in recent times, there is the new phenomenon called *polyamory* or simply, *poly*, sometimes described as 'responsible non-monogamy'. While the definition of polyamory is not always absolutely clear, and can include open relationships as well in its ambit, it is distinguished from swinging, because it's seen as encompassing sexual, emotional, romantic and spiritual dimensions. The basic understanding here is that anyone is capable of having simultaneous, multiple, deep, intimate relationships, and that the 'distracting' elements of marriage, like jealousy, exclusivity, power imbalances, etc., are squarely removed from the equation, thereby creating opportunities to grow as human beings.

However, jealousy does appear every now and again, and the successful poly is one who has been able to conquer this emotion and replace it with what is referred to as *compersion* (the opposite of jealousy, where you experience genuine happiness that your partner finds fulfilment or joy from somebody or something other than yourself). Fidelity, loyalty, honesty, equality, respect and transparency are big virtues among polys, for no relationship takes place in the absence of consent and consensus. If ever consent is withheld, the reasons have to be substantial.

Polyamorists may engage in long-term relationships in triads, quads or networks. They would still tend to have a 'primary' relationship and one or several 'secondary relationships'. They are a growing movement in the United States (apparently there're about half a million polyamorists there) and also participate in Pride parades to highlight the legitimacy of their cause. *Polyfidelity* is a more controlled method of engaging in multiple relationships. The partners that one can choose from are limited to members of a group, network or commune. And fidelity to this group is demanded at all costs. Otherwise, the dynamics are similar to polyamorous relationships.

Many multiple-relationship paradigms have assumed great popularity ever since the 1960s, when the sexual revolution took place, and flower power was at its peak. Also, the women's liberation movement played a significant role, for it was believed that the institution of marriage oppressed women and was therefore an unjust one. Great philosophers, feminists and political writers like Engels, Simone de Beauvoir, Jean-Paul Sartre, Germaine Greer and many others of their standing, came out strongly against the imbalanced power structures in man-woman relationships and these have all played a role in the genesis of multiple-partner relationships. While many went on to settle down to companionable monogamy, some have stood faithful to their philosophy and remain committed to not only practise it, but also to preach it. And they seem to be getting more and more converts with each passing year.

There is no law against multiple relationships, although there is no legal protection for them either, in that such relationships are usually not considered a valid marital contract for legal purposes, for legally, marriage remains a union between only two people. Some research into multiple marriages is under way, but it's too early to tell whether it is a viable and sustainable alternative to monogamy.

You can imagine Rakesh's excitement when I told him all this. A lot of this information was new to him and he was thrilled beyond words, even though his enthusiasm was dampened when I reminded him that all these changes were taking place primarily in the most experimental of world cultures—the United States. In our own country, multiple relationships seem a far cry. We're still debating the issue of arranged vs. love marriages.

I have found my 'soulmate' and I don't want to let go

The more romantic among us tend to be always on the lookout for the near-mythical 'soulmate', for there is a belief that for every human being, there is one such, lurking around somewhere in the world. Even people who are reasonably comfortable in their marriages may also be looking around for their soulmates. The most active quest for soulmates takes place over the Internet, in social networking websites, chat rooms and the like. Sometimes it may be a perfect stranger, or it may be someone from one's past, who suddenly pops up to play a new role in our lives. Or it may even end up being someone you know socially, but never had the occasion or the opportunity to get to 'really know', until you found each other in a relative unguarded moment dealing together with a crisis or on the Internet. And once the soulmate is recognised, things generally proceed rapidly.

I told Rakesh of Bhavna, a thirty-eight-year-old homemaker, married for twenty years (yes, she got married at the age of eighteen), mother of two teenage daughters, aged nineteen (yes, she had her first child within a year of getting married) and seventeen, who met her soulmate, Arshad, in an Internet chat room. After several weeks of correspondence, they exchanged phone numbers and started talking on the phone and grew emotionally very close. They'd seen each other's pictures, had video chats on Skype and had once even engaged in Internet sex using webcams (Rakesh was, by now, getting more and more excited; obviously I was expanding his horizons substantially). They couldn't meet because he lived overseas. She knew he was fifty-nine years old, but didn't mind this at all, for with soulmates, you don't fuss over details. Bhavna decided that she had to be with her soulmate and despite the protests of her husband, her family members and her teenage daughters, demanded and eventually secured a divorce. Soon, she left the country to join her soulmate, leaving behind a family in tatters, teenage daughters severely traumatised, and an embittered husband. When I last heard, she was still with Arshad, although nobody could tell me how they were faring. I thought Rakesh would be impressed with the story. He was, but not in the way I'd imagined. He found Bhavna's courage and determination absolutely admirable and wished that he had even a fraction of Bhavna's gumption. He felt she sounded like she could be *his* soulmate.

What about history?

I was waiting for Rakesh to remind me that historically, affairs have been considered most acceptable and that even religious myths refer to polygamy and polyandry and that gods and goddesses had enjoyed multiple-partner relationships. But he didn't go down that road, since, as I later found out, he was an atheist and didn't believe in mythology. And as far as history was concerned, he had little truck with it. So what if the kings and queens and nobility had engaged in mindless fornication? He felt there had been little else to do in those days. This was probably one of the few things Rakesh and I agreed on all evening. But what of concubines? Particularly in Eastern cultures? He seemed only mildly interested. He dismissed these as status symbols. He'd much rather have a Mercedes or a BMW. Probably cheaper than maintaining a concubine, he felt.

In many Eastern cultures that saw pretty rigid patriarchal dominance, particularly in China, the Far East and the Indian subcontinent, it was considered both a sign of prosperity as well as virility for a man to have a concubine or two. After his needs for having a family and propagating his DNA were taken care of, and he had established himself successfully in his professional endeavours, it was considered appropriate for him to take a concubine, predominantly for sexual gratification, since his wife, having borne multiple children, was likely to have become sexually unattractive and therefore, uninteresting. For those who couldn't afford maintaining a concubine, there were still other opportunities available: the *oirans* of Japan (not to be confused with the geisha), the *yiji* of China, the *kisaeng* of Korea, the *tawaifs* of Mughal India and of course, the *devadasis*. Courtesans were not an Eastern preserve and Western history is also full of stories of English royal courtesans, the French *grisette*, the Greek *hetaerae*, the Hebrew *pilegesh* and so on. Of course, courtesans were not like concubines in that there was no expectation on the part of the man to undertake any responsibility for the woman, but sexual favours were on offer on a fee-for-service basis.

Rakesh was, however, dismissive of the courtesan. Going to one was not really like having an affair, it was just like going to a hooker, he felt. Moreover, society was okay with it. So, where was the thrill of the chase, the seeking and finding of the forbidden fruit, he demanded. He wasn't overly enthused when I pointed out that, although it has become relatively uncommon to have concubines in most parts of the country, even today in some parts of Tamil Nadu and Andhra, for instance, it was not uncommon, if not particularly legal, for a man to have more than one establishment and the woman that ran each was referred to as a 'wife'.

In parts of Tamil Nadu, this practice has some degree of societal sanction and the second establishment is generally referred to as *china veedu* (literally translated, 'small house') even if often there is nothing really small about the house. Rakesh had heard of this, of course, but anything that had social approval did not really enthuse him. And what was more, it was too patriarchal for his liking, since the same opportunity was not available to women. He wanted a level playing field. A truly modern pleasure-seeker, our Rakesh.

However, unlike Rakesh and his lofty principles about extramarital involvements, many of those engaging in sex-seeking affairs (Chapter 4), do tend to engage with the relics of the courtesans and devadasis of the past, who are readily available in contemporary life in various forms. They may or may not consider this an affair, since it's a purely business transaction meant primarily for sexual release. It was more common in the past, for single men to frequent sex workers, but in modern India, it seems to be easier for young people to find unpaid sex, and sex workers of both genders (this might please Rakesh, for there's nothing patriarchal about this) seem to be dealing more with married people who seek, for whatever reason, sex outside their marriage. The usual justification is that it's happened from historical times and isn't it the 'oldest profession', after all?

Everybody's having one, so why shouldn't I?

Rakesh smirked a bit when he asked me this one. He thought he'd got me. Again, there is some truth to what he said. It's incredible that so many people, particularly among the middle and higher socio-economic classes are having affairs. It's like everybody's taken a token and is awaiting their turn. However, when one looks at actual numbers, one realises that we are not really dealing with an epidemic of infidelity at all. Unfortunately, there's hardly any data from our country on infidelity rates and most of what exists is gleaned from clinic or hospital-based samples, and this certainly doesn't reflect how many people who don't go to a therapist or to a hospital, are actually having affairs, just as the number of marriages registered in a year at a registrar's office is no indication of how many people in the community are actually married, since only a small proportion of married

couples in our country actually register their marriages. In
the United States where a little more organised data is
available, the estimates of infidelity rates, and I
emphasise the word *estimates*, for even in that country it's
hard to get accurate data on the subject of infidelity, range
from 10 to 30 per cent of all marriages. Which mean
that 70 to 90 per cent of married couples are faithful to
each other.

In our country, all one can say is that attitudes to
infidelity seem to be changing. A survey conducted by
India Today and AC Nielsen-ORG MARG (published in
India Today, issue dated November 22, 2010), polled about
5,369 people (2,705 men and 2,664 women) of various ages
and socio-economic classes from twelve major cities in
the country on various aspects of sex and relationships.
The survey revealed that close to 30 per cent (29 per cent,
to be exact) found the idea of extramarital relationships
acceptable or somewhat acceptable.

Needless to say, men constituted more of this figure,
for 43 per cent of them, as opposed to 15 per cent of
women, felt this way. There was hardly any difference
between different age-groups, socio-economic classes and
between those who were married and those who were
single. Those who were remuneratively employed were
more comfortable with the idea (39 per cent), probably
because they had more opportunities, as opposed to those
who were not (14 per cent). Obviously, co-workers are
more attractive than neighbours and friends. The survey
is silent on whether or not these people were actually
having extramarital relationships, but even if they were,
they might not have said so, mightn't they?

You might argue that affairs are not necessarily such a
big deal since only under a third of the population feels
comfortable with the idea of having them, and of these,
several could perhaps change their minds after a few

years into the marriage. True. But equally, those who find affairs unacceptable could also cross over. To me, the fact that just under a third of the respondents don't find it unacceptable to have an affair, says something: many couples are approaching marriage not necessarily as an exclusive equation, but are keeping their options open. And while the numbers are not actually scary at this point of time, and anyway survey data can't always be relied upon to make trend predictions (since they are usually plagued with a lot of methodological issues, response accuracy, etc.), it still does make one think.

Rakesh had obviously read this issue of the magazine and was feeling delighted with the emerging trend and the implications he was drawing from it. However, he was a little disappointed by the fact that only 15 per cent of the women were okay with having an affair. Look at his odds—how was he going to deal with those 43 per cent of men who were all in the same race? So, I guess even if 'everyone's looking to have an affair', there don't seem to be as many takers. For the moment, the likes of Rakesh will have to settle for plain and simple fantasy, I suspect. It needs to be remembered that this assumption that everyone's having an affair is probably more a myth than anything else. It's hard enough coming to conclusions based on survey data, but you're on a really slippery slope when you start relying on grapevine data to justify your peccadilloes.

The long arm of the law

Rakesh was genuinely horrified when I delivered my coup de grâce. He had no idea that extramarital relationships were punishable by law in our country. Of course, the law refers to it as 'adultery' and is very clear on who's punishable. The 'adulteress' is not prosecutable or punishable, in accordance with Section 497 of the Indian Penal Code and Section 198 of the Code of Criminal Procedure. The only person who can be prosecuted is the woman's paramour, provided that she is married and her husband had no idea of the affair. And the only person who can prosecute the paramour is the husband of the 'adulteress'. The cuckolded husband is seen as the only aggrieved party in this situation and the wife as the victim.

As defined by this law, a woman cannot commit adultery. It's only the male 'outsider who breaks the sanctity of the marital home' who can be punished if found guilty. In other words, if Rakesh has an affair with a married woman without her husband's knowledge (it's hardly likely, of course, that he would be doing so *with* it) and his paramour's husband finds out and can furnish evidence of the affair that will hold up in court, instead of going after Rakesh with a shotgun, the cuckolded husband can set the law on Rakesh, who if found guilty, faces up to five years in prison. And however angry the husband maybe at his wife for having an affair, she cannot be prosecuted even as an abettor to the crime.

However, if Rakesh's wife, Reema, had discovered the affair, she could legally do nothing about it, unless she persuaded the paramour's husband to prosecute Rakesh. But, since this could mean a five-year jail sentence, she might have thought twice before doing that. Of course, there are other legal recourses open to Reema like Section 498A of the Indian Penal Code which deals with cruelty against a woman by her husband or his relatives. She could also file for divorce on grounds of adultery under the relevant Marriage Acts, but even if she's really angry with Rakesh, she can't initiate criminal prosecution against Rakesh on grounds of adultery alone, because she's not seen as the aggrieved party in the affair. Only the cuckolded husband is. Nor can she prosecute Rakesh's paramour, for the latter is also seen as only a victim of the affair, even though she had seduced Rakesh. Of course, Reema might never be able to bring herself to see it quite that way. But there it is. That's what the law says.

One could argue about the rationale behind the laws on adultery, and there are several initiatives to amend them by providing women, too, the opportunity to prosecute their unfaithful husbands and so on, but I somehow can't view infidelity in the light of a criminal offence. Yes, it does cause a lot of pain all around, but somehow I feel that there are better ways to deal with it than by straining the already over-burdened criminal justice system, all because one is mad as hell that the marital vows were breached. However, I did succeed in giving Rakesh quite a jolt, even though I was not sure I'd succeeded in changing his mind, for the Rakeshes of the world don't really change their positions so easily. I honestly can't see him reading this book, for instance.

The morality of infidelity

Rakesh hastily left me to myself after he realised that he, if ever he wanted to, could have affairs only with single women (and since he was middle-aged, pot-bellied and balding, the odds of finding someone single were remarkably loaded against him) but not before muttering something about there being nothing immoral about affairs. Unfortunately, before I could say I agreed with him, he had disappeared. It's true. Affairs, surprising as it may sound, are not necessarily immoral acts, unless they're engaged in principally with the object of hurting one's partner.

Of course, everybody who has affairs does know that, if their partners ever found out about the affair, they would be hurt beyond belief, which is why secrecy is such an intrinsic part of infidelity and people believe that those who have affairs, do so knowing full well what the consequences could be and that they are therefore, 'culpable'. They certainly are culpable, because they always had the choice not to do it, which they *chose* to ignore. But culpability for an inappropriate choice doesn't make a person immoral. From my experience, I can confidently state that most affairs happen in certain contexts (we'll be exploring these a little later in the book). Of course, this does not justify having affairs, but it certainly does make the act of transgression a little more understandable. And the majority of people who engage in an affair, do experience a sense of guilt and remorse, indicating that their fundamental values regarding affairs have not changed. In other words, they are still 'moral' people even if they perhaps let themselves, and inevitably, their partners, down.

Which reflects, essentially, the fallibility of the human organism. Also, the fact that the majority of people don't have affairs, doesn't put them on a morally superior plane, for who knows what else they're doing that could give rise to a judgement of immorality against them? And what's more, when dealing with an institution like marriage, which is more of a social institution than a sacrament (although many people do think of it as the latter), the question of immorality is certainly a debatable one.

That affairs detract from a marriage is unarguable. That they cause a lot of hurt and emotional pain for everyone involved is indubitable. That they constitute a breach of the marriage vows is undebatable. But that they reek of moral turpitude is questionable. Those who think of marriage as a sacrament will certainly take a moral position on affairs. But those who think of marriage as a social institution, even one that has been developed for the common good, will appreciate the argument that just as tax evasion is an illegal act, though not an immoral one, so too is infidelity when it comes to the issue of marriage. It is a divorceable and in some situations, an illegal act, but not necessarily an immoral one. An affair can never be 'right', but it is 'wrong' only from the point of view of the marriage, for it definitely does cause harm to it, but the individuals in the marriage can and will survive it, regardless of what pain they may go through. Which is why I plead the case that we shouldn't get too judgemental or moralistic when it comes to infidelity, for if we do, we have no starting point to survive it, deal with it, heal from it or begin afresh.

We also do need to remember that there are many couples who don't see infidelity as an act of betrayal, and are as comfortable having an affair as they are of overlooking it when their partners return the compliment. Obviously, this book is not for them, for they have personally redefined the boundaries of the marital relationship and don't feel that affairs detract from their marriage, nor do they experience the pain of betrayal.

And hey, if it works for them, who am I to tell them that they shouldn't be doing what they're doing? But for couples who believe that affairs are acts of betrayal, then they certainly are acts of betrayal. The problem occurs when one partner feels that they are, and the other disagrees. If they are unable to see eye-to-eye on this one, despite their best efforts, I guess they'll have to make some hard choices. But those of you who are in synch with each other—and with me—that an affair constitutes a breach of faith, trust and respect, but is not a consequence of moral turpitude, read on.

2

'We're Just Friends, We're Not Having an Affair'

*B*efore getting in to discussing how to survive infidelity and affairs, we need to be clear what precisely an affair is and what exactly constitutes infidelity, just to make sure we're on the same page, otherwise you could be reading into what I am saying things that I never meant in the first place. Since the rules of the institution of marriage are being re-written, there is much confusion on what precisely infidelity is. Depending on how exacting your moral perspective is, or how stringent your value systems are, you could consider any perceived or potential violation of your marriage vows in thought, word or deed to fall within the ambit of infidelity.

I think we need to get a little more clarity than that and try and get a working understanding of what an affair is. So then we need never get into nit-picking, hair-splitting discussions on whether or not something that you or your partner is doing constitutes infidelity.

There are many definitions of infidelity developed by researchers in the field, but perhaps the most elegant and comprehensive of these is the one offered by American psychologist and researcher, the late Shirley P. Glass, who's often referred to as the 'godmother of infidelity research'. She defined infidelity as:

> *a secret, sexual, romantic, or emotional involvement that violates the commitment to an exclusive relationship.*

I think the definition is absolutely clear and needs little further elaboration. Dr Glass has also classified affairs into three categories:

- primary sexual involvement with no meaningful emotional involvement
- primary emotional involvement with little or no sexual involvement
- combined sexual and deep emotional involvement.

She's also observed that men have more of the first type of affairs and women more of the second and third. The third type is more likely than the other two to end up in divorce. She differentiates extramarital emotional involvement from platonic friendships in that the former involves emotional intimacy, sexual chemistry and secrecy. Internet affairs (which I have later described as e-affairs) are, in her opinion, 'the prototype for extramarital emotional involvement'.

Based on Dr Glass's definition and some other research findings, I have, after working intensively on infidelity in our country over the years, recognised five hallmarks of an affair, which I would like to elucidate on.

The famous five: Hallmarks of an affair

Most, if not all affairs, are characterised by the presence of at least two, if not more, of five hallmarks that serve to differentiate them from casual or even close friendships between two people of the opposite gender: *emotional intimacy, sexual involvement, secrecy, guilt and needy dependence.*

Without you, life would be meaningless: Emotional intimacy

The first of these hallmarks is emotional intimacy. I know that one can experience intimacy with a friend and that it can therefore be hard to distinguish this intimacy from that of an extramarital affair, whether you are the transgressor, aggrieved or paramour. But in truth, it's not all that difficult to do so.

Shaila and Ajay had been married for twelve years and had weathered all the storms that, every now and again, happen unannounced in most marriages. They both had good jobs and were generally happy with the way things were going. The only thing that made them feel incomplete was that they had no children. Despite having gone through several cycles of assisted reproductive interventions and despite having tried in-vitro fertilisation, nothing had happened.

Shaila had conceived twice, but miscarried both times. The infertility experts finally concluded that her eggs were not hardy enough and recommended surrogacy, which neither of them was comfortable with. They were talking very seriously about adoption, something she was still not ready to accept, for she, in some way felt very responsible for their state of childlessness. Ajay's reassurances didn't seem to help, however hard he tried.

At the infertility clinic they had met another couple, Shailesh and Aruna, who were going through the same issue, except in their case, the 'fault' lay with the husband's sperm. The two women didn't quite hit it off, but their husbands did and soon they started occasionally socialising with each other. Shaila liked Shailesh, not merely because their names were similar, but he seemed like such a good and decent man. That he was good looking also helped, even if she found her own husband more attractive. She couldn't understand why he'd chosen to marry 'that wretched Aruna', who, in her opinion had not even a single redeeming feature. She was unattractive, clingy, histrionic, had terrible taste and was nothing that Shaila was, but she tolerated her since she liked Shailesh so much.

Anyway, since they met only occasionally, Shaila could put up with Aruna's presence, but not for very long. Although she would have liked to spend more time with Shailesh, his wife was always around. Ajay was amused by Shaila's antipathy towards Aruna, but since he shared at least some of Shaila's sentiments, he was not particularly disturbed.

Entirely by accident, Shaila one day bumped into Shailesh at a bookstore where she was trying to kill time between client meetings. Shailesh was obviously a regular visitor at the store for he seemed to know the staff there. He was having a cup of coffee at the cafe attached to the store and invited her to join him. They spent almost two hours in animated discussion on a variety of subjects. Shaila had to rush when her infuriated client called up demanding an explanation for her absence at the meeting. Ordinarily, she would have been very agitated if such a thing had happened, but that day she was feeling good about life, so she managed to calm ruffled feathers and turn things around effortlessly.

For the next few days, it seemed to Ajay that Shaila was on a high. But, since it was an infectious sort of high, he just went along with it. Shaila found her thoughts incessantly going back to her chat with Shailesh. About how they spoke about so many things in just two hours.

His wry sense of humour. His crooked smile. The tuft of hair sticking out of his nose that she had an absurd impulse to trim. She added his email id on her chat buddy list and was happy when a little bubble popped up while she was at work on a boring presentation. Obviously, Shailesh had done the same, and soon they started chatting regularly, exchanging all sorts of little thoughts, quotations and ideas. He was able to help her with her work for he had worked in the same industry a few years ago and still maintained a network.

And inevitably, they came to talk of their childlessness and how each felt completely responsible for their sense of incapacity to parent a child. Shailesh told her he stuck it out with Aruna only because he felt he had failed her and that she never let him forget this. Shaila was very sympathetic of his situation and told him that she wished Ajay would express his anger and dismay to her, but he did everything to make her feel that it was all right, even when she knew that it wasn't. If only he would scream or shout or something like that. She could then deal with it. So, over their mutual feelings of inadequacy, Shaila and Shailesh bonded.

Shaila had told Ajay about her initial meeting with Shailesh and the ensuing chats and telephone conversations, but at Shailesh's request didn't tell him about their confiding in each other and sharing things with him that she hadn't even told Ajay about. Shailesh felt that if she told Ajay of their comfort level with each other and the depth of their friendship, Ajay may inadvertently make some reference to this in Aruna's presence and if this happened, all hell would break loose. Shaila thought this was certainly likely, even if she felt that Ajay would have no problem with their friendship at all, since he was pretty cool about most things she did. Anyway, she went along, because she felt that as much as there was nothing to hide, there was no compelling necessity to share either.

And so their friendship strengthened and deepened. They spoke to each other every day, chatted frequently on their instant messengers, sent each other funny, sentimental and inspiring emails and smileys, talked about work and met for coffee at least a couple of times a week. It never occurred to Shaila that she was not telling Ajay much about what happened during her day like she used to. Sometimes she thought she had already told him something she'd wanted to and was surprised that he didn't remember, until she realised that she'd mentioned it to Shailesh, not Ajay.

On his part, Ajay was going through a very busy period at work and was maintaining punishing hours, so he barely noticed that there was a slight, but subtle change in their emotional comfort with each other. They were not holding each other as much. There had been no sex for weeks. No text messages dotted with emoticons. No entwining themselves when they slept. No little notes around the house. When he did think of it, he attributed this to the demands of his work and decided that, after his work crisis was behind them, he would take Shaila on a holiday to Bali, something both of them wanted to do. He mentioned it at breakfast one day, but he was in such a hurry, he didn't realise that her response, enthusiastic though it was, lacked the usual excitement that normally accompanied such suggestions from him.

Shaila had no qualms about her relationship with Shailesh, because she felt that it was pure friendship. There had never been even a suggestion of a sexual innuendo or double entendre in their conversations. Just good, clean, healthy fun. And anyway, she didn't find Shailesh sexually attractive, nor, she assumed, did he her. Actually, when she thought about it, she didn't find anyone sexually attractive any more. Not even Ajay, with whom she'd shared a very active and enthusiastic sex life. She couldn't bear the thought of having sex now, with Ajay, or with anyone else. Maybe it was her hormones, she concluded. Anyway, the important thing was she didn't find Shailesh sexy. So theirs was just a friendship. A very special one.

But obviously, not everyone else thought the same way. Not Aruna, for instance.

When she was in the middle of preparing her department's annual budget, her laptop told her she'd received an email from Ajay. She couldn't imagine why he'd be sending her emails. Anyway, she opened it and was shocked by the contents. Ajay's message was only one line: 'WHAT THE HELL IS HAPPENING?' He never wrote in upper case unless he was really mad. Or had he pressed the caps lock key by mistake? She was all at sea. What could he possibly mean?

Then she noticed the little paper clip sign indicating an attachment. She opened it and found her entire relationship with Shailesh on the screen. Their chat transcripts, their emails, even copies of their SMSes. At the end was a note from Aruna to Ajay: 'Keep your wife's dirty paws away from my husband, if you are a man.' Angry as hell at Aruna, hurt by the suspicion in Ajay's tone, she called up Shailesh at once. Aruna picked up the phone and told her menacingly that if she didn't stay away from Shailesh, she'd have her beaten up. Shaila could well believe in her threat. Aruna came from a politically-backed family and had the necessary clout. Shaila backed down, all her anger melting into fear.

Over the next few days, however hard she tried, Shaila couldn't convince Ajay that she and Shailesh were only friends, not lovers. They'd never even thought of sex or love or anything like that. But Ajay's riposte was, 'People who are not in love don't SMS each other twenty times a day, chat for three to four hours online when they're supposed to be at work, call each other "sweetheart" and "dearest", send each other mushy e-cards, or sign off their emails with "I love you."'Of course, she was having an affair.

She tried to explain that whatever she was being accused of, was perfectly 'normal behaviour' between platonic friends in the twenty-first century. Then why hadn't she told him she felt so strongly about Shailesh? Why the secrecy? There was nothing to hide and there was nothing to tell him either, she argued. Did he tell her everything that happened in his life?

But there was nothing much that happened in his life, was his response.

She couldn't do anything about that, could she, she countered.

Then how come Shailesh knew stuff about Shaila that Ajay didn't?

Well, at least he was there to listen to her. Could she help it if Ajay was unavailable? And wasn't he making too big a deal of Aruna's paranoia?

It was not paranoia; there was hard evidence.

Rubbish! A few emails and chat transcripts do not constitute evidence. And what's more, she hadn't had sex or any form of physical contact with him, so there!

Yes, but had she had sex with Ajay when he wanted to? She obviously couldn't bear to have sex with anyone else.

Rubbish! It was a purely hormonal thing. Maybe she was getting menopausal.

At the age of thirty-five?

It's been known to happen, or maybe she was going through a depression or a midlife crisis or something.

Was she behaving like someone going through a depression? Laughing and smiling all the time?

Okay, but she hadn't had sex with him.

How could she explain the diamond earrings Shailesh was planning to buy her for her next birthday?

Surely friends can gift each other things?

Things that cost fifty thousand bucks? Had she lost it? It was just a friendship.

No, it wasn't, it was much more than that. Even now, she was defending her boyfriend and not understanding the pain her husband was going through. She was not defending Shailesh, she was defending herself. See, she didn't even refute him when he called Shailesh her boyfriend.

Oh, shut up!

And so it went.

Were Shaila and Shailesh having an affair? Probably not—yet. But could something have happened at some later time? Can't say, but quite possibly. For both of them were obviously experiencing an intensity of emotional connectedness that neither was currently feeling for their respective spouses, whatever the reason. One could argue that Shailesh was never very emotionally connected with Aruna, and so when he got an opportunity to relate emotionally to a friend of the opposite gender, he grabbed it and enjoyed it.

In other words, if one is in an emotionally unfulfilled marriage, it is likely that one will search for emotional contact elsewhere. But what of Shaila? She and Ajay were perfectly happy with each other, except for the fact that he didn't appear to be completely in synch with her when it came to her experience of responsibility for childlessness. She wanted him to show his emotions, but he was focussed only on casual reassurance. So, at least on this issue, their emotional connectivity was a little low. And this probably opened up some of the other cracks in their relationship as well.

Of course, she was convinced it was only friendship because she had never even contemplated having sex with Shailesh. But the absence of sex does not mean an extramarital relationship is not taking place. Emotional intimacy is often an indicator of a potential affair, even if there's no sex happening. As couples get closer emotionally, at some point of time, some enchanted evening, a line is likely to be crossed.

Also, one of the first signs of emotional connectedness with someone other than the spouse is that it becomes increasingly difficult to have sex with the spouse. This, of course, does not mean that every time your spouse pleads a headache when you want to make love, an affair is either incipient or is happening. There are many reasons why sex doesn't happen in marriages, and an affair is not the only one. However, when everything seems by and large fine, and one is getting emotionally closer to someone other than the spouse, the marital sex life does get impacted upon. If Shaila didn't *consciously* find Shailesh sexually attractive, it was probably because she *unconsciously* didn't want to, for she was not yet ready to acknowledge what she was actually feeling for him.

And for the record, platonic friends, even in the twenty-first century, don't whisper, text or email sweet nothings to each other. While the term, 'I love you' continues to be bandied around in all sorts of situations, when a man and a woman use it and when they find themselves saying things like, 'I love you, but I'm not *in love* with you', then believe me, a lot of rationalisation is taking place. It's pretty much like the 'There's nothing between us, we're just good friends' line that celebrities regularly throw at reporters.

And the final clincher in Shaila and Shailesh's relationship is that it was detracting from their respective marriages. They were thinking less of their spouses than of each other. They were sharing more with each other than with their spouses. Surely, that says something?

Blistering Heat: Sexual involvement

Shaila and Shailesh didn't have sex, or even talk about having sex. But Rattan and Shilpa did. In fact, they had a *lot* of sex.

Rattan was, he thought, comfortably, if not happily married to Anita. Until one day, Shilpa, an old flame of his, joined his sales team. She was smart, attractive and voluptuous, in fact more than Rattan remembered her to be when they were in school together. And she was single. The minute he set eyes on her, Rattan realised he simply had to have sex with her. He couldn't really relate to her emotionally, because he found her too flirtatious and aggressive, but sexually, he couldn't get her off his mind. He was careful not to mention her or anything about their history at school to Anita, for he knew she would be jealous as she usually tended to get when any woman paid a little too much attention to her husband.

Since Anita wasn't really particularly friendly with his office colleagues, she had no idea of Shilpa's presence in her husband's life. And anyway, she was too preoccupied with her children, managing their home and her work at the school she taught, to really notice any difference. All she saw was that her sex life with her husband had improved dramatically. From weekend sex, they were having almost daily sex and there was an urgency in their love-making that she'd never experienced before.

Little did she know that while he was with Anita, Rattan only had fantasies of Shilpa on his mind. All sorts of fantasies about locations and positions he never thought he was even aware of, took over most of his waking thoughts. And when he finally had sex with

Shilpa, at the first opportunity that presented itself (during a sales conference at a resort), it was even more mind-blowing than any of his fantasies.

Shilpa, though not sexually experienced, was very eager in bed, game for anything and willing to experiment with abandon. They talked very little. They just had passionate sex. There was no talk of love, relationship, commitment, the sort of things that couples usually speak about. There were no SMSes, emails, save for what was related to their work. There were no demands by either to have cups of coffee, spend romantic evenings together and so on. Whatever time they could create for each other, was spent having sex. Neither wanted a relationship. They were just enjoying each other's bodies.

The thing is, soon after his sexual relationship with Shilpa started, Rattan's ardour in lovemaking with Anita cooled off. She was a little befuddled by this and even asked him about it a couple of times, but did not really press the point. Being a naturally suspicious person, she secretly went through his SMSes, his emails, his chat transcripts and his Internet history, but found nothing to confirm her suspicions.

Until, one day, rummaging through his packed suitcase just before he went on one of his innumerable sales trips, she found, hidden deep in the pocket of one of his neatly pressed trousers, a packet of condoms, that he should have had no use for, since Anita had undergone a tubectomy after the birth of their second child. From then on everything went downhill for Anita, Rattan—and for Shilpa, as well.

So, there you have it. Seeking sex outside your marriage, even with a person you're strongly attracted to, is going to get you into trouble sooner or later. Some people manage to conceal their sexual peccadilloes from their spouses quite successfully for several years. But rarely does pure sexual chemistry last that long. A few days to a few months is usually par for the course.

Unless, of course, what started off as a sexual affair slowly becomes an emotionally-bonded one. While Shilpa and Rattan's sort of affair is not at all uncommon, it is more common for both men and women to seek one-night stands, paid or unpaid, if sex is what they're seeking. The idea, of course, being to reduce the risk of being found out (it's harder to be caught out by your spouse on a one-nighter), as well as to obviate the likelihood of emotional entanglement. However, nobody, not even Rattan and Shilpa, will ever doubt that both one-night stands as well as Rattan and Shilpa's sort of equation, would constitute infidelity, even if one may not be able to take such a clear stand when it comes to the sort of equation that Shaila and Shailesh had.

This is largely because, most of us equate extramarital sex with 'straying'. There are no explanations or rationales that can get Rattan out of the dock. If his sex life with Anita was bad, or she was completely disinterested in it, he could have had some basis, admittedly a weak one, for coming up with reasons. But he had none. Except that his hormones took him over completely. Not surprisingly, after giving him a hard time for several months, Anita finally forgave him, rationalising it by blaming Shilpa, 'the temptress', for the whole episode. I say 'not surprising' because this has been the consistent finding of research in the field of infidelity. Women are able to forgive their husbands for having a purely sexual affair, but find it much harder to do so when their men get emotionally involved with another woman.

For men, it's the other way round. They can deal with their wives having an emotional equation with another man, but find it unacceptable if she goes to bed with him. However, the India-Today Nielsen survey of urban

Indians that I'd quoted earlier seems to indicate that things are changing in contemporary life. Only 38 per cent of the women as opposed to 59 per cent of the men polled felt that emotional infidelity was tantamount to an affair. Of course, what they would do, if emotional infidelity actually happened in their lives, can only be a matter of speculation. But on the assumption that attitudes do reflect future behavioural patterns, it appears that women are becoming more tolerant of emotional connectedness than conventional wisdom and research findings from the West would indicate, and that men are more wary of their women getting into emotional comfort zones with men other than themselves.

Don't ask, won't tell: Secrecy

The third hallmark of an affair is secrecy. If you remember, one of the things that Ajay felt was a giveaway was the fact that Shaila kept her relationship with Shailesh away from him, even though he had never given her reason to believe that he was a jealous or suspicious sort of person. Probably, the fact that hurt Ajay the most was that in that emotional quadrangle (Ajay, Shaila, Shailesh and Aruna), he was the last to know of the 'special' relationship that his wife was engaged in. Shaila tried to blame his preoccupation with work as the reason she never told him anything about the friendship and also felt that since there was nothing to hide, there was nothing to tell either.

She might have got away with the latter argument if the level of intimacy and emotional communication in the marriage had been hitherto low. But it hadn't been. Shaila and Ajay were generally close and she had a habit of sharing every little detail of what happened in her life and thoughts with him, whether or not he was interested.

The only thing she had not discussed in as great detail with Ajay was her relationship with Shailesh.

But why *did* she keep her friendship away from her husband? Certainly not because he was busy at work, for she found the time to share other things with Ajay even during his busy periods. Basically, she was unsure at an unconscious level as to what was developing between her and Shailesh and more importantly, since she was developing a bond of comfort with him, she extended to her 'special relationship' what one normally does only to the marital partner—privacy.

The minute one feels the need to accord an exclusively private space to a relationship with a friend of the opposite gender, one ends up, in effect, 'protecting' that relationship from one's partner. This is not to say that every detail about the content of the friendship needs to be shared with one's partner. I am sure the partner is not really interested in all of these. But, if there's nothing really to hide, why hide it? When one has a friend, it is perfectly normal to tell one's spouse something like, 'Hey, I had coffee with so-and-so today and I've got a juicy bit of gossip to tell you.' But if one feels, 'Why should I "report" everything I do to my spouse?', obviously, the emotional closeness in the marriage is not quite what it should be. In such cases, 'passive secrecy' (*Don't ask, won't tell*) is in operation.

On the other hand, if one feels, 'I better not mention to my spouse that I met so-and-so for coffee, or there'll be hell to pay', one is engaging in 'active secrecy' (*What you don't know won't hurt you. Or me*).

Some people go to extraordinary lengths to keep their special friendships away from their spouses. Of course, there's usually a reason for this, and oftentimes this can backfire on them, for friendships or relationships can rarely be kept secret for long.

As Pradeep found out. His wife, Lekha, was a generally suspicious sort. More than your garden-variety possessiveness-suspicion sort of thing. Even though they'd been married for twenty-odd years, she could not bear him talking to any woman, even his female cousins. This did upset Pradeep, for he had been particularly close to one of his cousins, Anisha, ever since their childhood. Even though she was a second or third cousin—he had never been really sure which—they'd been neighbours through childhood, had spent a lot of time with each other and shared a lot in common. Everybody thought they'd get married when they grew up and everybody was happy about the prospect.

Everybody but them, that is. They never had such feelings for each other, and never once contemplated a life together. After college they'd gone their separate ways, had both fallen in love with different people and had got married to their current spouses. Lekha, of course, knew of this history and had never liked Anisha, despite Pradeep's best efforts to get the two women closer to each other. In her turn, Anisha didn't care much for Lekha either. So Pradeep had given up and everyone had got on with their lives. Until Anisha's husband, Vidyut, died in a road traffic accident, uninsured, leaving Anisha with the responsibility of bringing up their two children and paying back whatever debts the two of them had accumulated.

Naturally, this brought out Pradeep's compassionate side and he decided, even without her asking, to help Anisha deal with this crisis. He knew that there would be no point discussing the matter with Lekha, for he could predict what vituperative comments she would lambast him with. So, after talking to Anisha about it, and swearing her to secrecy, he started helping her financially and emotionally to deal with the crisis. He took great care never to visit her at home for he didn't want Lekha ever to know of the continued association.

He placed Anisha on the rolls of his company and even though she didn't have to show up at work, she would receive a monthly salary cheque. She had only to sign the salary vouchers using a fictitious name and, to make things seem completely aboveboard to his staff, she signed in the name of Anish (Pradeep's imagination, as you can see, was a bit limited). He explained this away to his accountant as helping out an old college-mate who was passing through a rough patch financially, and since the accountant was being well compensated, he was expected to overlook the deception. The accountant felt that his boss was siphoning away money from his business to a *benami* account and since he was used to this practice, didn't think twice about it.

Pradeep arranged to meet Anisha only at locations Lekha would never be seen dead in, those times Anisha wanted to discuss something with him about the children or cry on his shoulder, which was not really very often. He never met Anisha's children for fear they would blurt out something at some family wedding or get-together. However, using his network, he found good schools for them, helped Anisha re-negotiate her bank loans, advised her on her investments, and got her finances back on track. He felt happy that he could help out his childhood friend in her time of distress.

And Anisha was extraordinarily grateful to him for the lengths that he was going to, to ensure that she was able to keep her head above water. Obviously, his efforts at keeping things away from Lekha were working, since she never had an inkling of suspicion of whatever was happening behind her back. Possibly because there was no emotional involvement on Pradeep's part with Anisha, his marriage didn't really suffer or change. He knew he was on a slippery slope, but felt pleased that, all things considered, he'd managed things rather well.

Until one day, the cat, as usually happens, was let out of the bag.

Lekha had gone to his office to collect 1,00,000 rupees in cash from the accountant, since their son's school had been pressuring her for a donation. When the pressure tactics didn't work, the authorities had started issuing veiled threats that got Lekha agitated enough to take action. All said and done, the school was one of the best in the city, and she couldn't bear the thought of looking for another one for their son. She'd tried calling Pradeep, who was overseas on a business trip, but his mobile phone, for some reason, was not reachable that morning. So, she went to his office and asked the accountant to draw out the money for her and discuss it later with Pradeep, when he was reachable.

The accountant apologised, saying the balance in the company's current account did not cover her requirement, since they were all waiting for their overseas buyer to transfer funds that were long overdue, which was the reason 'Sir' had made this trip. There was some money, of course, but these had all been committed to suppliers and if any of their cheques bounced, 'Sir' would be in a lot of trouble. But he suggested that maybe 'Sir' could give her the money from the 'Anish account'. What on earth was the 'Anish account'?

Didn't she know? Sir was setting aside money in that account for the last two years, about 50,000 rupees or so every month, and there should be enough there. From there, it didn't take a determined and astute Lekha very long to figure out what exactly was happening. And Pradeep's bubble was unceremoniously burst.

So, there it is. This is a situation when secrecy was certainly not on account of an affair (none of the other hallmarks were present), but try telling Lekha that. Moral of the story: You can't keep a self-respecting cat in a bag for very long.

Is what I'm doing okay?: Guilt

Guilt and secrecy are closely linked. Most people engaging in infidelity or incipient affairs keep their feelings as well their relationships secret, because they either consciously or unconsciously experience a sense of guilt. The manifestation of the guilt may range from passive secrecy, through a nagging sense of disquiet, to an active experience of discomfort for betraying a partner.

There are also, of course, those who try and brazen things out. However, the vehemence with which they protest that they've done nothing wrong, or that theirs is not an affair, is usually a telltale sign that there exists some uneasiness in their minds about whatever is happening. An inner sense of guilt can come about even if they consciously believe there's no need to feel guilty for their act.

To me the presence of guilt is a good sign, for this means that since the affair goes against their inner sense of appropriateness, then sooner than later, they are more likely to make this a conscious train of thought and are likely to do something about it.

Samarth had known Rati only a few weeks, after they were thrown together on a project that the multinational company they both worked for deputed them to. They were both very professional in their approach to their work. They came from different cities, different backgrounds and they were different people. Samarth had a stable marriage and loved his wife, Asha, very much, and felt that they'd worked through all the normal niggling marriage issues they'd expected to confront. Rati was in an unhappy marriage, and despite being able to manage her professional life impeccably, found it next to impossible to make any headway in her personal one. Her husband was violent, abusive and generally nasty to her, but she could neither leave him, nor could she get used to the idea of living in fear. So she led a compartmental existence.

One day, after she'd had a bitter quarrel with her husband, she broke down in her cabin at office, when Samarth walked in. He asked her what was wrong, they began to talk and Samarth started playing the role of counsellor, which came naturally to him, for he had helped many of his colleagues and friends deal with these and other crises in their personal lives.

However, with Rati, it was different. He started developing feelings for her. And she for him, since they spent nearly twelve hours a day at work to meet punishing deadlines. One day, almost naturally, he held and kissed Rati, who reciprocated with equal spontaneity. This set off a tornado of guilt in Samarth's mind, and even though nothing more than a kiss happened, he felt he had violated his marriage by doing what he did. He felt he had let Asha down inordinately. He acknowledged to himself that had Asha done the same thing, he would definitely have seen it as a breach of their marriage vows. He couldn't sleep for several nights. He tried to keep an emotional distance from Rati, which was hard to do, since they were forced to spend so much time together.

Rati, too felt unhappy at the twist in their relationship, for she didn't like playing the role of the 'home-breaker'. She had very strong views on this since her parents' marriage had ended in divorce on account of one such 'home-breaker'. However, she had never felt as safe and happy in her entire life, as when Samarth had held and kissed her. She wanted more, but knew that she could never ask for it. Conflicted by her thoughts, she too tried to keep an emotional distance from him, but found the going increasingly difficult. Rather than risk any further such episodes, she, on the advice of her girlfriend, requested a transfer. Samarth was happy to endorse her decision, even though he had no say in it. Within a week, she managed to get an overseas posting that she accepted with alacrity so she could put as much of distance as possible between the two men in her life and herself.

Samarth, relieved though he was that Rati was out of his life, continued to feel wretched. He couldn't sleep, was tormented by thoughts of what he had done and how he had let his wife down, even though nothing had really happened. Asha realised something was troubling him and tried to be as loving and supportive of him as she was capable of, which was quite a lot. This made Samarth feel even more guilty, and one night he broke down and confessed his boundary violation to Asha. He felt the great sense of relief that confessionals usually provide to those who'd been suppressing guilty thoughts a while. But he could never have anticipated Asha's reaction.

She broke down completely, moved progressively away from him, and went into a major depression that required psychiatric intervention. They coped with it and are today making extraordinary efforts to get their marriage back on track. I am happy to report that they're doing a good job of it.

Not everyone experiences the kind of guilt that Samarth did, even though, fortuitously, he had not allowed any further lines to be crossed in his relationship with Rati. But realising how close he was to doing this, his inner sensibilities kicked in and he tried to face the situation, 'like a man', as he once said. Did he overreact? Perhaps he did, but in this sort of situation, overreacting is possibly better than under-reacting, for it helped

Samarth pull back just in time. However, whether he could have kept it away from his wife, and spared her the agony, particularly when nothing much had happened, is something that most of us would have a view on. But whatever we think, Samarth couldn't have done anything else, for that's the kind of person he is and that's the kind of relationship he and Asha shared. Transparency was obviously a very important part of their template, and I'm sure Asha would have done the same had the roles been reversed.

You might imagine that Rattan, the one who had a blistering sexual affair with his colleague Shilpa, experienced no guilt. Perhaps he thought that the affair wouldn't last and that he would enjoy it as long as it did. I feel he wasn't really allowing himself to think. His hormonal drive was so great, it probably took him over. Typically, in the sort of affair where sex is the primary element, the element of guilt is much less and sometimes not in evidence at all. And to a large extent this is because, oftentimes, it's men who engage in this sort of affair. Men can compartmentalise themselves much better than women. Sex can function in one compartment and the marriage in another. As a result, they don't consciously experience much guilt.

However, at some point guilt does tend to take over, particularly in the case of those men who do feel a sense of loyalty, love and commitment to their wives. As far as Shilpa is concerned, she was footloose and fancy free and was just enjoying her sexual romp until she found a man she could fall in love and settle down with. Usually, women, single or married, do eventually develop an emotional intimacy with their sexual partners, but contemporary Indian women, by virtue of a new consciousness regarding their sexuality, can sometimes function as effectively in compartments as do men.

However, had Shilpa been married, even if she was sexually deprived in her marriage, she would, more likely than not, have been hard-pressed to engage guiltlessly in an affair. But, that is just a matter of speculation.

There are certainly some people, men more than women, who are such skilful liars that dissembling is practically their second nature. Usually such people experience little or no guilt vis-à-vis their affairs. They may end up having multiple relationships, usually more sexual than emotional. As far as they're concerned, they can lie their way out of any situation, and typically, their consciences, if indeed such exist, are pretty under-developed. However, such people tend to be found out a little easier, since the index of suspicion in the spouse's mind is pretty high, because they have learned how to sniff out their partners' lies through years of having to live and deal with them. For, such people usually lie about a lot of things, not just their affairs.

I ache for you: Needy dependence

Dependence is something that is present in most, if not all relationships, whether the relationship is a casual or an intense one. You miss a friend who's unavailable to you for a while. You look forward to seeing your parents whom you've not seen in some time. You keep in touch with some, though not all, people whose love and support you're dependent on, and so forth. However, the dependence I am now talking about, the type that is the hallmark of some affairs, is slightly different.

Whether it's an emotional affair, a sexual one or a romantic one, the dependence on the paramour is based on a deep sort of *need* and a felt *void*. Sometimes, people engaging in affairs, feel an aching sense of need if, for whatever reason, they're not able to be in contact with their paramours. Normally, we would miss our other loved ones when we're not able to see them or be in touch with them. But we would rarely ache for them unless we're passing through a crisis or are emotionally a bit down and feel the need for their reassuring presence. But the sort of needy dependence that one experiences when having an affair, often results in aching longing when the paramour is unreachable. This sort of needy dependence exists in both emotional as well as sexual affairs and probably peaks in combined type of affairs.

To a large extent, this sort of aching dependence is experienced for two reasons. The first of these is that one rarely gets to spend as much time with the paramour as one would like, particularly since secrecy is involved. In order to keep the affair away from one's partner, one needs to carry on with one's other chores and discharge all other responsibilities including spending time with the spouse. The other reason is related to guilt. When one is not with the paramour one does experience some form or other of guilt about deceiving the spouse, and the only time this guilt can be assuaged is when one is with the paramour and can put one's spouse and marriage out of one's mind. As a result, one counts the minutes that one can be with the paramour again, in order to feel complete and 'normal'. If, however, one's life's situation permits, such as if one works with the paramour, whereby one gets to spend as much or even more time with the paramour, reverse guilt comes into operation, where one feels guilty for not spending enough time with the spouse and the family.

So people in extramarital relationships constantly struggle to find the right balance of time between spouse and paramour, and this by itself increases the sense of needy dependence. Who said 'forbidden fruit' is easy to digest?

So, if two out of the above five hallmarks are present, one can rest fairly assured that an affair is happening. However, there's one caveat. Even in the absence of the other four, if one is engaging in a sexual relationship with somebody other than one's spouse, then it definitely constitutes an affair, even if the person engaging in the affair does not experience emotional dependence, is not particular about secrecy, and feels neither guilt nor a sense of needy dependence on the paramour?. Such is the power of sex when it comes to breaking marital vows.

3

Some Myths & FAQs about Affairs

*A*lthough most people are pretty clear about their thoughts and views on affairs, there are still several areas of doubt and confusion in many minds. Hopefully, the next few paragraphs will help them resolve this.

Affairs take place only in 'bad' marriages

You'd think so, wouldn't you? The most surprising finding in infidelity research is that affairs happen even in 'good' marriages. Marriages which both partners would consider reasonably safe and stable. However, it also needs to be said that all 'good' marriages don't end up dealing with infidelity. Only less than a third of them do. It's not always that people go out and seek affairs; sometimes affairs just walk through the door unannounced. And when they do, they can be stunning and wholly unexpected even to the transgressing partner.

Remember Ajay and Shaila? They seemed to be quite comfortable, loving and supportive of each other. But

Shaila still got emotionally involved with Shailesh. Hers was not a 'bad' marriage by any stretch of imagination. But the affair happened anyway and did not reflect on the 'badness' of the marriage. So, if your spouse has had an affair, it doesn't mean that your assessment of your marriage as a good one was way off base.

The way to look at it is that all marriages, even good ones, do have their little chinks here and there, and given a certain set of circumstances, human vulnerability can take over and lines can be irrevocably crossed. The only way to affair-proof a marriage is to accept and understand that this risk or vulnerability always exists. All human beings are going to, at several points in their lives, feel attracted to people other than their spouses. How they deal with this attraction is what determines whether an affair is going to happen or not. Obviously, one can't jump into bed with every person one is attracted to. As long as one is conscious of this reality and is able to build reasonable strategies to affair-proof the marriage (discussed in Chapter 17), one can consider one's marriage reasonably safe from collateral damage.

Affairs kill marriages

This too, surprising as it may seem, is a myth. Most marriages which have had to deal with infidelity do not end up in divorce. Nor do they end up as marriages of convenience (I have dealt extensively with marriages of convenience in *The Fifty-50 Marriage: A Return to Intimacy*). In fact, what happens is that many couples use affairs as wake-up calls and once they have healed from the trauma of infidelity, work on addressing hitherto unresolved issues in the marriage. Yes, affairs do traumatise marriages. Of that there can be no doubt. But traumas do heal, if both partners are committed to the healing process.

I am sure that couples like Shaila and Ajay, Rattan and Anita and Samarth and Asha, will pull through and their marriages will be much the better for it. In fact, some couples in research projects have stated that, much to their own surprise, the affair actually ended up improving their marriage. Although this is still an isolated finding and has to be interpreted with caution. It doesn't mean that all of us have to go out and have affairs to get more out of our marriages, nor should this finding be seen as something that can legitimise the affair.

However, some marriages do break up after an affair. In fact, infidelity is often cited as a ground for divorce and the accusing partner generally has an upper hand in the divorce proceedings if infidelity is provable in court. Very often, marriages that break post-infidelity are those in which schisms were already very deep to begin with and the affair just served to set a seal on the irreconcilable differences between the partners. Sometimes, marriages break up because the aggrieved partner is simply unable to come to terms with the act of betrayal, perhaps because of very deep-seated and strongly-held value systems or because of the choice of paramour—usually someone the aggrieved spouse hates or is an enemy of, or someone who is closely related, or someone who belongs to a different socio-economic background, like a maidservant or chauffeur.

As a rule of thumb, cuckolded men tend to break off marriages more than aggrieved wives, when infidelity is in evidence, but this has largely been because of the influence of patriarchy and the economic dependence of women. In other words, men lose their sense of masculinity when their wives have affairs, and to save face have no other social option but to punish them terribly by divorcing them. And women, because they're economically dependent on men, have no option but to stay in the marriage, for they have nowhere else to go.

But, with the rapid changes in urban social mores, this too has changed, for neither partner feels as compelled to stay in the marriage as did their parents, and therefore do tend more often than earlier to use divorce as an option to deal with infidelity. These, though, remain in the minority.

Once a person has one affair, then more will surely follow

This too, is a popular, though fallacious belief. How widespread it is can be evidenced by the number of people who refuse to respond to couples therapy following infidelity.

Like Manpreet, who had gone in for couples therapy with her husband Manjeet after she had discovered that he'd been having an affair with their eighteen-year-old live-in maid. The affair had come to light after the maid had tearfully confessed to Manpreet that she was pregnant with Manjeet's child. Initially, Manjeet refused to accept his role in the pregnancy and insisted he was being framed by the girl, who had been hired to look after their young child since both Manjeet and Manpreet worked. Initially, Manpreet believed her husband, but the girl's pleas were also hard to ignore. Manjeet had insisted that she must have got involved with one of the drivers in the building, which Manpreet thought was a plausible explanation.

Still, the question of what to do with the girl was something they had to face. The obstetrician they went to took pity on the girl, for she believed the girl was telling the truth. The maid was able to describe in detail whatever Manjeet had done to her and even went to the extent of describing some anatomical peculiarities of Manjeet's genitals that she could never have known unless she'd seen them. Manpreet confronted Manjeet together with the obstetrician (who was her mother's friend), but he continued to resort to stout denial, until the obstetrician suggested that a DNA test of the foetus could clinch the diagnosis. Unable to protest any more in the face of possible scientific evidence, Manjeet broke down and confessed that he was the one to blame for the pregnancy. Manpreet was devastated, not only because Manjeet had slept with the maid, but because he had succeeded in convincing her that he was being framed. He was perfectly willing to slander the poor girl just so he could get off the hook. All her assumptions of Manjeet and his 'decency' and the halo he had acquired in their community for all the service he did for the poor and deserving, were shattered, for he had revealed himself to be a 'low-down' sort of man.

Following a medical termination of pregnancy, the maid was sent back to her village. Manpreet quit her job, refused to hire any more live-in maids, and went into deep depression. For the sake of their children, she didn't want to publicly humiliate her husband, as a result of which she had suffered alone. Unwilling to give up on the marriage, for a variety of social reasons, she suffered her husband's presence in the house and forced herself to act normal in front of the kids.

Manjeet, on his part, was initially belligerent, saying that since she refused to 'give him sex', he had to seek it outside. It was true that she'd been passing through a phase over the past year when she'd been completely off sex. He had claimed to understand this. She had never been a person with a particularly high sex drive even in the early days of the marriage, and this too, she thought, had been okay with him. Over the weeks, Manjeet became very remorseful and ashamed of what he had done, and begged her forgiveness. He spoke to his uncle and had him speak to Manpreet too, asking her to forgive her 'weak' husband who had now seen the light. Manjeet spent a lot of time in prayer to rid himself of his demons.

Manpreet was still not convinced and, despite several sessions of couples therapy, remained in doubt. She seemed simply unwilling to move on. Her therapist realised, from other aspects of her behaviour, that she had healed but was unwilling to let Manjeet off the hook and resume normal married life. On further probing, she revealed that she had been told that once a man had an affair, there was every likelihood that he would have more, particularly if the wife forgave him. So, she was very fearful that if she ever let him forget this episode, he would stray again.

Manpreet's is a legitimate fear, of course, since the last thing she had expected was that her spouse would ever betray her. However, it is more likely than not, a baseless one. There are some people who do have multiple affairs, but those who do, do so regardless of whether their spouse has forgiven them or not. In fact, the spouse's refusal to forgive can well be rationalised as the very reason for the next affair (*Okay, so you refuse to forget and forgive, so I'll seek solace in someone else's more appreciative arms*).

Nevertheless, the number of people this applies to is miniscule. The majority of transgressors, particularly those who feel genuine remorse for their infidelity and want to fix their marriage, rarely, if ever, have another affair in their lives. I hope Manpreet recognises this sooner than later, and allows herself to relax her vigil and start living a normal life again.

Trust, once broken, is impossible to rebuild
(Will I ever trust again?)

This is the question that Uma still asks herself two years after she discovered that her husband, Ganesh, was having an affair with her younger sister, Rama. Uma had come home unexpectedly early one day, and found her husband and Rama in a passionate clinch with their clothes off. Rama and her husband, Bharat, lived next door to them and the two sisters, while being reasonably loving to each other, could not really be considered close. There was an age difference of about ten years that separated them, but they did spend a lot of time together because Bharat travelled a lot on work, and since Rama had neither children nor a job, had little to do to keep herself busy. So she did help Uma a lot, since Uma had to manage not only her household chores, but also two children, as well as her job at a nationalised bank.

But, after the discovery of the affair, Uma was shell-shocked. She could see only one thing in her mind's eye: the vision of her husband and her sister together and the abandon with which they were enjoying each other. She heard in her mind's ear the passionate sounds they were making and the things Ganesh was saying to Rama, things he had never once said to her in all their married life. For three days, she didn't come out of her room despite her children's pleas and Ganesh's implorations. Her sister wisely stayed away.

When Uma finally emerged, she felt she knew what had to be done. She called for a family meeting. Her parents and two other siblings rushed to town, another sister hooked herself in on Skype since she lived overseas, and a bemused Bharat was asked to bring his parents without Rama's knowledge. When the day of the meeting arrived, an unprepared Rama was dragged into the meeting where she and Ganesh were humiliatingly denounced and roundly abused by Uma as well as the horrified family. A lot of drama followed over the next few days with Rama attempting suicide, and a semblance of normalcy was restored only after Bharat decided to shift out of town with his wife in tow.

It's been two years since all that happened, but even today, Uma cannot bring herself to trust her husband. She monitors all his activities, checks his emails and mobile phone twice a day. He has to report to her where exactly he is whenever she has a doubt in her mind. She questions him closely about all his work colleagues, especially women. She insists that he have sex with her every day and say the things to her that she heard him telling Rama. She has taken long leave from the bank and is still reluctant to resume her career, since she fears that her husband has not seen the error of his ways. She believes she can never trust him again. 'How can I?' she moans. 'With my own sister?' She feels that she's a victim of a double whammy. Not only had her husband strayed, but to do so with her own sister was, in her opinion, a criminal act that only very depraved men would engage in.

Actually, the spouse's sister or cousin or other member of the family are the most favoured choice of paramour among the middle classes in our country. This is largely because their social network largely comprises the members of the family or extended family. It's easier for people in this situation to get intimate with someone from an existing social network than try to forage around outside and run the risk of being rebuffed. This, of course, doesn't mean that Indian extended families are abuzz with extramarital relationships. What I'm saying is that if Uma and Ganesh belonged to a more urbane social environment, and if one of them was to have an affair, they would probably have chosen someone from their social network to have it with. In Ganesh and Rama's case, since their primary social network was their extended family, they chose to have an affair with each other.

Trust is one of the pillars of any marriage. When one gets married, whether or not it is explicitly stated, it's certainly implicit that either partner can trust that the other will maintain exclusivity when it comes to the spouse and not get involved with any other person, emotionally, sexually or both. So when a breach of trust occurs as it does in situations of infidelity, is it possible to ever rebuild that trust? Is the hurt so deep that the aggrieved partner can never trust the betraying partner again?

The short answer: Yes to the first and no to the second. Yes, a breach of trust has taken place that both partners will have to heal from, but the scars of infidelity are never so deep that they can never heal. Anybody who's ever been in a situation of infidelity and has healed from it will remember that they too went through this phase of fearing that they would never trust their partners again. But trust, while being a non-negotiable commodity, is certainly recoverable, provided that 1) both partners agree that a breach of trust has occurred, 2) that both partners agree that the said breach of trust occurred during a period of vulnerability, 3) that the transgressor feels remorse for the breach of trust, 4) that both partners are equally committed to the rebuilding process and 5) that there is never a repetition of the breach of trust again.

What did I do wrong? Am I so undesirable?

This is another question that many people ask themselves when their partners have affairs. Let's be absolutely clear about one thing. The affair happened not because you did anything wrong or were undesirable in any way. It happened because your partner chose to have an affair. There may be issues in your marriage, many of them unresolved too, but this does not mean that you're responsible for the affair. Some partners do tend to put the blame on the aggrieved partner saying something like

'If you had not done this or that, maybe I wouldn't have felt the need to have an affair'.

This is absolute tosh. Even if what your partner accuses you of is true, having an affair is not the appropriate response. There are many different ways to deal with unfulfilled expectations, and having an affair is not one of these.

So, even if you've let yourself go and put on weight in recent times, or are not looking as attractive as you did when you got married, believe me, these are not reasons enough to justify an affair. It is conceivable that your partner may have warned you to look after yourself, lose some weight or whatever, and you may not have paid attention to these. However, even so, if your partner attempts to justify the affair on the basis of these warnings, please don't get on the back foot, for this is not an acceptable way of legitimising an affair. I'm not suggesting you occupy the moral high ground because you didn't have an affair, but the affair happened not because you did something to make it happen or that there was some terrible lack in you that forced your partner to have an affair. It happened because your partner chose it to happen.

After an affair, the marriage is never the same again

Again, not true. More often than not, if couples work on their marriage after infidelity has taken place, the marriage actually becomes better. However, if you choose to just overlook the affair and not do any work on the marriage to strengthen it, then the marriage may stay in the same place it always was, or even take a couple of steps back. It's only when couples use the affair as a vehicle of control that the marriage begins to deteriorate.

Like Kartik did when his wife Shubangi had an affair after almost twenty-six years of marriage. During all the years of their marriage, Kartik was the prototypical hen-pecked husband. Shubangi was firmly in control of their lives and the marriage, and to maintain peace in the home, Kartik went along with her decisions. She was careful not to take everything away from him, and gave him some room to do 'manly' things so he wouldn't feel emasculated. He was far from being a wimp, but he was too afraid to have an affair even though, on a couple of occasions, the opportunity did present itself.

Surprisingly, the one who had an affair was Shubangi. Unable to resist the advances of a mutual friend of theirs, she went headlong into an affair that she had neither planned nor bargained for. Unfortunately, their daughter had seen her at a coffee shop, giggling like a teenager and batting her eyelids at Uncle Sarvesh and generally, in her daughter's words, 'making a thorough mess of herself'. She told her father about it and together the two confronted Shubangi who, being a generally straightforward person, confessed everything. Overnight, the equation between Shubangi and Kartik changed forever. Kartik was now the injured party, a role he'd never been allowed to play. He became the magnanimous and forgiving husband, something that saw his esteem rising sharply in their daughter's eyes.

As well as those of Shubangi. She couldn't understand how she could have been so stupid, how she could done something so unlike her and behaved like a teenager in love. She also knew, if the roles were reversed, she would never have been so generous to Kartik, and therefore, felt even more grateful to and humbled by his strength of character. Very understatedly, but very definitely, Kartik took Shubangi and their marriage over. He started calling the shots and every time she protested, he would make subtle references to the affair that would immediately silence her. He was, for the first time in their marriage, in the driver's seat, and deep within him, although he would never confess this to anyone, he was grateful to his friend Sarvesh for having seduced his wife.

Their marriage did change inalterably after the affair. From Kartik's point of view, this was for the better; from Shubangi's standpoint, she'd lost everything she'd carefully built over twenty-six years. But since neither had worked through the affair or their issues, their marriage still remains a controlling marriage, though the controller's position is now occupied by a new incumbent. In most other affairs, though, this is not the case. Some people do let the marriage slide terminally, but many people, in my experience, do try and get their marriage to a better place.

Only men have affairs

Who do you think men are having affairs with?

Although there's no hard data on this subject and although even in surveys women tend to find affairs less acceptable than do men, from professional experience I can tell you that even over twenty-five years ago (when I first started working with couples), large numbers of women too did have affairs. Infidelity is not testosterone-related at all. Granted, men in the past have had more opportunities to have affairs, but this is one area in which women have not been too far behind. It's of course more common for men to have primarily sexual affairs and for women to have more of the emotional or combined type of affairs. For women, sex is only an extension of the emotional equation, whereas for men, by and large, the emotional content happens, if at all, after the sexual liaison has taken place. Of course this is a generalisation, and current generations of urban men as well as women do tend to have more of the combined sort of affairs. The point is, both genders engage in infidelity.

There is nothing that has yet been convincingly demonstrated to show that either gender is more hard-wired to engage in infidelity. A lot of animal experiments are being carried out to see whether something in their DNAs could predispose either gender to have more affairs than the other. But at the moment all of this is too experimental to even bear describing. And if I have even mentioned it, it's only for completion's sake and not with the idea of raising the hopes of people that they could one day rationalise their propensity for infidelity as being in their DNA. For the moment, this too is a myth.

Having a fantasy is the same as having an affair

This might seem a bit much, particularly for those of you who enjoy a bit of fantasy. However, there are some people who believe that if their partners have even so much as thought of another person either romantically, emotionally or, worse, sexually, it would definitely constitute infidelity. Such people usually maintain the same standard for themselves as well, and if ever such a thing happens, they feel that they have betrayed their marital vows and go through untold agonies.

I personally feel they have set the bar too high—for themselves as well as their partners. It's very hard to go through life without feeling attracted to someone else. And the minute one recognises the attraction, some form or other of sexual, emotional or romantic arousal takes place. It's not uncommon for people to meet someone special, someone of the opposite gender, and wistfully ask themselves, 'Now why couldn't my spouse be like that?' or feel an immediate sexual arousal when they're around that person.

To some extent, this sexual attraction is chemically driven. What one can expect one's partner to do, is to not act on the attraction and get involved with the person in question. That's certainly reasonable. But to expect them not to feel attraction itself, is way too high a standard, and one impossible to sustain. I understand that you don't want to hear about who your partner's attracted to. But, every time you go out, if you're looking to see who your partner's looking at and assuming some sort of mental infidelity is happening every time you catch your partner looking at someone of the opposite gender, it is only going to end up pushing both of you away from each other. I would recommend some slack being cut here.

If you remember the story of Asha, Samarth and Rati (Chapter 2), although nothing major happened between Samarth and Rati, they did cross a line; they hugged and kissed each other. Of course, Asha went through a cataclysmic reaction when he told her about it, but at least one can understand that Samarth and Rati did, even if in a small way, act on their mutual attraction. But if Samarth had merely fantasised about doing this, and Asha had reacted similarly, then she might have been going over the top a bit.

I do understand the dynamic in operation here. The fear is that today's attraction could result in a line being crossed tomorrow. And the expectation is that the best way of preventing oneself from boundary violations is to not get attracted in the first place. However, this goes against natural forces, and one must trust that however attractive one's partner finds someone else of the opposite gender, lines are not necessarily going to be crossed. In the final analysis, we need to have more faith in our partners as well as in our own selves.

4

Why Do People
Have Affairs?

It's hard to tell why people have affairs. What makes them, in that brief moment of vulnerability, cross a line that they have hitherto respected? What is happening in their minds and perhaps in their married lives, that either enables or helps them rationalise, rightly or wrongly, to withdraw the exclusivity they have agreed to provide their spouse, and allow someone else into their lives? Even though each story has its own inherent dynamics and explanations, one still needs to be able to view the larger picture clearly in order to fit our piece of the jigsaw into it. Perhaps, an understanding of the different situations and contexts in which people cross their boundaries, may help in giving us a clearer picture.

In the following few chapters I propose to explore the different situations and contexts in which infidelity takes place, as well as the dynamics of some of these. The idea is to give you some sort of understanding of why you or your partner engaged in an extramarital relationship. Let me make it clear that I am not legitimising or helping you legitimise the act of infidelity, but only giving you a sort of template with which to view what happened in your marriage.

I will be addressing different types of affairs in the three predominant contexts that American infidelity researcher, Dr Shirley Glass again, has classified infidelity patterns into—the predominantly sexual type of affairs, the predominantly emotional type of affairs and the combined type of affairs (Chapter 2). Aside of these, I will be exploring some special types of affairs which have a psychological basis to them, as well as some that may not have a deep-seated psychological basis but still need to be dealt with differently. There may be some situations that I haven't covered, for I propose to address only the most common variations. However, on reading the following, you might get a fair idea of how to interpret your own situation.

5

The Predominantly
Sexual Affair

*T*his is the commonest variant of affairs, and would constitute, I imagine, at least 40 per cent of all instances of infidelity. You would expect that more men than women would engage in this sort of affair, and you would by and large be correct—with some caveats. Contemporary urban women who have, in recent times, become more in touch with their sexuality, are not averse to seeking a purely sexual relationship outside their marriage, particularly if they are dissatisfied with their marital sex lives. But what starts off as a purely sexual involvement for women, may end up more likely becoming an emotional involvement as well. In the past, women in low-sex marriages too sought sex outside their marriages. However, in view of the fact that they were economically dependent on their husbands, they had to make sure that it would not end in emotional involvement and would invariably choose partners whom they were unlikely to become emotionally involved with.

Typically, in those days, such women would find younger sexually deprived partners, who had no intention of getting into a committed relationship, but wanted sexual gratification. The stereotype of adolescent boys and young adult men losing their virginity to older married women does have some basis and was probably more prevalent till the 1980s or so. In current times of sexual liberation, though, teenage boys don't look to older women for sexual gratification, when they can seek it with teenage girls.

The 'not-enough-sex-at-home' affair

The garden-variety of the predominantly sexual affair is when—and this is a no-brainer—for whatever reason, there's either no or not enough sex happening in the marriage. It's not as if the mere absence of marital sex is going to immediately result in a search for it elsewhere. I have known couples whose marriages have not been consummated for long periods (five years and longer) still waiting it out, hoping things will change. The critical determinant of whether sex is sought outside the marriage is whether the non-functional partner is willing to do something about it or not.

As in the case of Sulekha, who had severe pain every time her husband, Rajan, tried to penetrate her. He wanted to take her to see a gynaecologist, but she refused to go along because she believed only in homeopathy and not Western medicine. Her homeopath (her aunt actually, and it is not known whether she was a trained homeopath or not) kept giving her medicines, but nothing seemed to change. Till things reached a point that Sulekha wouldn't even let Rajan attempt sex. She started talking about adopting a child.

A frustrated Rajan had a torrid sexual affair with Sulekha's single friend, who was trying to mediate between the two and allowed herself to get sucked in to a sexual vortex because she was as sexually deprived as Rajan was.

In Ayesha and Maqbool's marriage, the situation was different. Maqbool's sex drive was never very high to begin with, so the sex in their marriage was occasional and he always ejaculated prematurely. Immediately after, he always turned over and went to sleep, leaving Ayesha aroused and very frustrated. He refused to listen to her entreaties to visit a sex therapist. Finally, after ten years of this, Ayesha had a sexual affair with her co-worker and eventually even got emotionally involved with him, leading to a humiliating marital breakdown for Maqbool.

In both these marriages, the issue was not that the sex was not good enough. It was that neither Sulekha nor Maqbool was willing to take remedial measures. Today, sex therapists (qualified ones, mind you, not the ones who advertise on walls and send out flyers) have a variety of simple solutions to most sexual problems. Also, if there is a deeper medical problem, this too can be resolved. So, seeing a therapist may not be a bad idea if your sex life is not what both of you want it to be. It's far easier and less painful than getting involved in a sex-seeking affair.

The 'variety-seeking affair'

The second reason why predominantly sexual affairs take place is when marital sex gets a little monotonous and one of the partners feels the need to spice up the sex life a bit. There is a belief that variety helps.

It certainly does. A variety of positions and approaches, that is. Not necessarily a variety of partners.

For, as many people like Manish realised, whoever you have sex with, it does become monotonous with them too, after a while. He had launched into a torrid affair with his friend's wife, Sharada, when his friend had been posted overseas for a couple of years. Sharada couldn't join her husband because she had a school-going son in the XI Standard, and neither wanted to disrupt the boy's education. So she had stayed behind, but since the sex had gone out of her marriage a few years ago, she was more than willing to engage in a romp with Manish, who had always fancied Sharada.

The strange thing was that he still had an active sex life with his own wife, Nishi, and didn't really have too many complaints really. It was just that sex with Nishi seemed a little boring. And he was very excited about having sex with a new woman. So, an affair commenced. Initially, it was wonderful, but when he thought back about it later, it was largely to do with the forbidden fruit thing. The anticipation, the wait to snatch time together, the anxiety not be seen by the neighbours, all culminating in explosive sex. However, after a few weeks of this, Manish's interest in Sharada waned. In fact he found sex with Nishi far more interesting, for his wife was an active lover. Sharada was not and was, in fact, more conservative when it came to love-making. So after the novelty of the new body had worn off, Manish started trying to back off from Sharada. He avoided her calls, didn't answer her text messages and tried to give her as wide a berth as possible when they did occasionally turn up at the same social gathering.

This Nishi found a bit strange. Although she had never suspected that the two of them could have been involved, she found Manish's shortness with Sharada and his anxiety to get away from her very uncharacteristic. She tried to ask him, but he dismissed her questions airily. Unfortunately, Sharada had fallen in love with Manish, and became more and more persistent. In a desperate, but ill-advised attempt at getting him back, she spoke about their affair to Manish's sister-in-law (his brother's wife), who was part of her kitty circuit, pleading with the woman to persuade Manish to come back to her. That blew the lid off the affair, once and for all.

Nishi walked out on him, refused any attempts at reconciliation, insisted on an immediate divorce and got her way. Manish today deeply regrets his sexual misadventure. He also realises that he has no one to blame but himself. And what was worse, the sex he had sought was neither very different nor better.

Sometimes, a variety-seeking affair takes place because the spouse is unwilling to engage in sexual experimentation and prefers to pretty much 'get it over and done with' in the tried and tested method that they'd always adopted. Not that there is no sexual enjoyment; it is the uncompromising nature of the spouse who refuses to engage in any variations that seems to be the contributory factor.

This is the situation Ramaswamy found himself in. His wife, Sivakami, with whom he was otherwise very happy, was by nature not particularly adventurous about anything, let alone sex. They'd been married for thirty years, had married off a daughter and had a son of marriageable age who was then away in the US on an 'onsite project'. They had the house to themselves and Ramaswamy, who had suppressed all his sexual fantasies all the years while the children were growing up, wanted to give vent to these.

It's not as if they didn't have a sex life. They still had sex thrice or four times a week, and Sivakami believed that she was 'cooperating' well with her husband's need for sex. Left to herself she would have been happy to conclude their sex life, for she had a vague feeling that after the age of forty, the very act was slightly depraved. But she didn't want to suffer what her older sister had gone through, when she had flatly refused her husband's sexual advances, only to find that he was having it off with anyone he could lay his hands on, bringing them much social notoriety.

So Sivakami dutifully complied. And she did enjoy it, in whatever manner she was capable of. But she put her foot down when Ramaswamy suggested that they change sexual positions, did it in every room in the house including the bathroom and watched pornography while they were at it. She thought her husband had gone mad and suggested he visit a psychiatrist. He didn't make things easy for her, suddenly appearing in the kitchen with his clothes off, waving his erection at her. Or sneakily inserting a pornographic DVD and switching it on just when she sat down to watch her favourite soap. Or inserting print-outs of pictures of porn stars having sex in various impossible positions into her magazines. Or reading aloud from a well-thumbed-through copy of *The Illustrated Kama Sutra* when she sat down to her prayers, insisting that the *Kama Sutra* was as much of an ancient Indian religious text as whatever she was reading aloud from.

And stuff like that. She was fed up with him and once, in a moment of exasperation, told him to go and find himself another woman who he could do all these 'dirty things' with. She never expected he would follow her advice, never having done so in all their years of married life. This time, though, he did. One doesn't know how hard he looked, but he soon found an impoverished young widow in the neighbourhood, plied her with gifts and affection, and proceeded to live out all his fantasies with the young woman, who found him a surprisingly skilled and enthusiastic lover, and started demanding more and more from him. Ramaswamy discovered Viagra and was stupefied to find what wonders it did for his sexual prowess. He started progressively increasing his dose of the drug, which he could procure easily from distant pharmacies in the city from smirking sales assistants. Sivakami, who was relieved that her husband had stopped behaving like a sex maniac with her, assumed that he had eased off the pressure owing to her threat of walking away. She was confident that he would never stray, for who would want an old, bald, overweight, unattractive man like him?

She was also pleased that their sex life had reduced to a manageable once-a-week. So she was shocked to her core when the neighbourhood grapevine gleefully informed her of Ramaswamy's affair with the young widow. She confronted him as soon as he came home from one of his energetic romps with his paramour. At the same time, she noticed he was not looking very well, and complained of some chest pain. Initially, she thought he was faking it just to get out of a confrontation. But, she also saw he was looking pale. So he was rushed to hospital where he spent a couple of days in the intensive care unit owing to a mild coronary insufficiency. His doctor, who was obviously experienced in such matters, asked him if he had been taking a lot of Viagra. When Ramaswamy sheepishly nodded his head, he got a lecture from the doctor, was put on a strict diet, and told never to go near Viagra again, if he wanted to avoid coronary bypass surgery.

A chastened Ramaswamy went home and neither he nor his wife talked about sexual variations, although they had a reasonably content unviagrated sex life for several years. The poor abandoned widow left the city and found herself a new life far away, but not before she had got her erstwhile paramour to give her some kind of a settlement to begin a new life with.

Variety is not always the spice of life.

I have known some women who, after a certain age, are quite happy to let their husbands seek sex elsewhere, and the husbands do precisely this. The only requirements are that the husband does whatever he wants to do with discretion (very hard to comply with in the age of GPS), that the paramour not be permitted to become demanding (equally hard to comply with) and that no diseases are acquired (easier to comply with thanks to the latex industry). And so it's no longer uncommon to see older men on the prowl looking for sex in the oddest places. I suppose, if this arrangement works for both partners, it's then technically not infidelity and one doesn't need to explore this any further.

The 'cybersexual affair' or the 'e-affair'

A variation of the variety-seeking affair is the 'cybersexual' affair that is becoming increasingly common in these days of increasing broadband penetration. Typically, people who are a little wary of getting involved with someone they can touch and feel, tend to engage in cybersex with relative strangers. Sometimes, these affairs can also be conducted with someone they know, who's far away and unlikely to be actively involved in their lives in the foreseeable future.

Malini, whose sex life was stable if not wildly ecstatic, spent a lot of time on the Internet, predominantly on social networking sites. Out of the blue, on Facebook, she hooked up with Tanveer, a former colleague of hers who was now overseas. This colleague was known to have had a crush on her when they were working together. Malini never reciprocated because she felt he was not really her type. However, to kill time, she got chatting with him and he seemed to have matured a lot after moving to Europe. He was recently divorced, and sent her pictures of himself. He had also filled out a bit and had become a bit of a dasher, but did not seem, by his own admission, to have much luck with women.

She also sent him pictures of herself in various poses. One day, entirely unexpectedly, he sent her a sexually provocative message, something about her breasts. She was appalled. And excited. Sexually undertoned messages flew back and forth on their instant messenger, and in the course of the next few days they were having cybersex. Soon, tiring of this, they started having telephone sex and then—no prizes for guessing—sex on video chat. Malini couldn't believe she was doing this, but enjoyed it nevertheless. Then Tanveer became greedy. He showed up one day at Malini's doorstep. An aghast Malini slammed the door in his face and refused to let him in. She was terrified to actually see him in the flesh. So Tanveer went back to Europe where he renewed cybersexual contact with Malini again. This time she responded, and they started their relationship all over again. How long this will continue, I have no idea.

Malini is not crazy about the idea of infidelity, but she enjoys the cybersex so much, can't bring herself to stop. Her husband suspects nothing, for he spends a lot of time away at work, and since he is not very tech-savvy (he's an up-and-coming politician), he's quite happy that his wife is not making a fuss about his absence from home. Whether he has sexual liaisons outside the marriage is not really known, but she is sure he does. And she rationalises her behaviour by saying she has not touched another man and therefore is still 'chaste'. She doesn't think that what she's doing is risky and doesn't fear anyone hacking into her computer (she says she uses an external hard drive when she's with Tanveer). She's not worried about media-hackers either, for she thinks her husband is too small-time a politician for anyone to care. She feels she has all her bases covered. Only time will really tell.

The 'thunderbolt' affair

The next reason why predominantly sexual affairs happen is on account of one of the partners being struck by the *'thunderbolt'*. Out of the blue, even when the marital sex is perfectly satisfactory, one of the partners suddenly meets someone so sexually attractive, that the hormones can't be kept under control, and launches into a purely sexual liaison.

This is precisely what happened to Rattan and Shilpa (Chapter 2). Despite having a mutually satisfactory sex life, Rattan was hit by the thunderbolt when Shilpa came back into his life. As far as she was concerned, she had nothing to lose (but whether the same thunderbolt struck her, too, is not certain, because I'm not aware of her side of the story), but Rattan did have a lot to lose, despite which he allowed himself to be overwhelmed by his hormones.

Although this sort of thunderbolt thing happens more commonly to men, it does to women too. Rekha, a fitness enthusiast, found she couldn't resist her well-sculpted trainer at the gym she spent at least a couple of hours daily. She thought of him night and day in purely sexual terms, even though she was having what could be described as an energetic sex life with her husband. She eventually persuaded her husband to set up a gym in the house, hired the gym guy as a personal trainer and proceeded to have her way with him—without much protest from him, of course.

The chap was not particularly skilled at sex, but she was intoxicated with his aura and smell and simply had to have sex with him every day. She ended up thoroughly exhausting the chap, who quit the gym, moved away to another part of town and changed his mobile number. Soon Rekha realised that the same trainer had been 'training' several other women in the same gym, and his absence was felt by many of his other 'trainees' who were commiserating with each other when Rekha overheard them. She was disgusted with herself, more so when she found a few weeks later that the only thing she had to show for her affair was an unpleasantly recalcitrant fungal infection. Nobody found out about her affair, but Rekha is still disgusted with herself for what she allowed herself to do. She's still seeing a therapist once a week to work it out of her system.

Whatever the reason behind the sex-seeking affair, it needs to be emphasised that sex, by itself, cannot be the basis of a sustaining bond. There are the 'swinging' couples (discussed in Chapter 2), who mutually enjoy sexual variations, and many of them report that it does wonders for them. As long as both partners are okay with it, there's no real problem. It's only when one partner goes behind the other's back that catastrophes ensue. And even if you're never found out, it leaves its mark, as it did on Rekha. There are, admittedly, many people, particularly those who engage in one-night stands with strangers or those who engage in paid sex, who do feel that a little experimentation with new partners helps a lot. But a life of seeking momentary thrills is not the easiest thing to sustain, and even such people, after a while, realise the futility of it.

Attraction to other people is inevitable—but *acting* on it may not get you what you were looking for. If the marital sex is not satisfying enough, there are better ways to deal with this than by seeking another partner. Because the one who starts off as a temporary partner may not be willing to stay that way. Or *you* may end up falling in love with your paramour. And before you know what's happening, your sex-seeking affair will turn out to be a combined type of affair.

The 'peer-pressure affair'

This sort of affair is usually of a predominantly sexual kind and does not really occur because anyone is voluntarily looking for an affair for the heck of it, but because most of the members of the peer group that the individual belongs to are having, have had or intend to have affairs. The pressure to belong to the group moves the individual in the direction of a fling, with the peer group members acting as cheerleaders. Often, having an affair is a rite of passage for 'membership' in the group, and the ones who don't engage in the sexual part of the companionship, may end up being isolated or marginalised by other members of the group. Although by and large men are the greater subscribers to this form of affair, in recent times, women belonging to the upper-middle and upper socio-economic classes too seem to be having their share of 'fun'. As far as men are concerned, peer-pressure affairs cut across socio-economic classes.

Arif, an area manager with a pharmaceutical company, had grown up in a conservative environment in a small town. He was a good and conscientious worker, and even though not overly innovative or dynamic, had attracted the attention of his top management who considered him a valuable employee and gave him regular promotions and incentives. His marriage to Tahira was a good and stable one. Arranged by their families, the marriage had both of them feeling blessed to be with each other, for Arif was a kind and respectful husband and Tahira a gentle and loving wife. They had two children who were being well educated in good schools where they did reasonably well. Arif and Tahira's sex life was mutually very enjoyable and neither aspired for more. In short, an unremarkable, comfortable, middle-class story that may have stayed incident-free until they died. However, Arif's elevation to the position of regional sales manager queered the pitch a bit.

All of a sudden, instead of dealing with medical representatives who belonged to his social and educational environment, Arif's peer group now consisted of better-educated people from all over the country, who were articulate, well-travelled and urbane. He could match them as far as his work was concerned for he had a firm grip on his region and his sales figures. But in other areas, he found himself wanting. He neither smoked nor drank and just didn't enjoy going out to pubs and nightclubs. He was generally considered a wet blanket by the rest of his peers who started teasing and mocking him, initially subtly, and later more openly. Even some of the top management felt he was too rigid and his national sales manager had, during the last appraisal, told him that he needed to lighten up a bit and be more of a 'team player'.

For the first time in his life, Arif felt stressed. Tahira couldn't help him because she shared his values and believed that he was doing nothing wrong. All she could advise him was to do his namaaz regularly and leave the rest to Allah. He did this too, but things remained the same. Fortunately, he was producing enough results for the management to be happy with him, but the marginalisation by his peers continued unabated.

Until finally, he had to attend a special sales meeting his management had convened for top performers in the company at Bangkok.

He allowed himself to be persuaded by his peers and seniors to indulge in a 'special Thai massage' organised

for all the participants at the meeting. He had no idea
that the 'special' involved sex with the masseuse, and was
quite shocked with what the pretty woman was doing to
him. Filled with pleasure, he was loath to stop her and
pushed aside all thoughts of Tahira from his mind. But
after the 'massage', he was filled with an aching pain and
disgust for what he had done. He was greeted by his
colleagues very warmly when he met them for dinner, for
they had found out from the masseuse what had
happened in his room. For the first time he felt a sense of
acceptance by his peer group and the ensuing bonhomie
encouraged him to ask for more 'special massages'.

His colleagues were ecstatic with this 'conversion' of
Arif from a party-pooper to a fellow-adventurer. He was
now on warm back-slapping terms with all of them and
basked in a new-found popularity that compensated for
the guilt he felt when he saw Tahira again. But the guilt
came back later and hit him like a cyclone, a few weeks
after he returned. He could not bring himself to confess
to Tahira, but found himself unable to sexually perform
with her. No amount of amulets, potions and pills could
do the trick. Not surprisingly, he could have sex with
hookers every time he went out of town on sales trips,
but not with Tahira.

Even though peer-pressure affairs have their adverse
consequences, not everybody reacts like Arif did, and
many people who engage in such romps rationalise the
whole phenomenon as a 'necessary evil' and get on with
their lives until they get found out or until they join a new
peer group where affairs are considered inappropriate. It is
also not uncommon for groups of male buddies who go
out on a vacation to visit strip clubs and have lap dances,
or a group of female buddies to hire a male stripper and
kick up their heels. But it needs to be said that not all sales
conferences in Thailand are about 'special massages', nor

are all vacations with same-gender buddies an excuse to indulge in extramarital sexual activity.

The 'sex-addiction' affair

Dasharat refused to believe that his wife, Nilima, was a sex addict. He thought he had married a 'sweet, simple girl' that he had met and fallen in love with when both were in Germany doing an on-site project for their software companies. They had been instantly attracted to each other and had almost instantly got sexually involved as well. She was enthusiastic and demanding in bed, but he had been able to satisfy all her demands and he had thought they were a perfect match. Nilima had generally simple needs and was very loving, caring and nurturing. She was not aggressive and generally deferred to him in all key decisions. He had no hesitation in proposing to her and she had no hesitation in accepting. Since they belonged to the same community, their parents had no problems either and they soon got married.

The first year was sexually blissful for both. They made love every day, sometimes several times a day. Each couldn't have enough of the other and felt they were perfectly matched. A few months later, Dasharat was posted to Germany again for six months. Unfortunately, Nilima couldn't accompany him since she had to do a stint in Mexico around the same time. She insisted that he buy her a vibrator so she could continue to derive sexual gratification during their time apart. He thought this was a bit strange, but did so without commenting on it.

After they were reunited, Nilima continued to be sexually demanding although, by now, Dasharat was beginning to fade a bit. Not that he didn't enjoy the sex, but he couldn't do it every day. He suggested that they have a baby in the hope that this might get Nilima off sex. She was quite enthusiastic and a year later they had a son. However, nothing could keep Nilima away from Dasharat. Even though the child slept in their room, she insisted on having sex until her husband lost it and accused her of being a 'nymphomaniac'. She withdrew from him, deeply hurt, and went into a shell. They did resume a sex life of sorts, but the searing passion had cooled down and soon they were having only weekend sex. Nilima seemed to have become happier and Dasharat started relaxing around her a bit. However, one day when he was using her laptop, he discovered a large stash of porn on it. Also a lot of chat transcripts of an overtly sexual nature with strangers as well as with some of their male friends. Furious, he confronted Nilima, who broke down and confessed to him that aside of porn and cybersex, she had also been involved with multiple sexual partners—strangers as well as friends—over the preceding year. She told him that she just couldn't do without sex and had to have sex at least once a day. For as long as he was having sex with her daily, there had been no problem, but once he stopped doing that, she started looking elsewhere, for the vibrator had stopped satisfying her a long time ago. She felt unhappy, wretched and distressed when she didn't have sex and felt considerably relieved after she managed to get her needs gratified by a man. She was not happy about the situation, but it seemed to be beyond her control. A horrified Dasharat took her to see a sex therapist who diagnosed Nilima to be a sex addict.

Sex addiction, though not really a common phenomenon, has generally been under-reported, since sex addicts rarely underwent psychotherapy or any other form of intervention. But recent celebrity sexcapades have brought the phenomenon under media focus. It is increasingly being considered a diagnosable mental condition akin to other addictions, and it appears that similar brain pathways may be involved in the problem. Sex addiction is characterised by an overpowering impulse to have sex, the denial of which results in withdrawal symptoms (as Nilima experienced). It's not as if sex addicts are addicted to seeking multiple partners. They are only addicted to sex and if the committed partner is able to meet their requirements, they have no desire to look elsewhere, for what they're seeking is sex and not variation. Nevertheless, it's often very difficult for their partners to give them what they need every time they need it, as a result of which they tend to seek it wherever they can. It's easier for women to find sex for there are more men out there who are willing to respond to the need for casual sex than there are women. Of course, celebrities of either gender have it even easier, for they have no dearth of takers.

Sex addiction is a serious clinical condition that requires to be treated. It shouldn't be confused with the high sex drive that some people have. Nor should it be used as an excuse for sexual profligacy. I have seen several people who engage in variety-seeking affairs trying to offer sex addiction as an excuse for their behaviour. They often back down when I suggest that they may need hospitalisation and medical treatment for their problem. Fortunately it is not a common clinical condition. All that needs to be remembered is that it can happen.

6

The Predominantly
Emotional Affair

It's not very often that affairs remain predominantly emotional, for when emotional involvement takes place, sex does usually enter the picture, more often than not as a consummation of the emotional engagement. There are some affairs, though, where the sexual line is never crossed, so the protagonists reason that they are not having an 'affair'. But as we had discussed in Chapter 2 and had seen in Shaila's and Shailesh's story, the emotional intimacy intense enough to detract from the marriage, the secrecy and the associated guilt provided clear evidence that an affair was taking place, regardless of their protestations to the contrary. Had it been undetected, Shaila's and Shailesh's affair may have progressed to a combined sexual and emotional affair or may have just petered out. Whether theirs would have remained a predominantly emotional affair or whether it was an interrupted combined affair-in-progress is hard to tell, because they had not yet reached the crossroads that many relationships reach: when both protagonists have to decide whether to take it to the next level or not.

It is customary to say that women engage more in emotional affairs than do men, but the fact that they choose to have their emotional affairs with the opposite gender obviates such a conclusion. All that can be said is that women do tend, by and large, to be attracted more emotionally than sexually—and may engage in sex more as an expression of love—but in contemporary urban India, this too may not stand up to scrutiny, for more and more women are quite comfortable engaging in sexual and combined affairs than before.

Perhaps a more interesting development is the emergence of the metrosexual man who, too, is quite comfortable in engaging in a predominantly emotional affair without wanting to take it to a sexual level, sometimes because of a lack of opportunity to do so, sometimes because he feels that doing so would diminish the purity of his emotions for his paramour, or sometimes because he fears that any possible sexual incompatibility may send their relationship on a downward spiral.

I would like to explore in this chapter only those affairs that usually remain predominantly emotional affairs and rarely, if ever, involve a sexual component. The ones that tend to end up as combined emotional and sexual affairs tend to follow their own distinctive patterns and will be described in some detail in the next chapter.

The 'soulmates' affair

In Chapter 1, we met Bhavna, a thirty-eight-year-old homemaker who left her husband and teenage daughters to pursue a relationship with Arshad, twenty-one years her senior, whom she had met on the Internet and who she felt was her soulmate. I am not referring to this sort of relationship when I refer to the 'soulmates' affair in this chapter, for Bhavna's and Arshad's relationship was a combined emotional and sexual affair, even though the initial connect had been an emotional one. The type of affair I now refer to is a purely emotional equation between two people who refuse to break away from their marital partners, but still insist on conducting an emotional relationship with each other because they believe they are soulmates and cannot do without each other. They expect their marital partners to accept this relationship because there is nothing sexual involved, and therefore they rationalise to anyone who cares to listen that what is going on between them is a sort of 'divine connection' and not a sordid affair. Needless to say, the marital partners are hard pressed to understand this soulmate thing (and often never do), but astonishingly, once they realise that there is no real threat to the marriage, are more likely than not, inclined to accept it and get on with their lives.

When questioned by his wife Shakira as to why he was spending so much time with their attractive neighbour, Rachel, Javed declared that he and Rachel were soulmates. And anyway, her husband, Chacko, didn't seem to mind, so what was Shakira's problem? Shakira hit the roof. She refused to accept the presence of another woman in their marriage and insisted they move out of the apartment immediately. She met Chacko and was aghast that he didn't seem to mind Rachel's relationship with Javed. 'They're only soulmates,' he laughed. 'They're not sleeping with each other.' He seemed sure that his wife would never get into a sexual liaison with anyone else. But Shakira wasn't sure that Javed wouldn't. Yet, in spite of all her dramatic protests, Javed refused to let go of his relationship with Rachel, for he genuinely believed that they would never get into a sexual relationship with each other.

He explained to Shakira, as patiently as he could, that he and Rachel were like brother and sister, that they just enjoyed each other's company and spent most of their time with each other talking about life, philosophy and the like, that they were both deeply connected to their respective religions and that neither would ever leave their spouses because of this. This Shakira could believe, because she knew that Javed was deeply involved with Islam and Rachel with Christianity. A devout Catholic, Rachel was actively engaged in a variety of church activities, was part of a Bible study group and did not believe in the concept of divorce. Javed did his namaaz five times a day, was a Haji, an active member of several mosque-related committees and volunteered time instructing young children in the tenets of Islam.

Finally, after several months of feeling angry, hurt and in some way, violated, Shakira accepted Javed's and Rachel's relationship. She could never get it out of her mind, though, that he spent more time with Rachel than with her. She was uncomfortable with the text messages and endearments that flew back and forth. She could still not come to terms with the idea that they could say 'I love you' to each other, particularly since Javed had rarely said this to her. She felt that their sex life was more mechanical than before, but he thought she was imagining it. They seemed to spend less time together than they used to and she felt terribly inadequate that she could not converse with her husband on the subjects that Rachel and he seemed so much at ease with.

On the advice of her mother, Shakira decided not to say anything more to Javed, accepting her mother's reassurance that after all, Javed was not talking of divorce and that she was still his wedded wife. And besides, where would she go, if she left him? She was a homemaker and had no other skills. Her parents couldn't look after her any more since they were old and dependent on their son, who was not particularly close to Shakira anyway. So, she dismissed all thoughts and decided to wait it out until Javed and Rachel lost interest in each other. Every day, she prayed for this to happen.

Not all spouses are as accepting as Shakira. When Phiroza found her soulmate in Sagar, her husband Minoo served her an ultimatum as soon as he found out about it. Phiroza had been passing through a phase of a lot of personal angst about her life, and was not happy with her work, marriage—and life itself. She had tried her best to come to terms with her marriage, but she felt Minoo was too earthy and pragmatic to understand what was happening in her mind. He could never relate to her feeling that she was at odds with the world ever since she was a child and that she was somehow meant for higher things than being a financial analyst. Her career was at a dead end; her children didn't need her any more since they were now teenagers; Minoo would have been happy with anyone who cooked a decent *dhansak* and gave him sex twice a week. And her only friend from childhood had emigrated a few years ago to the United States.

She had seen a doctor and a psychologist, but was unable to get anywhere in her life. Until she came upon, by accident, a neighbourhood *Soka Gakkai* group. She had been persuaded by her friend Renu to just attend one chanting session and see if it made a difference to her. It did. And soon she was hooked to this Buddhist group, where she met Sagar, who became her self-appointed mentor. Gradually, Phiroza and Sagar began to feel that they were connected at a spiritual level and their mutual dependency started to grow.

Initially, Minoo had tolerated Phiroza's involvement with the Soka Gakkai, even though he found the whole thing bizarrely esoteric. As long as Phiroza was not intending to give up her Zoroastrian faith, he was okay with all her idiosyncrasies. But when she began to neglect her 'wifely duties', he grew annoyed. And when he realised that she was spending her Sunday mornings chanting with Sagar at his residence instead of going to the Soka Gakkai group sessions, he was really angry. In a showdown, he accused her of carrying on with Sagar.

She was very calm, since she had just come back from a chanting session, and told him that she was not having an affair but that she had found her soulmate in Sagar. This enraged him and he forbade her from having anything to do with Sagar. He was uncompromising. She had to choose between Sagar and Minoo. After much thought, chanting and discussions with Sagar and other Soka Gakkai members, Phiroza chose to stay in her marriage, and her brief, but intense relationship with her soulmate came to a premature end.

It isn't at all uncommon for soulmates to connect on only one or two aspects that each seems to find missing in their respective marriages or lives.

Ramila and Naresh had been married for close to twenty-five years when he found himself a soulmate. Theirs had been a reasonably comfortable marriage, though Naresh always felt that this was because he went along with most of Ramila's irrational wants. Their lifestyle had been dictated by the way she wanted to live. Their social network consisted of people she wanted to be friendly with. Their vacations were planned on the basis of where she wanted to go. Their children were brought up the way she thought was appropriate.

This was not the way Ramila experienced the marriage. She maintained that before any decision was taken, she and Naresh had long discussions, and whatever decisions they took were mutually accepted ones. She didn't see herself as the prima donna he was making her out to be.

That he had married above him was evident to both of them as well as to everyone in their respective families. He came from a lower middle-class background and had studied in a village school in the vernacular until he came to the city to do his college education, which is when they met each other. She was city-born and bred and came from an upper middle-class professional background, and it astounded everybody in their respective social networks when they announced to the world that they were going to get married to each other.

Their parents were too stunned to offer any valid objections, so they soon got married and emigrated to the United States, where they, to everyone's pleasant surprise, had an uneventful marriage and two children. There was never any indication that anything was wrong in the marriage, and in truth, there wasn't. While not ecstatic, they were certainly happy and had some very good times with each other. But over the last year, Naresh had become a little withdrawn and moody and seemed to be pining for India. So she suggested that they come back to India for a year or two and see how comfortable they were here. They had the usual teething problems in a new place, but found they were able to slip into a reasonably comfortable routine.

A couple of months after their return, Naresh was approached by some old friends from his village to help in renovating the temple there. On one of his visits, he met Sita, also a former resident of the same village, a few years his senior, who now lived in the city and was anxious to do something for her village. Sita was overweight and unattractive, but made up for these shortcomings by being a sunny and cheerful person. Naresh and Sita found a lot in common with each other, specifically their passion for old Hindi film songs, Vedanta, and traditional Indian recipes. Naresh had been able to share none of these with Ramila who was more 'urban-Westernised' in her taste.

Soon, Naresh and Sita started spending a lot of time with each other and had long conversations on the phone as well. He kept this relationship from Ramila since he felt that she would never be able to relate to Sita who was from, and remained, in a completely different social and economic class. Needless to say, Ramila found out soon enough about Naresh's soulmate with whom he exchanged sweet text messages, the most incriminating being one in which he had quoted some lines from an old Hindi film song to the effect that since he had given her his heart, he would also give her his life.

Ramila flew into a rage and went to meet the woman her husband was getting mushy with. She was aghast when she saw Sita. 'How could you think that cow is your soulmate? Did I marry a cowherd?' was her repeated question to him. He weakly tried to defend Sita, at which point, six months before their silver wedding anniversary, Ramila walked out on Naresh, was uncompromisingly unavailable for any effort at rapprochement and divorced him as soon as she was legally able to. Naresh is now single and unhappy because Sita refuses to leave her husband because 'he is a good man, and there has never been a divorce in my family'. But they continue to remain soulmates.

Obviously, Naresh was missing some elements in his marriage, as a result of which he never felt completely connected to Ramila. When he married her, he knew what he was getting into, but the excitement at being accepted by such a desirable woman—who was the college belle and clearly someone whom a country bumpkin like him could rarely have aspired to marry—was overwhelming at the time. Also, in fairness, she had done a lot to smooth over potentially awkward situations and had loved him for who he was without overtly trying to make him over. But when he met Sita, some long-buried needs of his had resurfaced and he had fallen headlong into a relationship with the kind of person he would have ended up marrying had not Ramila accepted him.

soulmate relationships are as threatening to a marriage as any other form of extramarital liaison, whether or not sex is involved. The perceived implication in a soulmate equation is that in some way or the other, the partner finds someone else closer to being a perfect match than the spouse. Put differently, but for the marriage, the two soulmates would have gladly made a commitment to each other and consummated their relationship. If the individual still chooses to stay in the marriage and pursue an equation with the soulmate, the spouse obviously feels 'second-best'—and who among us is prepared to accept such an evaluation?

If indeed the paramour is a soulmate, why stay on in the marriage? Why not pursue that relationship more openly? These are the questions that can be—and often are—legitimately asked by the aggrieved partner. The transgressing partner usually comes up with some rationalisation in response, but never really a satisfactory one. Of course, some people, like Bhavna, feel the need to be true to themselves and end up marrying the soulmate. Unfortunately, they often end up finding that the soulmate is not such a great marital partner after all, for marriage requires more than just a 'soul connection'.

But again, a lucky few find that their decision to take up with the soulmate was the best one they've ever made and worth the pain they suffered and caused, when they tore themselves apart from their erstwhile marriage and family.

Even those like Shakira who compel themselves to accept their partners' soulmate, do so only because they don't have viable alternatives, for remaining in a marriage where they feel second-best diminishes them and the marriage. Just think of it. Always knowing that although your partner has sex only with you, the soulmate is the preferred choice when it comes to emotional and intellectual connectivity, can't be easy to live with. Shakira saw herself principally as a sex object, the mother of Javed's children and the keeper of their home. Hardly ingredients for a substantial sense of self-worth, don't you think?

The Cyber-emotional affair

This sort of affair is not much different from the cyber-sexual affair, except that the focus is on emotional connectivity, not sexual expressiveness. The dynamics are similar in that both affairs are conducted exclusively in cyberspace, perhaps owing to the discomfort that one or both of the participants experience in conducting a face-to-face relationship. There seems to be some sort of security in the feeling that the paramour is more virtual than real and this, in a strange way, serves to elevate the relationship. It's pretty much like having a 'phantom lover', and both participants end up vesting in each other qualities and attributes that the other may not really possess. And yet the feeling of being loved and cherished is very real and this is the buzz that both partners are looking for.

At some point of time, the cyber-relationship too, much like any other relationship, does grow and then the partners have to decide where to take it from there. Has it become too close for comfort? Should they dump each other and move on, always remembering this brief sojourn in their lives with affection and warmth? Or should they meet and see if the emotional chemistry exists in real life too? Unfortunately, unless they are extraordinarily tech-savvy, the cyber-paramours soon end up getting 'caught' by their spouses, and taking a call on their relationship is forced on them. That said, it is not uncommon for cyber-relationships to proceed to consummation as happened with Bhavna in Chapter 1, but for the most part they seem to peter off after a point.

It is very rare for a cyber-relationship to become a long-term one, but I have known this to happen typically when both participants in the relationship know each other beforehand. But when the cyber-partner is a relative stranger whom one has met more by chance in a chat room or some such space, the relationship tends to be short-lived when the need it served no longer exists.

As happened with Harsha and Mala. Harsha was an investment banker by profession but a novelist by aspiration. He had written a novel but was unable to find a publisher and was quite disheartened. He had dreams of quitting investment banking and becoming a full-time writer, but his lack of success in placing his first novel was a huge stumbling block. He found little support from his prosaic wife, Nimmi, who did not share his dreams. The last thing she wanted to be was a writer's wife. She had chosen him because he was an investment banker, and she frequently quarrelled with him saying that had he so much as hinted that he wanted to be a writer, she would never have linked her lot with him. She was convinced that writers made a pittance and she was too much a creature of comfort to ever swap her financial security for something as ephemeral as creative satisfaction.

'A Chetan Bhagat comes along only once in a blue moon,' she frequently admonished him. A frustrated

Harsha put up some excerpts from his novel on his blog, hoping some bored publisher would come across it and it would make publishing history. His blog was not a very popular one, but his novel did excite the curiosity of a random visitor, and Mala entered his life. She, too, was an unpublished writer and soon they were sharing each other's writing, giving each other constructive criticism and generally supporting each other through their bleakest moments. When they had exhausted the subject of their writing woes, they soon started crying on each other's shoulders about the insensitivity of their respective spouses. The relationship progressed rapidly and they exchanged pictures and stories of their lives, some of which even their spouses were unaware of.

Since Mala lived in Australia, they didn't have the opportunity to meet each other, but their love for each other grew. Sex never entered the picture, for both were incurable romantics and were as much in love with the idea of unconsummated love as they were with each other. Mala had to go off cyberspace for several months when she went through a nasty post-partum depression (Harsha did feel a stab of jealousy that even as she was in love with him, she was sleeping with her husband and having his child). During this period, Harsha's novel found a publisher (through an investment-banking friend) and was not merely published but went on to become a bestseller. Since writing a bestseller in our country gets you well known, even though it doesn't really pay too many bills, Harsha continued with his job and started on his second novel.

What changed most in his life was Nimmi's attitude to him. Amazed by his success, a newfound respect for Harsha and his capabilities was aroused in her and almost overnight she became very supportive of his second novel, giving him the space to write and offering to take on a boring but well-paying job herself so he could give full vent to his creativity. Harsha had never been happier.

When Mala eventually recovered from her depression and re-established contact, with a long email describing the woeful time she had had, he quickly deleted it from his inbox and added her to his blocked senders list. He also unfriended her from his social networking accounts and deleted her from his buddy list on his messenger. Till today, Nimmi has no clue of this cyber-affair that her husband had. And what Mala must have gone through, I have no idea. But the relationship had served its purpose for Harsha and he hopes one day to acknowledge her as tangentially as he can in one of his forthcoming novels.

The love-addiction affair

Love addicts are not very different from sex addicts except that they are addicted to the buzz of falling in love, and sex is not really what they hanker after. While, unlike sex addiction, love addiction is not considered to be a psychiatric disorder, *love junkies* do exist in larger numbers than one would imagine.

Arjun's and Priya's marriage had been arranged by their parents and they felt comfortably compatible with each other for the first year. After this their marriage became less than tolerable for each had expectations that the other simply couldn't fulfil. Priya fell in love with a co-worker, who she felt was more compatible with her than was Arjun, and soon launched into a torrid affair with him. Arjun soon found out and the affair was abruptly terminated after a family panchayat was summoned at Arjun's instance. Arjun felt that, although he was the wounded party, he must be generous and take Priya back for the sake of the family prestige. So he did.

Nothing much changed in the marriage, though. They continued to be distant and unconnected but performed whatever roles were expected of them, including 'duty sex' every now and again. But Priya was painfully unhappy. Never having been in love during her sheltered teenage years (save for the regulation adolescent crushes on Shah Rukh Khan and Sachin Tendulkar), she had for the first time in her life experienced all the heady emotions and the neurochemical buzz (principally a chemical messenger in the brain called dopamine) of romantic love and she just couldn't get enough of it. She held out for several months, after which she fell madly in love with one of Arjun's friends who had been trying to hit on her ever since she'd been married. Fortunately, fear of discovery, and the fact that he was too much like Arjun for her comfort, ensured that this didn't last long. She fell out of love with him, but was pining to be in love again.

Soon, after seeing a movie called *Dhobi Ghat*, where the protagonist is a dhobi, she fell in love with the young boy who came to their house to do their ironing. She fell *out* of love with him soon enough when she realised that all the young man wanted was sex. Over the next few years, she fell repeatedly in love with different people— mostly co-workers, friends' husbands, husband's friends, a distant relative—only to fall out of love again.

With some of them she had sex; with most she didn't. Most of her love episodes remained undetected, save for three for which she had hell to pay. Even today, Arjun refers to her as 'the slut at home'. She seems to be 'cured' now in that she has been love-free for the last two years, and I hope she stays that way, for her love addiction has caused a lot of emotional harm to herself, her husband, her two sons, her parents and her siblings as well.

As described in *The Fifty-50 Marriage: A Return to Intimacy*, the experience of romantic love is related to bursts of secretion of certain chemicals in the brain called the substituted phenylethylamines, of which dopamine and noradrenaline are primarily implicated as the 'love chemicals'. They produce a sense of euphoria and well-being just like the synthesised substituted phenylethylamines such as amphetamine ('speed') do. So it is but natural that those of us who are prone to addictions may get addicted to these 'love chemicals' and seek to be in a perpetual state of love to experience the 'high' associated with it. Sadly, since romantic love dies sooner rather than later, love junkies tend to fall in love again with someone new to get their 'fix'. However, it needs to be remembered that not all people who have multiple partners are love addicts. Many of them simply enjoy the illusion of self-worth, power and control that accompany multiple relationships. That they pass this off as love addiction is merely a clever excuse.

7

The Emotional &
Sexual Affair

Most of the affairs described earlier, regardless of whether they started off in search of only sexual release or soulmates, have the potential and the propensity to 'graduate' into combined emotional and sexual affairs. Many don't. Some do. And both transgressor and paramour end up feeling that they have at last found 'true love'. Whether or not they were in search of true love is hard to tell, but there does exist that romantic streak even in the most prosaic amongst us, for did not most of us grow up on a staple diet of film songs that extolled the virtues of the loved one, movies where the boy almost always gets the girl, poetry that celebrates the joy of loving and being loved, and tales of legendary and star-crossed lovers who did heroic things for love?

Of course, all this was also accompanied by healthy doses of mythological stories that dwelled on responsibility, obedience and reverence to elders and the family, accompanied by admonitions that only one's parents could choose our life partners. As a result of this many among us chose responsibility over adventure and ended up marrying partners who were relative strangers and with whom we were expected to fall in romantic love sometime after the knot was tied. Obviously, romantic love is hard to synthesise on command and it's only a lucky few who fall in love with their chosen mates. Most of the rest develop some form or other of love with their partners over the years and end up building stable and caring relationships. But the experience of romantic love remains a matter of lore to them. Unless, some enchanted evening . . .

The 'true-love' affair

It's very hard to define what precisely 'true love' is. And I'm not even going to try to. All I will say is that it is easier felt than described. People who go through the experience of true love genuinely believe that they can find lasting happiness with each other, and *only* with each other. Particularly when they fall in love as mature adults, not teenagers or young adults. That they behave like teenagers and young adults even when they find true love as mature adults seems to somewhat detract from the credibility of their argument, but that they experience a feeling of content and calm that are elusive to teenage and young adult love, does compel one to listen to them with a little more seriousness.

In an ideal world true love would happen before one makes a commitment and gets married. But, since a large bulk of the population tends to get married in their early twenties, when they're still young adults and arguably, not yet mature enough to make lasting long-term choices, they may be visited by true love a little later in their lives. Also, since most Indians still have their marriages arranged by their families, the question of finding true love in their arranged partners may not always arise. That a fair number of couples in arranged marriages do end up truly loving each other is a bit of a bonus, but the process of selection being what it is, it is more luck than anything else that determines such an outcome.

The good news is that urban Indians are not rushing to get married. The age at marriage has been steadily increasing in the last decade or so, what with both men and women wanting to settle down a bit in their careers and build up some decent savings before marrying. Although no hard data is readily available, a rough estimate indicates that urban women tend to get married when they are twenty-six or older and urban men when they are twenty-nine or older. This means they may be more mature when they get married, thereby increasing the possibility that 'love marriages' in the twenty-first century may be based more on true love than infatuation or immature love. A corollary to this could be that less people will then seek true love outside of their marriages.

Not that this seems imminent because most of our marriages are still family-arranged, where the chances of finding true love even in more mature minds is still hit-and-miss. It seems possible, therefore, that those of us who are romantically inclined and have given up on finding true love within the marriage, may find it outside even if we don't actively seek it, thereby making life more difficult for ourselves and everyone around us.

Akshay is a serious-minded nephrologist who got married in accordance with the wishes of his family when he was twenty-one years old and doing his internship in medical college. His wife Darshana was eighteen at the time and had just entered college. He was keen that she pursue her education and so, through the early days of marriage, she balanced home and college fairly well, acquiring a degree in visual communication. They shared a lot in common and were seen by all as a very close and very-much-in-love couple. They weathered a few storms and managed to stitch together a comfortable marriage, although a few years into the marriage they both realised that there were far too many differences between them. They had decided to 'compromise' on some of their needs so that they could have a harmonious home life. The needs hadn't gone away, but their commitment to their marriage saw them through—until fifteen years after they were married. When Darshana was thirty-three, she fell in love with a man she had met while on a flight back home from a meeting with a client of the public relations company she worked for. He seemed perfect for her and she to him.

As their relationship grew so did her conviction that she had found her true love. They had desisted from getting their relationship on to a sexual plane, for she was convinced that if they made love, she would have no choice but to abandon her family. They came close on several occasions, but he, too, pulled back. He was divorced but didn't want to be the reason for her divorcing her husband. She knew she wanted to spend the rest of her life with her paramour, but couldn't find any 'real reason' to divorce Akshay since he was a decent guy and theirs was not really a bad or 'toxic' marriage. Also, there was her son to be considered. And her family. She felt stuck. Her one big chance at 'true love' was staring her in the face, but she was in a major quandary. Should she focus on her own needs or should she tear apart several lives that were so closely intertwined with hers?

A true dilemma, and a very hard one to resolve. Obviously, Darshana had not gone out looking for true love, but she found it. Having done so and having realised that this would be the only reason for her breaking her carefully constructed world, she found herself looking at it from the point of view of Akshay, their son and the rest of the family. I really don't know what she finally did, but she struck me as the kind of person who would have stayed back in the marriage. Unless, of course, Akshay or somebody in their family had found out about her relationship. In which case, it's quite conceivable that she may have walked out and married her true love rather than stay and bear the ignominy of the 'fallen woman' label.

Sometimes, people in affairs, especially those unable to decide what to do, tend to take a lot of risks as they unconsciously want their affair to be discovered, in order that the decision gets taken out of their hands. Once the spouse gets to know about the affair, there is always the possibility that the spouse might want out of the marriage, thereby clearing the way for the true lovers to get together. This method is a very risky one, for there's no telling all that can go wrong. I think it's best to take a decision before it is taken out of one's hands.

Even if one is not in a stable marriage, true lovers can face a similar dilemma. Like Shravan, who had a very toxic marriage with Shyamlee, did. He couldn't remember any period in their arranged marriage that was truly memorable. They had fought over everything that could be fought over and had come close to divorce on three distinct occasions. Each time, their families rallied round and cobbled together patchy resolutions that kept them going in peace, if not harmony, for a few months. A few years into their marriage, they had decided that, come what may, they would stick together for the sake of their two daughters who had begun to show signs of stress-related behavioural disorders at school owing to the tensions at home.

After this, things had settled down and although Shravan couldn't claim to be happy, Shyamlee had stopped harassing him and vice-versa. They had no sex life at all and there was a tacit understanding that each could seek their sexual needs outside of the marriage, provided they were discreet about it. He had several not-wholly-satisfying sex-seeking affairs. Whether Shyamlee had done the same, he had no idea, for there was never any indication or murmurs in the grapevine to this effect.

And then, he found 'true love' when he met Sonia, a tarot card-reader, who had come to deliver a talk at his Rotary club. Sonia was an attractive widow who was used to fending off men hitting on her, but she found herself drawn to Shravan like she had never been to any other man, including her late husband whom she had loved dearly. Soon, Sonia and Shravan were in love with each other and couldn't bear the thought being with anybody else. Sonia realised that it wouldn't be easy for Shravan to get out of his marriage even though she wanted him to. So, wisely, she didn't push him. But the rumour mills soon got into the act and the city was abuzz with gossip about the Sonia-Shravan relationship.

Shyamlee hit the roof when she heard about it. This time the family meeting was unable to effect a rapprochement, so firm was Shravan's steadfastness about his love for Sonia. Shyamlee demanded an outrageous settlement and refused to budge from her position. Sonia received threatening phone calls and emails, which further strengthened Shravan's resolve. He was still negotiating with lawyers on the settlement amount, when his older daughter, all of thirteen years of age, fell into a deep depression and attempted suicide. She may have died but for Shyamlee's timely intervention. Shravan was distraught. His daughter told him clearly that she would do it again if he ever threatened to leave her mother. Shravan was cornered. He could see his chances of ever marrying Sonia slowly vanish for he could never do anything that would jeopardise his precious daughter's life. Nor could he expect Sonia to wait for him until his daughters were old enough to understand. So, even though his marriage was a toxic one, Shravan couldn't get away from it.

Sometimes it is the children, sometimes the family, sometimes religious beliefs and sometimes even the health status of the spouse, that can hold people back from taking that final step. And so they stay stuck in a twilight zone unable to proceed one way or another.

Shravan's story is not an unusual one by itself— except for the ending. He had underestimated Sonia and her love for him. She waited for nine years, until he could get his daughters to understand, until Shyamlee had eventually accepted the inevitable, and until they could get divorced by mutual consent. Sonia and Shravan got married a year ago and by all reports are extremely happy with each other.

While I have no problem with true love and am also aware that it's impossible to know beforehand whether the love one feels is really true, it only becomes an issue when it happens in an extramarital context. If the marriage is an unhappy one, one could argue that at least one of the spouses gets an opportunity to pursue a happy relationship. But, as Shravan found, this is not easy to do either. Children are involved. Families are involved. Responsibilities are involved. And in the final analysis, when one breaks a marriage to pursue another relationship, however appropriate or justifiable the latter may be, one ends up creating trauma all around, and the guilt of this is bound to impact on the true-love relationship whether one likes it or not. I know you'll tell me that love doesn't take all of these into consideration when it makes its unheralded appearance. I agree, but experiencing 'true love' with someone other than your spouse is not only fraught with more obstacles and complications, but also constitutes an extramarital affair. And your spouse has every reason to feel aggrieved, even if your marriage has not been a happy one.

Many people in true-love affairs find it extraordinarily difficult to make a decision as to which way to go. This is understandable because it represents a huge struggle with the conscience and since we, as a nation, have been brought up to prioritise our duties and responsibilities over our personal desires, it makes the conflict harder to deal with. But it has to be dealt with. And soon. When it's dragged out it causes even more pain and heartache, and delays the healing process quite considerably.

Shravan's extramarital relationship dragged on for nine long years before it became a marital relationship. I have no doubt that it caused much trauma for his daughters and other members of his family. His justification were the Shakespearian adages that 'the path of true love rarely runs smooth', and 'all's well that ends well'. Unfortunately, when it comes to relationships, the ends rarely justify the means. And don't throw that old 'all's fair in love and war' argument at me. Even in love and war, there are fair and unfair ways of doing things.

If indeed you find that you are truly in love with somebody other than your spouse, there are only two choices available to you. Dump your spouse and go to your paramour or give up your paramour and concentrate on mending your marriage. I agree that you have to choose between a rock and a hard place. But it's your rock and you can make the hard place softer if you so choose. The longer you hover in no-man's land between these two choices, the more irreparable will be the damage you cause not only to yourself but to all those around you.

8

Affairs in Certain Special Situations

Some affairs happen in certain special contexts and may have deeper psychological dynamics to explain their occurrence. They could be emotional affairs, sexual affairs or combined affairs. The reason why they happen may not be as clear as some of the affairs described earlier, but as in the case of most affairs, there's always an explanation.

The revenge affair

Although marriage is not supposed to be a battleground where warring partners play out their respective conflicts, in some marriages at least, this is sadly the case. Spouses haven't learned to resolve their conflicts using rational means and end up seeking revenge on each other for slights, imagined or real. One of the methods used to exact revenge on the spouse is to have an affair. Not that it is carefully plotted out or strategised. It is an unconscious mechanism that some couples use, for it is hard to actually go and sleep with someone merely to annoy your spouse. Since revenge is the dynamic that exists in their relationship to resolve conflicts, it becomes second nature to use it as a weapon of aggravation.

Sometimes, the reason for seeking revenge is that the spouse has also had an affair in the past. But this need not necessarily be so. Oftentimes the reason for revenge is the way one partner is treated by the other. Let's say one partner is controlling and aggressive, perhaps even violent, then the subdued partner may end up having an affair just to hit the spouse where it hurts most. Sometimes, it happens that one partner suspects the other of having an affair but is unable to prove it.

Like Shweta was.

She was sure that her husband Pratap was having an affair with his executive assistant. She had no evidence to prove this, for Pratap was usually a very careful person and, try as she might, she could find no trace of any hanky-panky. All she knew was what her woman's instincts told her. The assistant's insolent manner to her that Pratap never checked her on and the comfort with which she and Pratap stood in each other's presence was enough to tell her that there was something on between them that went beyond the confines of a boss-employee relationship. Added to this was the fact that the girl came from a financially straitened background and was unattached despite being very attractive. Shweta knew Pratap was a sucker for sob stories and was convinced that he had walked into the girl's trap. But she had no way of proving it. All his telephone bills were clean. His mobile phone had no incriminating messages. Nor did his laptop. Every time she confronted him with her suspicions, he dismissed them with a laugh. She took to dropping in at the office unexpectedly but never found anything she could latch on to. She made some unusual sexual demands of him that he duly complied with, even though he never initiated anything. She had never been a highly-sexed person and he had been, at best, a workman-like performer.

She even set detectives to tail Pratap and his assistant but called them off after a fortnight of fruitless expense. But the suspicions refused to go. She was positive that an affair was happening under her nose. She could literally smell it, but reluctantly had to give up on her instincts, which she concluded, with disappointment, had let her down for the first time in her life.

Even though she was forced to stop voicing her suspicions, she still seethed inside. She confided her fears and doubts to her closest friend, who in turn shared it with her husband. The man was very sympathetic and tried to do whatever he could to prove the alleged affair. But he too failed. But Shweta was very grateful to him for believing in her instincts and one day, when she was alone in his company, completely unexpectedly ended up kissing him and going to bed with him.

Shweta was shocked by what she had done. She knew she had to somehow undo the damage. So she confessed to her friend, who expectedly cut her out of her life. She also confessed the fling to Pratap who was surprisingly cool about the whole thing. He calmed her down, gave her a pill and, when he thought she was asleep, left the room.

She was too agitated to fall asleep because she felt Pratap's reaction had been too 'gentlemanly'. She knew he was very emotionally controlled but she wanted him to express his anger and hurt. Maybe, she thought, he was actually experiencing these emotions, all the time presenting a stoic exterior so she could calm down. So she got out of bed and looked for him, finally finding him on the balcony. She was about to say something when she realised he was on the phone. She eavesdropped on a conversation that he was having with someone all about her affair. And he didn't seem angry or hurt about it. He was in fact chuckling and telling the unseen person that now that Shweta had done this, and Pratap had a hold over her, he could get away with anything and 'they' needn't be so careful in future. Shweta was stunned, but also bewildered, for she was sure that his mobile phone was still on their bedside table. She checked to make sure and, slowly, the penny dropped. Pratap had another phone that he used exclusively to communicate with his paramour, which is why his 'official phone' was squeaky clean. Shweta and Pratap were divorced the following year.

You might wonder whether this was really a revenge affair because Shweta didn't set out to take revenge on her husband. But, as I said earlier, a revenge affair rarely happens consciously. Just look at the situation. Shweta was sure her husband was having an affair, although she had no evidence. This meant she was going through the emotions that a genuinely aggrieved partner does. Naturally, when this is the emotion you experience, you're hardly in the mood to consciously play the transgressor, since this would mean that you are no better than your partner. She had never been attracted to her friend's husband. She was also not the type of person who would offer sexual favours merely out of gratitude. And yet she went to sleep with her childhood friend's husband, knowing this would cut her off from her friend. She could well have kept quiet about the whole thing and dismissed it as an indiscretion that she would never engage in again, thereby sparing her friend as well as herself unnecessary emotional pain. But she went and told everyone, including Pratap.

Obviously, part of her mind wanted him to feel the pain she felt and she was disappointed enough that he didn't seem to, to follow him to see how upset he really was. Yes, she did have a revenge affair and came out of the whole thing as a victim rather than a perpetrator. And, in the process, proved her point. But the question is, at what cost? Now she has to not only live down her husband's deception, but her own as well.

The 'parental-patterns' affair

This is a tough one to understand and come to terms with as it involves a deeper psychological mechanism than do the other variations of affairs. However, since it is a relatively common reason for infidelity, I would like to explore it in just a bit of detail.

When children know that one or both of their parents have had affairs, and have gone through the emotional trauma of dealing with the consequences of this, they are at risk, unless they are careful, of ending up repeating this behaviour pattern when they become adults, and the opportunity presents itself.

Margaret was only nine when she and her father caught her mother in bed with their driver. Her father had taken her out shopping and they had finished much earlier than expected. Since she didn't feel like eating a pizza as they had planned to do, they decided to come home earlier than they'd planned. Their driver had not accompanied them since Margaret had insisted that her father drive her as a special treat, to which he had readily agreed. For years after the event Margaret held herself responsible for her mother's affair, for had she not insisted on her father driving, the driver would have come with them and none of that stuff would have happened. To this day she could never forget the scene. Her father had thrashed the driver thoroughly and then turned his attention to her mother. This was the first time she had seen a man naked and she had stared in horrified fascination at the man's penis until her father had kicked her out of the room. She begged and pleaded with her father to not beat up her mother. Her father had stomped out of the room kicking the driver all the way to the gate, gone out, got drunk, come back and given her mother the thrashing of her life despite Margaret's entreaties. Fortunately, her mother survived, her father calmed down after a few months and the rest of her childhood passed off reasonably smoothly. Nobody spoke about it again, but Margaret did think a lot about it.

The first time she had sex with David, whom she eventually married, the images of the driver and his penis flashed through her mind, and it took a lot of effort to get them out of her system. They did go away, eventually, as she and David hunkered down to married life and had, from all descriptions, a very affectionate marriage. They had three sons along the way and even though there was not much money, they all got by fairly well. David's engineering business started flourishing when he started manufacturing automobile spare parts. Very soon, a lot of money came their way and the quality of their lives rose dramatically. They bought a house and both husband and wife had their own cars since Margaret had to ferry the children to school, tuitions and other activities. All this came at a cost, though, because David had to work very hard to maintain his company's position in a highly competitive environment. He now had 300-odd employees and their families to think about. He had developed blood pressure and was on medication for that. He didn't control his diet, drank too much and smoked about twenty cigarettes a day. Despite Margaret's pleas he refused to change his lifestyle. They had hardly any joy or closeness in their lives any more. He was crotchety and didn't want to hear her 'small woes' as he described them, particularly when he had so much on his plate.

Not surprisingly, he collapsed one day at work and an angiogram revealed major coronary insufficiency, for which he had to have bypass surgery. After this he was asked to slow down, stop smoking, control his diet and not do anything that caused him stress. He started taking it easier, delegating work responsibilities and going later to work than he usually did. He hired more staff to reduce his burden and, much to every one's surprise, this also included a chauffeur. He had hitherto not allowed anyone to drive his prized BMW, but now realised that the stress of the city traffic was too much to handle. Margaret was not used to handling so much staff—cook, maids, a gardener, chauffeur, bearers and a general factotum whose job description nobody was clear about— but she managed. Things seemed to be going well—until one day, David came home early and found Margaret in bed with the gardener.

Even if one argues that Margaret and David had drifted far apart anyway, and that their lifestyles had changed dramatically, which is why Margaret had an affair, the question remains, why choose the gardener as her paramour? Given that they were socially active, she could have an affair with the dozens of people in her own social circle who had hit on her. Was it because she thought the gardener was a safer bet? Not really, because he was relatively new and she had no way of knowing whether he would keep the affair a secret. Was it because she had seen him several times looking at her lustily and because he was young and firm-bodied? Again, not really, since she was not unaware of men looking at her wherever she went, and the driver too looked at her the same way. The truth is she was replaying her mother's affair with their driver.

When a child realises that a parent is engaging in an extramarital relationship, there is a period of confusion in the child's mind. The fact that the discovery of the affair produces such a traumatic reaction, or the fact that sometimes children get drawn into lying on behalf of the transgressing parent to cover up the affair, tells the child that what is happening is 'wrong'. Otherwise, why keep the affair a secret? And why should the other parent get so upset? No child likes to think that a parent could do something wrong since parents are seen as the moral authority that the child derives value systems from. So, the event is buried deep in the unconscious mind, but never quite goes entirely away. And later in life, in an effort to legitimise the parent's behaviour, the child, now an adult, engages in similar behaviour. The easiest way to legitimise our parents' unacceptable behaviour is to incorporate it into our own repertoire. That's why Margaret had an affair, and that too with her gardener, not anybody else from her social network, although she had a wide range of potential paramours to choose from.

This pattern repetition applies not only to affairs but any behaviour on the part of the parent that the child regards as unacceptable. Which is why we sometimes catch ourselves saying 'Oh God, I'm turning into my father (or mother)', when we engage in a behavioural pattern that we thought was inappropriate in our parents.

Another thing that parental affairs teach us, particularly when the parents make up and get on with their lives, is that affairs can be survived. Of course, if the affair led to their divorce, we may think differently. Sometimes, some children are privy to multiple affairs that a parent had, and are even abettors in the process, as when a child feels that one parent is treating the other badly and is very protective of the abused parent. If the abused parent ends up having an affair or two, the protective child internalises this as acceptable behaviour and may eventually repeat this pattern as an adult, particularly if the spouse shows behavioural traits of the abusing parent.

However, it needs to be unequivocally stated that the vast majority of children of parents who had affairs do not have affairs of their own. As a rule of thumb, the younger and more impressionable the child was when the affair was discovered, the more the child knew about the affair, the more the child abetted the parent's affair, the greater the likelihood that the child will grow up to have an affair, unless a conscious attempt is made, when entering into marriage, to process and deal with the trauma of infidelity.

The exit affair

In toxic or unhappy marriages, where one or both partners feel trapped in the marriage and don't see a way out, since there doesn't really seem to be a 'solid enough' reason to separate or get divorced, the 'trapped' partner may have what's referred to as an 'exit affair'. As its name suggests, the purpose of the affair is to find a 'legitimate' reason to exit the marriage or get the partner to exit it.

Like Subroto did when he found that his eight-year marriage to Kalyani was not going anywhere. Their fathers had been classmates and buddies since their school days and they had resolved to get the two married to each other as early as when Subroto and Kalyani were in school. The two were not particularly friendly with each other during their childhood days, since they moved in different circles, despite the fact that they had a lot of occasions to meet and get to know each other. They didn't particularly dislike each other, but there was not much chemistry between them.

When Subroto finished his chartered accountancy and found a job in a leading auditing firm in the city, his parents suggested he get married to Kalyani. He was not particularly averse to the idea, since he had not found anyone else over the years. Kalyani was working in a stockbroking firm and just recovering from a broken relationship with her college friend who had been two-timing her for almost a year-and-a-half. She was disenchanted with men but allowed herself to be persuaded to marry Subroto only because he was at least a 'known devil'. Not the best starting point for a marriage, you'd imagine, but I've seen many successful marriages start on even less promising premises.

But not so in Kalyani's and Subroto's case. They trundled along, never very happy, never really hostile, just somewhere in-between. They did whatever was expected of them, but their marriage never really took off. Subroto felt Kalyani was a chronic depressive and she found him a bore. They had dutiful sex every now and again, but never felt any real passion for each other. Despite the best of medical intervention, a child was just not happening. Their careers were not doing brilliantly, but not too badly either. They bought an apartment in the suburbs and commuted to the city like everyone else did, but they seemed to function best when they were away from each other.

After eight years of this lacklustre existence Subroto wanted out, but there was no way he could propose divorce to Kalyani, since nothing that she was doing could, by even the most extraordinary stretch of imagination, be considered inappropriate. Since Subroto did not have too many friends, he couldn't really talk to anybody about his dilemma. He wanted a happy marriage but had no clue how to convert his marriage into one such. The status quo was taken care of by the arrival of Kalyani's cousin, Parvati, who came to spend a month with them, since she had to attend a company training programme in their city. She was bright and lively, even if much younger than Subroto. But this did not prevent him from getting worked up over her. He fetched and carried for her like he'd never done for Kalyani. If Kalyani noticed this, she didn't seem to care one way or another. About ten days after her entry into their lives, Parvati and Subroto had passionate sex with each other. Both enjoyed the experience so much that they felt compelled to repeat it every day since Parvati would have to leave by the end of the month.

He started taking risks to make it happen. Parvati protested, fearing Kalyani would catch them at it, but he was beyond caring. In fact, he hoped she would. 'Nothing will happen' was what he repeatedly told Parvati as he came into her room every night after Kalyani had gone to sleep. The inevitable happened a few days before Parvati was due to leave. Kalyani, wakened by the noise Subroto and Parvati were making, interrupted them in the throes of passion. Nothing was said. Everybody just sulked for a couple of days. A few days later, Subroto and Kalyani separated and initiated civilised divorce proceedings, despite the parents' exhortations to give each other one more chance.

There are, of course, many better ways to deal with marital unhappiness than to have an exit affair. Since lack of intimacy is not a valid ground for divorce, it's not unusual for somebody wanting out of a marriage to consciously or unconsciously engage in an extramarital relationship. In such a situation, typically, the choice of partner is such that the paramour becomes irrelevant once the purpose is served. So, invariably, exit affairs are dead-end relationships where there is little possibility of the relationship advancing to a higher level. Also, the level of risk taken in conducting the affair is pretty high, since discovery is the objective. Of course, not all exit affairs end in civilised divorces. It is more common for the aggrieved partner, who probably also wants a divorce, to raise Cain and milk the situation with as much drama as possible in order to either procure a good settlement, or wriggle out of any settlement altogether, as the case may be.

The office affair

Nagesh's team was on a roll. They had achieved their sales targets for each of the last six quarters and were considered the stars of the FMCG company he worked for. All his team members knew that a large contribution to this success was the performance of Kritika, a member of the team. All his team members also knew that Nagesh and Kritika were having an affair for the last year-and-a-half. But nobody seemed to particularly care, as long as the targets were being met and the team incentives were rolling in.

Nagesh's and Kritika's affair began when they came together on a key project with stiff deadlines. They formed a good team and worked very well together with an almost instinctive understanding of what was required. They could anticipate each other's thoughts and were really on high charge when they were around each other. After the project was completed and hailed by everyone in the top management, an excited Kritika and Nagesh found themselves in a tight celebratory clinch at the office after everyone else had left. They consummated their relationship then and there.

After this there was no stopping them. Kritika was single and career-driven. Nagesh was married and career-driven. They realised that they would probably have made a lousy marriage, but for as long as they were in each other's company at work, they were perfect together.

Nagesh's wife was a simple, straightforward woman and a homemaker. She had no clue about what he did at work and had never met Kritika. Both Nagesh and Kritika preferred to keep it that way. The company management, realising their chemistry, and not really concerned about what went on after office hours, ensured that they always worked together with an eye on the company's bottom-line. Working together energised them and the sex energised their working together. Neither of them ever assumed that they were in love with each other, but realised they were very dependent on each other professionally.

But since there was a lot of pressure from Kritika's family for her to get married, she eventually succumbed and married a corporate trainer. Neither of the lovers was worried about this eventuality, for they had decided that whatever happened, their affair would continue. Sadly for Nagesh, Kritika fell in love with her husband, and slowly started moving away from Nagesh. After a few months she persuaded her husband to accept a long-term assignment overseas and as soon as the visa formalities were complete, she resigned her job and joined him there, and a made a clean break with her past.

Her past, unfortunately, was not so lucky. He was shattered, his performance plummeted, he was sacked from his job, and went through a depression that his in-the-dark wife lovingly nurtured him out of.

Given the amount of time we spend at work and the fact that we sometimes have more quality-time with our work colleagues than with our spouses, it should come as no surprise that office intimacies are on the increase. In a typical day, we spend about ten hours at work, at least two on our commutes, about six at sleep, on an average two doing household chores, at least one attending to after-office phone calls, one updating our Facebook pages and idle Internet surfing, and two in front of the television. On weekends, we party, recover from our partying, sleep and do the weekly shopping. Where's the time for the marriage?

Obviously, not all couples feel this way, and despite working punishing schedules, still manage not to have office affairs, even if marriages are placed squarely on the backburner, to be attended to only during the annual vacation which are inevitably taken in the company of friends. Surely, we can do better. And then we wouldn't run the risk of office intimacies getting in the way of our lives.

While office intimacies are fine before marriage, and in fact, many offices today have become better match-making locations than even Internet marriage portals, post-marriage, they can be, and often are, potential minefields unless one is cognisant of this and takes necessary precautions. It's easy to impulsively jump into an office affair. But it's not so easy to deal with its consequences. Don't say I didn't warn you!

The homosexual affair

'How do I deal with this?' was the question that Binoo asked of me when she came to see me. 'If he was in an affair with a woman, I'd at least know what to do. But with a man! How do I deal with it?' Binoo had the previous week caught her husband Jatin in a sexually compromising position with their neighbour's twenty-one-year-old son. The boy used to hang around at their home, constantly wanting to spend time with Jatin and ask him questions about engineering. Binoo has assumed that since the boy's father was a master mariner in the merchant navy and spent nine months a year at sea, the boy was missing a father figure and was seeking out Jatin, even though Jatin was only about ten or so years older. She had never in her wildest dreams imagined that the two of them could have any other form of relationship, certainly not a gay one.

Of course, she had always suspected that the boy was gay, but she had no problems with that for she considered herself a liberal modern woman and was not especially homophobic. But she never thought her husband could be gay too. He seemed straight enough to her, although, in hindsight, she recalled that she found it peculiar that he preferred to watch Salman Khan than Katrina Kaif. She had assumed that this was because he was also into body-building. Once, she had seen some gay porn on his laptop, but since there was a lot of heterosexual porn as well, she didn't think too much about this. And their sex life, though occasional, was seemingly okay, although she was not a very sexual person and had no way of telling. Anyway, they'd had enough sex to produce, at his insistence, a son within a year of getting married. But now she was stumped. Part of her was glad that he was not rejecting her for another woman, but the other part was absolutely aghast. And she had no clue how to move forward.

In truth, Jatin knew he was gay even as a teenager. But took a long time to come to terms with it. As a young adult, he had a string of gay partners but no steady relationship. He despaired of finding someone he could love and live with. He tried immigrating to the United States since he knew there were more opportunities there to pursue a gay life, but had his visa application rejected three times for reasons he was still not clear about. His family and his friends put a lot of pressure on him to get married. He was against the idea of an arranged marriage and managed to postpone it for as long as he could.

When his father ultimately threatened suicide, Jatin, in desperation, found Binoo, who worked in another company in the same building as his, and whom he had given an occasional ride home, and proposed to her.

She was stunned into accepting his proposal even though she barely knew him. She was not attractive and had a large birthmark on her forehead which seemed to put potential suitors off. Not being able to afford plastic surgery, she had thought she was doomed to a life of reluctant singlehood. And here was a good-looking man proposing marriage. So, they did get married and had a son as well. And now this.

Gays and lesbians have a very hard time in our country. Most people neither realise nor understand that they're as normal as straight people, except that they prefer to be in an intimate relationship, both sexually and emotionally, with a person of their own gender. They are victims of homophobia, social ostracism, pejorative comments and until recently, even the long arm of the law. As a result most gays and lesbians are afraid to 'out' themselves and to live openly gay lives.

The biggest problem they face is the great Indian marriage obsession. Everybody pressures them to get married. It's only the brave few that manage to resist. Even if they are still closet gays, they prefer to remain so than get married to a person of the opposite gender. However, very few are as brave. Invariably they succumb to the pressure, get married and engage in, at best, inadequate relationships with their spouses. I have known people to get married, like Jatin did, to somebody who may not have otherwise find a spouse easily, so they could use their marriage as a smokescreen, leaving them free to pursue their gay lives. I have also known gay men to marry lesbian women with the understanding that both use the marriage as a cover.

Lesbians find it easier to 'fake' sexual interest than gay men. But almost invariably, somewhere along the way, their inner needs assert themselves, and they engage in homosexual affairs. Taking precautions to disguise their gayness comes naturally to gay people since they have lived with covering up their secret from their adolescence onwards. As a result, many of them may never be discovered to be gay. There are many spouses who have gone through their married lives never realising that their partner was gay or lesbian all along. Some people are bisexuals and are sexually comfortable with either gender. People belonging to this group generally tend to have more successful marriages than gays or lesbians who have forced themselves into matrimony.

So what does one do when one finds that one's spouse is a closet gay or lesbian? First off, one must realise that people who are gay cannot be 'converted' into becoming heterosexuals. They can't be 'treated' for their homosexuality either, for gayness is not an illness. Even if some doctors, psychiatrists or religious gurus offer to 'treat' or 'convert' your spouse, please don't accept this, for this is simply not possible. I don't intend for this to become a treatise on homosexuality, but all I can say is that the only way to deal with spousal homosexuality is to accept it as a reality. There is nothing you or anybody can do to change it.

The perfect solution is for the gay or lesbian partner to be freed to pursue a relationship with someone of the same gender. But, in our country, where will they go? There are very few spaces for gay people to engage with each other. However, if both of you decide to stay married for whatever reason, even if the sex goes out of your marriage, you are perfectly justified in expecting fidelity, for this is what marriage is all about. I know it's a tough call. But sadly, it has to be made.

The midlife affair

People often wonder whether the much-written about 'midlife crisis' really exists or whether it has been made up just to rationalise some erratic behaviour that people engage in when they hit their forties or thereabouts. Given that this is a phenomenon that cuts across cultures and ethnic groups, and given that it is often accompanied by symptoms of menopause and andropause (the male menopause), one must conclude that it does indeed exist.

When men and women in the mid-forties find that they are ageing and are uncomfortable accepting this, they may end up behaving like younger people, and do things uncharacteristic of their age. They dress younger, they push themselves harder physically, they party more, they may undertake long treks, buy a flashy new motorcycle, prefer the company of younger people and so on.

And they may also have affairs.

Lajju hated turning forty. In order to delay it for as long as she could, she celebrated her fortieth birthday when she was actually forty-four. All the invitees knew this, of course, but they all ignored this little detail. She had a wide social network and was socially very well connected in the city. She was a well-known painter and her arty soirees were generally very well attended. Her husband Bunty, who was pushing fifty, was amusedly tolerant of her reaction to the forties. 'Whatever you do, don't have an affair with a toyboy. Or you know the consequences,' he chided her gently.

Lajju had never thought of having one, always considering that affairs were tedious, sordid and plebeian. Everybody she knew was having one and she didn't want to reduce herself to their level. But have an affair is exactly what she did. And that too with a toyboy. She didn't go out looking for one, but a toyboy found her nevertheless. He was a twenty-two-year-old fashion model, who tried to supplement his income by posing for artists. He was empty-headed, devoid of conversation or aesthetics, but he had a terrific body and he seemed to desire her, for she thought she saw an erection when he was sitting for her. Also, when she asked him how old he thought she was, his unhesitating reply was 'Thirty-five'.

So, she had an affair with a toyboy, which energised her immensely—at least initially. She then tired of him and wanted to get rid of him, but he refused to go away, until she was forced to introduce him to a fashion designer friend to give his career a boost. She had not wanted to do this, for she wanted to keep her affair a secret. But her fashion designer friend ferreted out all the details from the toyboy and the city's gossip circles had a field day. Fortunately, the gossip didn't reach Bunty's ears, and she didn't have to deal with any of the consequences he had threatened her with.

Often, midlife affairs are more like flings and are conducted with younger people, in an illusory attempt to regain a sense of lost youth. Sometimes, they can be intensely emotional as well, and it is not unknown for people to suddenly leave their marriages after growing besotted with a much younger man or woman, and to deeply regret their decision a year or two down the road. During the midlife period, when the sex drive wanes a bit, people, instead of accepting this as an inevitable phase of life, tend to panic and try and restore their sexual vigour by having an affair with an attractive person of the opposite gender just to tell themselves that they are still virile or feminine, and desirable as well. Often these affairs are short-lasting and peter out very soon. Many of them are never discovered, but since Indian cities still function like clusters of villages, the grapevine sooner than later queers the pitch, with devastating consequences.

Well, now you know why people have affairs and the different ways in which affairs happen. I don't mean to explain away affairs, or expect that, now you have an understanding of affairs, you will, in some magical way, forget all about it and move on with your lives. Understanding infidelity is one thing, but surviving it requires a lot more than just understanding it. Whether you are the transgressing partner or the aggrieved one, there is still some work to do before you can bury the affair and forget about it. If you're reading this to pick up a few tips on how other people have affairs, it might be a good idea to get your spouse to read the remaining sections of the book.

PART II

SURVIVING INFIDELITY

9

Discovery of the Affair

*I*t's an extraordinary fact of contemporary Indian married life that the majority of affairs are discovered sooner rather than later. Whether this is because transgressors take more risks than before, or whether it is because the very same technology that facilitates the smooth conduct of affairs, facilitates discovery as easily, or whether because the intuition of the modern married person is much more sharply honed to discover affairs with ease, is hard to tell. But it's axiomatic that the only people who believe the affair to be a well-kept secret are those having the affair.

It is true that some affairs never get discovered, particularly the one-night stands and the purely sex-seeking affairs which are intense and are of short duration. However, if an affair continues for any length of time, the chances of it being discovered are particularly high. If the transgressors are not tech-savvy, the incriminating tech trail that they leave behind will, in all probability, let them down every time. First-time affairs are at even higher risk, for neither the transgressor nor the paramour is experienced enough to ensure that they leave no trail. Serial short-term transgressors may be harder to catch, but they too make careless mistakes and the truth does come out. The bottom line: If you think you've covered your tracks, think again. You're likely to be found out.

I do not intend this to be a manual on the ten or twenty things you need to do to discover whether or not your partner is having an affair, for simply put, there is no surefire formula with which you can do so. I am simply going to share with you some of the usual ways in which affairs get discovered. Typically, in our country, affairs get discovered in one of five ways:

Caught in the act

In the past, this used to be the commonest method of discovery of an affair. In the absence of available venues in which to conduct an affair, most protagonists would do so at either the transgressor's or the paramour's home, when they believed that the coast was clear. But given that they lived in joint or at least extended families, it was very rare for the coast to be absolutely clear. Invariably somebody would stumble upon them and their game would be over even before it began.

But in contemporary times, there are many more spaces where people can conduct affairs, as a result of which getting caught in the act is relatively less common. Homes are generally inhabited by nuclear families and it is not uncommon for a bored housewife having an affair inside her house to be able to get away with it. Until the neighbours' curiosity is piqued enough to initiate an investigation into the identity of and the purpose behind the stranger who visits regularly. Unless, of course, the paramour is also the neighbour. In which case, there's always the security personnel or another neighbour who dislikes the paramour or the transgressor, whose nosiness can be counted upon.

If the affair is being conducted outside the home, the chances of being caught in the act are generally far less, unless the cruel hand of fate takes over. As it did when Ramona was romancing her paramour in a park, a distance away from home (where her mother-in-law's presence obviated the possibility of an extramarital tryst). Both of them used to visit this park regularly since it was considered a lovers' haven and they were surrounded by many other couples who had eyes only for each other, as a result of which they were relatively undisturbed.

Unfortunately for them, they chose to meet there on Valentine's Day. A TV crew chose that particular park to record a clip on how love was in the air, and deeply engrossed in a loving hug, Ramona and her paramour did not notice that they were being recorded along with a dozen or so other couples. Since this was a local TV channel that did not particularly believe in the value of privacy or concealing their subjects' identity, the unexpurgated clip was telecast that evening when Ramona, her husband and the family was sitting down to watch television after dinner, and changed her life forever.

Husbands and wives coming home early and catching their spouses *in flagrante delicto* still does happen, but it's worse when a son or daughter or a parent-in-law is the discoverer. As happened to Margaret when she was a child (Chapter 8, p 126). When a spouse catches a partner in the act, it is even more difficult to deal with the affair, as Uma realised when she saw her husband Ganesh in bed with her sister Rama (Chapter 3, p 68). For, you have to deal not only with the thought or the idea of your partner having an affair, which is hard enough to do, but also the visual image that is often exceedingly difficult to erase from your mind's eye. I have found that healing is the most difficult if one spouse catches the other in the act.

Sometimes, catching people in the act may not be actually seeing a couple in a compromising position. It may also have to do with overhearing a romantic conversation between spouse and paramour, or spotting them in a restaurant, or at the movies when the spouse was supposed to be busy at work or someplace else. It's also not uncommon for a friend to report that the spouse was seen cosily ensconced with a paramour at the movies or at a restaurant or any other public place. Many transgressors do manage to get away from being sighted by a friend or anyone else, by casting aspersions on the motives and machinations of the friend in question, and since most of us don't want to believe that our spouse could be having an affair, we end up accepting, even if our suspicions are aroused, our spouse's version, sometimes even terminating our relationship with the hapless friend. But when one does the spotting of spouse and paramour oneself, there's no way the spouse can slip out of that one.

Technology to the rescue

This is the most common method of discovery of an affair. As has been said *ad nauseam*, technology helps in the conduct of affairs, but it equally aids in their discovery. Usually it's a stray text message that the aggrieved spouse comes across that brings down the fortress of secrecy created by the paramour and the transgressing spouse. Initially, most participants in an affair are very careful about sending coded text messages to each other. Often, the paramour's contact information is stored in a different, and more innocuous, name by the transgressing spouse. But the number of calls or text messages between the transgressing spouse and the paramour (which usually gets logged either on the phone or by the service provider) is revelatory. The itemised mobile phone bill has spelled the death of many an affair, especially if the aggrieved spouse is in the habit of checking the itemised bill to make sure the service-provider has not over-billed by error or design.

Usually, in a reasonably comfortable marriage, spouses don't go around checking each other's calls or text logs, and so there's no index of suspicion. However, if by happenstance (and happenstance happens more often than we expect it to), the transgressor's mobile phone is within the aggrieved spouse's reach or if the transgressing spouse happens to be in the shower when the text arrives, and the text just happens to appear to suggest an unusual familiarity between sender and receiver, bubbles are easy enough to burst.

For some reason, when people have affairs, they seem to feel compelled to send late-night or early-morning text messages ('I want to be the last person to say good night and the first person to say good morning'). And even if the phone is on silent mode, it does tend to flash or vibrate, or does something to catch the attention of anyone near the phone. And if this 'anyone' turns out to be the aggrieved spouse, well, you know what's likely to happen. Since it would appear really weird if the transgressing spouse carried the phone around everywhere including the shower (some people tend to do this regardless), there are always unguarded moments that nobody can anticipate.

The other common way technology plays a role is by means of email and chat transcripts. Many couples do share each other's email passwords and there's nothing wrong with this. But rarely do they bother to log into each other's email accounts. Unfortunately, if circumstances warrant that they do, well, the cat is soon going to escape.

Madan was usually very well prepared for any eventuality. On one occasion, though, he had forgotten to take an important piece of information with him for an outstation meeting. The file was on his desktop computer at home. He asked his wife Sharada to email it to him, but Sharada told him she was unable to access her email account, since the email service-provider's servers seemed to be down. Since he was in a hurry, he asked her to access his email account and send the file as an attachment in an email to himself. He texted her his precious password, resolving to change it as soon as his meeting was over. But it was too late.

Which spouse who has been denied access to her partner's email account and who suddenly gets an opportunity to get into it, is going to pass up the opportunity to do a bit of snooping? Not Sharada anyway. It didn't take her long to find a folder unimaginatively titled 'Love' and read a whole lot of torrid emails between Madan and his distant cousin, Karishma, who lived overseas and visited every three or four months. Being sure that Madan would change his password and she would never see these emails again, she took printouts of all the emails, so she could confront him when he returned that evening.

The same could happen with chat transcripts, which seem to get saved somewhere or the other and can be retrieved by any tech-savvy person nosing around one's hard disk. And the most tech-savvy people in the world are children. I can't tell you the number of children who have found sizzling evidence of their parents' amorous shenanigans and have rushed to spill the beans. What a way to get an education! So, however tech-savvy the transgressing partner is, it is not particularly difficult to be found out.

Acting on intuition

There was a time when a woman's intuition was considered something to be feared, particularly when the husband was having an affair. While this continues to hold, in recent times, men aren't doing too badly either. Nobody would have suspected that Hari had anything close to an intuition. He always gave the appearance of being a pleasant enough chap, but not quite there. He was very much a family man and very dependent on his wife, Sushma, who was a generally more vivacious person and enjoyed interacting warmly with people around her.

Through most of their married life, she felt stifled by Hari, for his demands on her time were so much, she had very little time for herself. Not that they did anything special together. But whatever Hari did, Sushma was expected to do with him. He never really nurtured his talented wife, for he didn't know how to. She was a trained classical singer whose career could have really gone places, but for Hari playing the role of the albatross around her neck.

One day, out of the blue, Hari asked her if she was having an affair with her percussion accompanist. She was shocked and had a row with him. How could he accuse her of such a thing? And that too without a shred of evidence. Hari agreed he had no evidence, but was absolutely sure that the comfort level she shared with the man when they rehearsed together, was of the kind that only intimate couples had. She was aghast and accused him of being paranoid and needing psychiatric help. In fact, everyone in Hari's family thought he was mentally disturbed when Sushma told them about it.

Two weeks later, Hari threw a sheaf of papers at her face. It was her itemised mobile phone bill that he had procured from her service-provider although he was not authorised to give this information to anyone but her. How could she explain the three-hour conversations and the forty-six text messages to her percussionist on a single day? She confessed.

While intuition does not always work, it can sometimes create the suspicion that the spouse is up to something, particularly when accompanied by uncharacteristic behaviour. Typically, the spouse appears more irritable, secretive, possessive of the mobile phone, suddenly takes long walks alone, looks guilty every time somebody walks in on a telephone conversation, has whispered telephone conversations, sends and receives text messages at very odd times, appears preoccupied with some deep issue and so forth. Of course, it's conceivable that all that the spouse is up to, is planning a surprise birthday or anniversary party, or is going through a depression or a crisis at work. But these are easily cleared up. But when this cagey behaviour persists, it is not uncommon for the intuitive aggrieved spouse to realise that something is going on that needs to be investigated. If the transgressing spouse is not forthcoming, then there are, of course, other ways to find out.

Now starts the snooping and the amateur sleuthing. If this doesn't yield any results, more spouses today than ever before, have no qualms about resorting to professional detectives, particularly if the intuition is strong and the index of suspicion high. Since most transgressing spouses are doing this for the first time, are not particularly good actors, and do experience some guilt at whatever they are doing (otherwise why the secrecy?), they are found out sooner, rarely later.

Grapevine buzz

The only time the grapevine played a useful role in Mussarat's life was when her husband, Muzaffar, was having an affair with his assistant. Mussarat was a gynaecologist and Muzaffar a cardiothoracic surgeon in the same hospital, but given their busy schedules, they hardly met at work. Hospitals have very active grapevines, but since Mussarat was never plugged into it, for she loathed it, it never came to her attention that her husband was having what is generally referred to as a 'roaring affair' with his attractive assistant, who never left his side while he was at work.

Finally, a sympathetic matron called her aside and broke it to her. Mussarat didn't believe it initially, but when the matron offered to take her right then to the doctor's rest room in the cardiothoracic department, Mussarat went alone. She didn't catch the lovers in a sexually compromising position, but he was resting on a couch, with his head in his assistant's lap. That was enough for her to demand a *khula* from him.

Confession

Although it may seem unusual, confessions are sometimes the way an affair is discovered. This typically happens after one-night stands or intense affairs of short duration engaged in by an individual whose guilt levels are high enough to prompt a confession to the spouse. This could be because the transgressor in question is by nature highly guilt-prone, or because the marriage is a stable and generally transparent one.

Generally, marriages survive confessed affairs far easier than if the aggrieved spouse had to literally dig out evidence of the affair. Of course, the initial shock is extremely high since it's so unanticipated, but as long as the transgressing partner does not demand brownie points for the confession, the aggrieved spouse usually does give some weightage to it, and the couple is able to heal faster.

Sometimes, confessions could come about for another reason. Shefalee was having an intense affair with her colleague Jaidev which happened to be discovered by his sharply intuitive wife, Carol. He managed to communicate this to Shefalee, who was put in a fix. Knowing how vindictive Carol could be, she decided that the best thing to do was to tell her husband, Sameer, about it before Carol got to him.

So that evening, over dinner, she made a full confession about her 'stupidity'. Of course, she overlooked telling him about Carol having found out about it. Sameer was stunned, but he gave Shefalee full marks for being honest. When Carol called to speak to Sameer, he coldly informed Carol that he already knew about it and had decided to forgive his wife for her indiscretion. Carol was unstoppable, and gave him a blow-by-blow description of how exactly she had discovered the affair and all of what her husband and his wife had been up to. Despite his dislike of Carol, whom he had always thought of as a coarse woman, Sameer heard her out. Shefalee ended up being the loser twice over for the twin deception. It took Sameer a long time to recover from this double whammy.

Sheer accident

Divya was, what is generally referred to in our country as a 'homely' wife. She had diligently taken care of her husband Anil and their family with a lot of love, patience and understanding. For their tenth wedding anniversary, more at his family's insistence, Anil had been persuaded to take her to Goa for a long weekend. Anil, being a creature of habit, booked them into the hotel he usually stayed at when he went to Goa on his innumerable business trips. At the lobby, when they were checking in, they bumped into the hotel manager who greeted Anil warmly. 'Your wife's not come with you this time?' he asked Anil, not noticing Divya's presence.

Homely or not, this was enough for Divya, who was much sharper than she looked, and Anil's bubble was well and truly burst. Had they gone to another hotel, or had they checked in an hour or so earlier, or if the manager were a little more sensitive, who knows? Anil may well have got away with it.

Chance discovery of affairs happens more often than one realises. Of course, one could hypothesise that Anil wanted to be discovered, or why would he be foolish enough to take Divya to the same hotel that he usually took his girlfriend to. Then, how about this one? Sheetal was sitting next to Pika on a flight and both the women chatted a bit. They were not really each other's types, so while they were friendly enough, they did not get into any form of personal conversation. Sheetal was cutting short a business trip to surprise her husband on his birthday. So when she got out of the airport, she was taken aback to see her husband waiting outside. She ran towards him not noticing that Pika too was doing the same thing. Pika beat her by a whisker and jumped into his arms. All he could do was to stare at Sheetal, stunned. It was not a very happy birthday.

Pure Bollywood? May sound like it. But take it from me, it happens. After hearing innumerable stories like this, I have developed a healthy respect for Indian scriptwriters. Yes, affairs do get discovered by chance. And when they do, the sense of betrayal is extremely high, for the questions topmost on the aggrieved partner's mind is, 'Suppose I hadn't been there, how much longer would the affair have continued? How could I have not realised that my spouse was cheating on me?' and the like. On top of the transgressing partner's mind is one just thought, 'Hell. What are the odds that this could have happened?' Whatever the odds, it has happened and has to be dealt with. The world works in mysterious ways.

10

Surviving the Affair

However much pain they may bring, affairs can be survived. Millions of couples all over the world have survived affairs. I know this is small consolation for those of you who are trying to survive your partner's infidelity, but please be assured that the pain you feel when you discover the transgression will go away. The affair may leave a small scar in your mind, but this too will heal. However, healing can be facilitated if we're able to understand the healing process and the rebuilding effort. For the sake of convenience, I have dealt with the process of surviving infidelity in the following pages by breaking it up into three stages.

The first of these is the *first confrontation,* in which one deals with the trauma of discovery and its immediate aftermath. We will explore the initial emotions and behavioural reactions of both aggrieved and transgressor and look at how the issues that crop up in this stage can be dealt with. This stage covers the first week to fortnight after the affair has been discovered.

We will then explore the *stage of healing*. A terrible trauma has assailed us, but we need to heal from it if we're going to survive it and reclaim our lives. You're probably mourning the loss of the marriage you believed you had, but at this stage, I'd recommend that you just concentrate on healing yourself. Don't worry about the marriage just yet. Once you have healed, you can decide what you want to do with your marriage and where you want to take it. This stage could last from anything between three weeks to several months depending on the connectedness of the couple, the type of affair, the duration of the affair, the identity of the paramour (stranger or friend), the strength of available support systems and the method of discovery of the affair.

And finally we'll turn our attention to the *stage of reason*, where both of you, having completed the initial healing and having put some distance between yourselves and the affair, will be in a position to rationally look at what happened and take some key decisions for what needs to be done for the future. Once we've done this, we'll also take a look at how marriages can be affair-proofed. But before we get down to all of this, we need to turn out attention to the first confrontation between aggrieved and transgressor.

11

The First Confrontation

This is a very important stage of dealing with infidelity for the tone for the survival process usually gets established right at the very beginning—the first time the couple actually talk about the affair. Until this point there may have been suspicions, accusations even, but no acknowledgement that the affair was in existence. There are no ground rules for the confrontation and you'll just have to go about in the manner that comes most naturally to you. It's hardly likely to be a civilised discussion over a cup of tea, but it needn't become a free-for-all either. I'm not going to give you a checklist of things you should and shouldn't do, for chances are that the discovery of the affair and the first confrontation have already happened, if you've come this far in reading this book, and anyway, you can't seriously expect to confront your partner with a checklist in hand.

Once the confrontation is over, there are only two possible outcomes. Either the transgressing partner admits to having or having had the affair, or refuses to do so.

Typically, if the transgressing partner has been either caught in the act or has confessed, or if the discovery of the affair is through the assistance of technology, it's hardly possible for the transgressing partner to deny the affair. But if the method of discovery is through intuition or through the grapevine buzz, then it's quite possible that the affair may be denied. If denial is the outcome of the confrontation despite overwhelming evidence pointing towards an affair, you'll have to take fresh stock of the situation and assess whether your accusations were without substantial basis.

When could one consider that the evidence clearly points to an affair? I feel three requirements have to be fulfilled. First, your partner's behaviour in recent times should have become noticeably and uncharacteristically secretive. In other words, there should be a distinct and demonstrable change in behaviour from before and not just a gradual drifting away from you.

Second, you should definitely have seen something inappropriate in your partner's possession which your partner actively keeps away from you. An example would be a mushy text message or email from a 'friend' or 'colleague' or anybody for that matter. Of course, definitions of 'mush' vary between people and merely texting 'I love you' may or may not constitute proof of an affair. But if such text messages are actively kept hidden from you or your partner gets very annoyed with you when you read them, there is a cause for concern. Another example could be a condom packed in the suitcase for a business trip that can't be explained satisfactorily. Of course it's possible that the condom was packed the last time you went on a vacation together and both of you may have forgotten about it. Some men use condoms to masturbate as well. But if it's a brand you don't recognise or if you haven't been on a vacation in a while, or your partner does not masturbate with a condom, then I guess this could be a telltale sign.

And the final requirement would be that your marital rituals have changed recognisably in the last few weeks or months and the explanations provided for these are weak or unconvincing. For instance, you've not had sex for ages despite making love two or three times a week earlier, or your partner has not visited your parents in several months although a regular monthly or fortnightly visit was the usual pattern, or the nightly calls you used to receive when your partner was on business trips seem to have altogether ceased. Each couple has their own rituals and it's hard to give a comprehensive list of such instances, but if your rituals have changed and the explanations provided by your partner are not satisfactory, you have a reasonable basis to wonder what's happening.

If you're a naturally suspicious person, you wouldn't need any of these to suspect that your partner's having an affair, but then you're unlikely to need hard evidence anyway. You'll probably harass your partner until you get a confession or ferret something out using other means. But if you're not a naturally suspicious person, the above three indicators may point you in the right direction. If, despite all of these, your partner's response to your repeated confrontations and entreaties is still stout denial, I think you have no choice but to wait for something else to happen that will give you more information to make up your mind, or take the matter to a person you feel may be able to help in coming to a conclusion (and I don't mean a detective agency!).

For one to survive infidelity, at the end of the confrontation, the following should have taken place:

A. Both of you agree that an affair is taking place or has taken place.

B. The transgressing partner expresses remorse about the
   affair and wants to survive it and rebuild the marriage.
C. Both of you agree that the transgressing partner either
   already has or will forthwith terminate the relationship
   with the paramour.
D. The transgressing partner has given an explanation of
   why the affair took place, whether or not the aggrieved
   partner accepts this explanation as a valid one.
E. The transgressing partner has answered whatever
   questions the aggrieved partner has about the affair.

From the foregoing it will become readily apparent
that if you're going to survive the infidelity, the basic
requirement is that the affair should be over or
terminated. If what you're dealing with is an exit affair or
a true love affair, then in all likelihood, the confrontation
could also signal the end of the marriage, for it's quite
possible that your spouse may want to choose the
paramour over you or choose to exit the marriage. But in
all other types of affairs, barring a few unpleasant
possibilities discussed below, it's certainly possible that all
the above criteria can be fulfilled.

When the transgressing partner refuses to let go of either the marriage or the paramour

Probably the most important conclusion of the first
confrontation has to be that the affair is over. It's hard for
a marriage to survive an affair that is ongoing. If the
transgressing partner agrees that a relationship is in
progress but it's not an affair, since no sex is involved, as
in say, a 'soulmate affair', and therefore refuses to give up
the 'soulmate', then more effort needs to be undertaken
to persuade the transgressing partner to give up the
relationship, provided it satisfies at least two of the five

hallmarks of an affair (Chapter 2). I know that it can be humiliating to sell the idea to your partner that the paramour cannot be part of your life. But I do know many people who value their marriage and their partners sufficiently to go through this. If this doesn't work, then the only option is to escalate matters to others in your network. I would recommend meeting a neutral person first, like a therapist or a counsellor, so that the matter can still be contained. If this doesn't work, there is no option but to involve family members and friends to undertake this on your behalf. But before doing so, I'd recommend that you tell the transgressing partner what precisely you're going to do, for if any escalation is done without the partner's knowledge, then you become party to a counter-transgression and therefore, likely to lose whatever regard your spouse might still hold you in.

Some people I know have tried talking to the paramour and either threaten or plead for the return of their spouse. It is also not unusual for the paramour to be at the receiving end of cyber-attacks or cyber-threats. For instance, one angry aggrieved spouse posted innuendoes about the paramour on a Facebook wall, and since there were a lot of shared friends on their network, the paramour had a very hard time explaining things away. Another gave out the mobile number of the paramour on a sex site, as a result of which the paramour was besieged with telephone calls from strangers wanting to have paid sex. I have also known aggrieved spouses threatening to tell the paramour's spouse about the affair, if the paramour is married, and indeed actually go and tell the spouse about the affair in an attempt to break it up. I would honestly not recommend any of these counter-deceptions at all. I wouldn't recommend them even if you were doing it with the transgressing spouse's knowledge. For these are actually very counter-productive. When the paramour is attacked, all the protective instincts of the transgressing partner become fully aroused, and whatever sympathy you may have had till now will be completely lost. As a result of your machinations, you will probably end up pushing your spouse and paramour even closer together.

If, despite your efforts at straightforward escalation to others in your social network, the transgressing partner refuses to acknowledge the relationship as constituting an affair and refuses to give up the paramour, then you have only two choices: Accept the relationship and wait for it to die down, or call your lawyer. There are many people who have chosen the former option, and the soulmate affair has petered out after a while for a variety of reasons. Those that have chosen the latter option have done so because their minds would not permit them to be in a triangulated relationship. I guess it's just a question of who you are, what you want and how much you're prepared to accept from your partner. There is no such thing as a right or wrong decision in this situation, as a lot of other factors will also determine what you finally decide.

Letting go of the paramour

If the transgressor has agreed to the existence of the affair, the first thing that has to be done is to let go of the paramour. In the case of an emotional or a combined emotional and sexual affair, this can be difficult for the transgressing partner to do, since some emotion has been invested in the paramour. Many aggrieved partners are okay with their spouses having a last conversation with the paramour so that closure can be applied on that relationship. Although they would like to listen in on the conversation. Now, this may be hard for the transgressing partner to agree to, but few aggrieved partners would like to permit their spouses one last emotional moment with their paramours in privacy. My usual recommendation in such a situation is that the transgressing spouse and the aggrieved spouse engage in a conference call with the paramour with the latter's full knowledge that the aggrieved spouse is part of the call, in the course of which the transgressing partner tells the paramour that the spouse has discovered the affair, that the affair is henceforth over and that there will be no personal communication between the two of them in future. I also recommend for the aggrieved partner not to say anything, for this could and often does make for a messy conversation. However, if the paramour is known to the aggrieved partner, then it may be difficult to prevent the latter from saying something. But if both spouses resolve to do this in as civil a manner as possible, things can be a little more contained.

If, despite this, the transgressing spouse still wishes to have one last conversation alone with the paramour, this need not be considered a further attempt at transgression because, in an emotional affair, it's hard to break up abruptly and in the presence of someone else. But any further attempts at communication can and should be considered unacceptable. Some transgressing spouses in an emotional affair may try and negotiate some time over which they will gradually taper off the relationship with the paramour. Honestly, this is unworkable. You can't reduce dependence by reducing exposure to a person. A clean break is critical. And cold turkey at that.

Some aggrieved partners insist on involving the paramour's spouse (if the paramour is married) as well in the whole process. Frankly, this is something I would never recommend. The paramour's marriage is not your business and this would certainly constitute, in my book at least, an infringement of the paramour's liberty, particularly if the paramour is unrelated. In the event that the paramour happens to be a close family member of the aggrieved partner, say a sister or a brother, then some other form of intervention may have to be planned, but this may not be the best time to do it.

When the transgressing partner acknowledges the affair, but feels no remorse

Remorse is an important emotion in surviving infidelity, simply because it establishes the fact that both partners are on the same page. The transgressing partner acknowledges responsibility for having had the affair and the fact that remorse is experienced testifies to the fact that the affair was an inappropriate act and not one that bears repeating. In other words, remorse establishes that both partners are equally clear that an affair detracts from the marriage. However, some transgressing partners, particularly those who've had sex-seeking affairs or those who are in toxic marriages, may feel that the experience or expression of remorse may put them in a one-down position and therefore may refuse to express any. They may rationalise the affair and expect that the aggrieved partner get over it at the earliest. Needless to say, aggrieved partners at the receiving end of this sort of behaviour would usually be hard-pressed to find it acceptable. Surprisingly, many do. Particularly if they are economically or emotionally over-dependent on the transgressing partner. That said, surviving an affair cannot proceed in the absence of remorse. At best, stoic acceptance can be the only outcome when remorse doesn't exist or even if it does, is not in evidence.

There are some aggrieved partners who do not accept whatever remorse the transgressing partner exhibits. These people have the mistaken belief that only if their emotional pain disappears does it mean that the degree of remorse experienced by the transgressor is high enough. So, they keep expecting even more remorse. Believe me, your partner's remorse won't take away your pain. It will certainly help in rebuilding your relationship, but it can't do more than that. Your pain will go away eventually, but it'll take a little while before it does. The aggrieved partner's pain and the transgressing partner's remorse together create the glue with which the marriage can be rebuilt.

When the transgressing partner finds it uncomfortable to talk about the affair

I am yet to come across a transgressing partner who can talk with comfort about the affair to the aggrieved partner. Understandably so. The transgressing partner is already experiencing guilt, remorse, shame and humiliation and dealing with all of these is not the easiest thing to do. This notwithstanding, I would still recommend that the transgressing partner communicate with the aggrieved partner either verbally or by writing, a broad description of the affair. Stuff like how they met, where they met, how often they met, how often they had sex, whether any commitments were made to each other and the like. There's no need to get into the lurid details or a comparative account of the marriage and the affair. If the transgressing partner finds it too uncomfortable or awkward or humiliating to do this, I would recommend you cut your partner some slack. You can talk about it if you still want to, at a later point in time. But if you, the aggrieved one, expect your partner to share all the details, so you have enough data to monitor the future and ensure that there are no possibilities for a repetition of the affair, my advice is not to do it. There's no way you can monitor everything your partner does.

Some aggrieved partners don't want to hear any details about the affair. They just want it to be over. In this case, there's no point forcing the person to listen to all the gory details merely so the transgressing partner can feel completely unburdened.

12

The Trauma
of the Aggrieved

By whatever means the affair is discovered, the event is probably the most traumatic one that each partner has ever faced. It is true that the method of discovery dictates the way couples deal with the affair, but the initial responses are usually not very different. Usually the aggrieved partner tends to believe that the transgressing partner, being the perpetrator of the 'crime', has no business being traumatised, but in truth both partners are traumatised by the discovery of the affair, and both have to deal with the situation in their own ways. I'd like to first explore how most aggrieved partners react during the first fortnight after discovery.

Shock & pain

The first reaction on discovery of the affair is numbing shock. Like it hasn't sunk in. Because one has always believed, felt or hoped that affairs happened only in other peoples' marriages, not one's own. And then the pain kicks in. Each of us reacts differently when we experience emotional pain. Some of us sob inconsolably, some of us withdraw into a stunned silence, some of us do mechanical chores, some of us take a pill and go to sleep, some of us get drunk, some of us lash out verbally or physically at the nearest person, some of us break things. There is no fixed pattern of dealing with the pain of discovery of the affair.

There is one rule, though. Express your grief if you can. The best way of expressing emotional pain is to cry. Whether you do so in your partner's presence or in private doesn't really matter. Do whatever comes naturally to you, but try and contain it to between you and your partner. I'll expand on this a little later.

If you're living in a joint-family situation, you might want to find a quiet place where you can express your initial emotion in privacy. If you feel like being held by your partner during your initial outburst, that's absolutely fine. It doesn't mean that you're 'sleeping with your enemy'. Your spouse is still your spouse, not your enemy. If the thought of being in your spouse's presence makes you cringe, find a private space in which to process your initial emotion. Some people I know try and deal with the situation calmly and rationally even immediately after the discovery. This is not real 'calm or rationality'. It's just part of the state of shock, the calm before the storm, as it were. For it's very hard to accept your partner's infidelity in a stoic and equitable manner, unless you've had or are currently having an affair of your own.

If feasible, try not to involve anybody else, say children or other family members, as soon as you've discovered the affair. With the best of intentions, they may actually increase your pain. Wait for at least forty-eight hours before you decide whether to involve someone else or not. You might feel too agitated to sleep, and might need a tranquilliser to calm you down. Whatever you do, make sure you don't take it for more than two or three days, for you're very vulnerable to getting dependent on them. Tranquillisers are not available as easily over the counter nowadays, since the laws are a bit more stringent, but they're still available. And given their addiction potential, they are best administered under medical supervision.

Anger

Anger is also a common first reaction upon the discovery of an affair. Breaking objects, throwing things at the spouse, hitting and causing physical hurt to the spouse, ranting at the spouse regardless of whether others can hear, flouncing out of home, driving recklessly, dashing off to the paramour's place or calling the paramour or the paramour's spouse are all things that many aggrieved partners do. We'll discuss handling the paramour a little later, but as a rule of thumb, containing your anger is not a bad idea, although it may not always be possible. For, as much physical pain as you cause to your partner with your anger, you cause physical pain to yourself as well. If you've tried hitting someone, you'll know what I mean.

Anger is a perfectly normal emotion to feel in this situation, but it's an emotion better expressed verbally than physically. That old aphorism that 'sticks and stones may break my bones but words will never hurt me' is patently untrue. Words have much greater potential to hurt, certainly in a situation such as this one, and I would encourage you to express your anger verbally. Whatever harsh words you utter should not be held against you, for your partner is likely to be aware of the pain you're going through and that the only way you can satisfactorily express it is in words, which you may or may not mean. Try not to go over the top, though. For, no matter how much you hurt your partner, your outburst is not going to make your pain go away.

Some people go into a 'cold rage' where they try and *freeze out* their partners, by refusing to talk to or engage with them. From the transgressor's point of view, cold rage is as difficult to handle as 'hot rage', but from the aggrieved partner's point of view, cold rage doesn't give you an opportunity to express what you're feeling and at the end of the day, increases the anger you feel. Also, people who get into a cold rage tend to be more impulsive when it comes to divorce decisions. In this frame of mind, divorce seems to be the ultimate punishment that one can deliver to the errant spouse. Fantasies of 'cutting her off without a single paisa' or 'taking him to the cleaners' abound at this time. I'll be discussing divorce and the timing of the decision a little later in the chapter, but for the time being let me say this: however tempted you are to call or rush to your lawyer to put together a divorce petition, please desist, for now is not a good time to do this. You are doing this largely because you feel the need to take some immediate action to deal with the situation (particularly if you're a person of action), but believe me, there's a time and place for everything, and this is certainly not the time for even considering divorce.

While you may remain angry for a few days, the explosive anger usually dies down after the first day or two. If it doesn't you'll find that you just can't get out of this stage and your whole process of healing will certainly be prolonged. Sustained anger is like picking at your scabs. Some people feel that if they communicate to the partner that they're no longer angry, the partner will stop feeling remorse, or worse still, may continue the affair. Believe me, if that's what the transgressor wants to do, that's exactly what will end up happening, whether you stay angry or not. It is certainly counterproductive to your own healing to communicate an emotion because you feel it will keep your partner under check. Just allow yourself to experience your legitimate emotions.

Feelings of inadequacy and rejection

Some people may not experience emotions of anger at all, and may straightaway feel inadequate and rejected by the transgressing partner. Even those who've been through the anger phase invariably tend to go through these emotions as well. The predominant thought is '*I must have done something wrong to have brought this on*'. Or, '*There must be something wrong with me for my partner to reject me.*' Or worse, '*Maybe I am simply not good enough. Or attractive enough. Or smart enough.*'

All understandable feelings, but absolutely baseless. The affair didn't happen because you did something wrong. Of course you must have done some things wrong in the course of your marriage, for all of us are imperfect and tend to screw up every now and again. But the affair did not happen because of this. The affair happened because your partner chose to let it happen. Even if you've committed your share of mistakes in the marriage, an affair is not the appropriate response on the part of your partner. While it may appear that you have been rejected in favour of somebody else, this too is not quite true. Otherwise why would your partner still be there in front of you?

If your partner has eloped or has asked you for a divorce in order to pursue a relationship with a paramour, that's another thing. Even in this situation, I wouldn't consider it a rejection of you, the person, but a rejection of the marriage both of you had. If your partner wanted someone else, it doesn't make you an inadequate person. It just means that you were probably too mismatched to meet each other's needs.

Also, why would you want to think that you're not smart or attractive or good enough for your spouse? It wasn't particularly smart of your partner to have an affair, was it? And it's not as if your partner is a paragon of virtue for you to think you don't measure up, right? If you've read the first part of this book, you'll realise that among the reasons people have affairs, finding a 'better partner' is not one. This has nothing to do with you or what you are. This has everything to do with your partner's ability, or lack thereof, to deal with an inner impulse that most human beings have, but don't necessarily act upon.

Jealousy & bitterness

'You've spent three hours on the phone with your paramour almost every day, but snap and snarl at me every time I call.' *'You've had sex with your paramour three times in one day, but for me you always have a headache.'* *'What does your paramour have that I don't?'* Take it from me, the only thing that the paramour has that you don't is no baggage. Since the paramour is relatively new, there is no history in that relationship. So everything seems new and shiny. But once baggage starts accumulating, as it inevitably does, believe me, the paramour is not going to be very appealing any more. And three hours of telephone conversation will come down to a snappy couple of minutes, and the sex will seem to vanish from that relationship too.

As I understand it, the issue here is not why the transgressing partner spent more time with or invested more energy in the paramour. The issue is, why didn't the partner spend more time with or invest more energy in the aggrieved spouse? This is certainly a legitimate question, and one that no transgressing partner will have a ready answer for. Again, it goes back to the baggage question. When couples allow a marriage to get to a 'been there, done that' situation, obviously there's not much energy in the marriage. Perhaps, neither is quite ready to look through whatever baggage has accumulated to do some spring-cleaning of the marriage. So, if the transgressing partner is doing with the paramour what rightfully should be done with you, it's only because the baggage is coming in the way.

Most aggrieved partners feel jealous of the fact that the partner seems to be doing with the paramour pretty much the same things that both spouses did together when they were courting or during the early days of their marriage. True, there's not much variation in the kind of things lovers do together. And while it does hurt that what you thought was exclusive to your marriage (some of the things you did together or the terms of endearments you used for each other) is now being shared with another person, what it also means is that your partner is reasonably consistent and knows only one way to express intimacy.

Nevertheless, there are some people who feel deeply hurt and jealous of the paramour who, they feel, has received far more elaborate expressions of intimacy than they themselves have. This is more true of arranged marriages where, in the early stages of marriage, awkwardness and gawkiness were more in evidence than romance, as a result of which there were not too many expressions of intimacy. As one woman told me, 'For me, he used to show his love by buying jasmine flowers to wear in my hair. But for her, he buys a diamond pendant!' I guess he couldn't afford a diamond pendant in those days. And, quite frankly, even if he had been able to, it would perhaps never have occurred to him to make such a romantic gesture.

Really, what your spouse did with the paramour should not embitter you, as long as remorse is in evidence. People do silly things when they think they are emotionally involved, and when they have an opportunity to reflect on it, they would give anything to undo what they did. But if you get into comparisons or a competitive mindset, it's only going to cause you more agony. My recommendation: don't do it.

Loss of femininity / masculinity

Each of us believes that we're feminine women or masculine men. But when our partner deceives us by having an affair, unless the affair in question is a homosexual affair, many of us immediately experience temporary feelings of loss of our essential femininity or masculinity as the case may be. This is purely temporary, but sometimes it can be intensely experienced. The question in our minds is '*Am I not woman / man enough to satisfy my partner?*' The truth is, just as the affair has nothing to do with your attractiveness or perceived lack of it, it has equally nothing to do with your being woman or man enough for your partner. The affair happened only because your partner chose to have one and has, let me say this as many times as it takes, nothing at all to do with who or what you are. If indeed your partner felt you were less feminine or masculine than desirable, then there are many different ways in which this could have been approached and dealt with. Having an affair was not one of them.

By and large, men are more likely feel a direct attack on their masculinity when their wives engage in an affair that has a sexual involvement. This has to do with cultural influences, where masculinity tends to be associated with sexual prowess and the capacity to 'satisfy and control' the woman. Interestingly, men don't feel as much of a threat to their masculinity if their wives have purely emotional affairs where she has not engaged in any form of sexual activity with the paramour. This doesn't mean that men don't mind their wives having emotional affairs. They do, very much, and won't stand for it, but they don't end up feeling emasculated in this situation. On the other hand women do tend to feel de-feminised if their husbands have an emotional affair with another woman, for many Indian women define the essence of their femininity in terms of how nurturing and loving they are of their men and their families. They tend to handle sexual affairs more easily, since there is a general cultural belief that 'men will tend to stray'.

In modern urban India, this distinction between the male and female responses seems to be getting slowly blurred and regardless of the type of affair, both men and women seem to react with the feeling of a similar dent to their masculinity and femininity respectively. Fortunately, this is a temporary feeling unless the transgressing partner has, in the past, made the aggrieved partner feel less feminine or masculine, by repeated statements or behaviour to this effect.

Feelings of humiliation

An affair is undoubtedly a humiliating experience for the aggrieved partner. Whether the affair was discovered by the active efforts of the aggrieved partner or by accident or through a confession, it is very rare for the aggrieved partner not to experience a feeling of being belittled. For one thing, there is always the belief that affairs happen to other people, not us. It's possible that this is a thought we have articulated to each other, and maybe even to others. It's also possible that we have been judgemental of other people who've had affairs—both the transgressor and aggrieved. We may have also been a tad self-righteous about others' affairs. So, when it happens to us, it's very hard to take and we feel that we are now at the receiving end of the sanctimonious judgements that we know other people will be making of us. For another, we may pride ourselves on being very sharp, and we have to come to terms with the reality that we had no clue that our partner was having an affair, or that we had ignored the red flags scattered along the way the last few months. So this adds to the feeling of humiliation and directly increases the anger we feel towards the transgressing partner.

In truth, we don't need to feel humiliated. Whatever positions you took against affairs in the past, remain valid even today, for an affair is not something you still think of as appropriate. Although you never imagined in your wildest dreams that this could happen to you, you now realise how vulnerable all human beings are, despite their best efforts. It's not much different from when a person leading a very healthy life, eating judiciously, exercising regularly, avoiding stress, still has a coronary at the age of thirty-five. It happens to the best of us, even if we do everything right, due to reasons beyond our control. I am not saying that we shouldn't lead healthy lives merely because we don't know what the future holds. We still need to do our best, but we need to be aware that occasionally, things can go wrong. Like it has now, in your marriage.

Further, the fact that you didn't discover the affair yourself or much earlier doesn't mean you were being an ignorant dufus. It just means that you're a trusting person and never expected your partner to deceive you by having an affair. And that's the only way to be, right? You can't live your life in anticipation of death. Equally you can't get into a marriage in the anticipation that you or your partner is going to have an affair. Makes for a terrible life and a terrible marriage if you do. I do agree that people who are trusting experience more pain when their trust is betrayed. But believe me, they also experience much more joy from their marriage than do suspicious people. That's not a bad compensation, actually.

Depression and anxiety

Having what is generally called a 'nervous breakdown' is nothing to be ashamed or embarrassed about, particularly when an individual has been traumatised. Many aggrieved partners may go through an episode of depression or agitation when they are coming to terms with the fact that an affair has taken place. When I talk of depression, I am not referring to the sadness and emotional distress that accompanies the discovery of the affair. Some of us may go through an actual emotional breakdown, what's sometimes referred to as a 'clinical depression'. Typically, such a person would manifest symptoms like extreme social withdrawal, total disinterest in everyday life, low levels of energy, loss of appetite, impaired concentration, repeated crying spells, difficulty in falling asleep, waking up early in the morning (around 3 am or thereabouts), thoughts of suicide, maybe even an aborted suicide attempt, restlessness and agitation. Some people may manifest signs of anxiety, with or without the above symptoms of depression. These would typically include the constant feeling of fear, inability to concentrate, panic attacks, sweating, chest pains and palpitations.

All these are normal during the recovery period. However, if the above symptoms persist for more than two weeks, or if suicidal thoughts or attempts are present, I would recommend consulting a psychiatrist and taking some medication to ameliorate the symptoms. I agree that the depression and anxiety have been brought about owing to the affair and that no pill, however effective, can make the affair go away. But if you're going to be in a state of clinical depression or anxiety, it's extremely hard to survive the affair, for your mind is in a benumbed state and not really responsive to whatever you need to do to heal.

When faced with any emotionally traumatic situation, there is a sudden decrease in the levels of serotonin and noradrenaline, which are chemical messengers in a part of the brain called the limbic system that controls our moods. Normally, within days the levels of these two chemicals bounce back, but in some of us, they don't return to the baseline levels, which is why we go through a clinical depression or anxiety. The medication prescribed by your psychiatrist will jumpstart your limbic system by delaying the breakdown of serotonin and noradrenaline, thereby increasing their availability in the brain. As a result, you get a level playing field, so you can then start dealing with the affair using your inner emotional strength. You'll need the medication for a very short period, usually a month or six weeks, unless there are other factors that are delaying your recovery, which your psychiatrist will be able to help you understand.

Disgust and loathing

In the immediate aftermath of discovery of the affair, it's perfectly understandable that the aggrieved partner feels disgust towards the transgressing partner. *'How could this be the person I married? How I hate my spouse!'* may be repetitive thoughts. The natural extension of this line of thinking would be *'Can I ever love my spouse again?'* The answer is, yes you can, and you will. If love was part of your marriage, it will come back, but at this time, owing to the feeling of betrayal, all you see when in your transgressing spouse is somebody you think you can't recognise any more. Someone you had mistakenly assumed loved you and cared for and did a lot of memorable things with you.

In truth, your spouse has not really changed. One imprudent act does not mean that your partner is no longer the one you used to love and who used to love you. You're probably thinking, '*Okay, my partner slept with the paramour once. I can live with that. But again and again? How could that have happened? Was there no conscience that kicked in? No application of mind at all? Was any image of me ever in my partner's mind when conducting an affair? And my God, we still had sex while the affair was actively on? What kind of a person would do that?*' Thoughts like these may make your partner completely repulsive to you.

Try and remember that your partner is likely as filled with self-loathing and is struggling to understand what on earth could have prompted such behaviour. For, when in the throes of an affair, one doesn't think at all. Most people who are having affairs tend to function in compartments. Which is why they don't really think of the consequences of what they are doing. Men generally compartmentalise more than women, but women too, seem to be catching up. So when they're with their spouses, they function in the spouse compartment and with their paramours, in a different compartment. Believe me, if your partner has shown remorse over the affair, the chances are very high that this is also accompanied by a feeling of relief that the affair's over, because functioning in compartments does take its own toll and expends a lot of mental energy in the process.

Once you have healed, the feeling of loathing will go away and you'll be in a position to re-connect with your spouse. If you still want to, that is. But until this happens, it may be prudent for you not to dwell on such thoughts, for the more you allow them to enter your mind, the more they will overwhelm you. And fill you with bitterness. Of course, if you always thought your spouse was slightly disgusting, then these thoughts will come to you easier and faster. However, in the interest of your own recovery, I would recommend you not indulge them, for if you do, it's your own healing process that gets delayed. And you need to heal not for your partner's sake or your children's sake or your family's sake or for the sake of saving your marriage. You need to heal to feel whole again, so you can make considered choices of what you'd like to do with the rest of your life.

Some things that aggrieved partners tend to do that are best avoided

Rushing to a divorce lawyer

Believe me, now's not the time to think of divorce, although there are many people who feel that they can't bear the thought of living with the transgressing partner anymore and rush immediately to their divorce lawyers. This tends to happen more often in toxic marriages than in reasonably stable ones, more when the woman is the transgressing partner on account of the feeling of loss of masculinity on the part of the husband, more when the woman is financially independent in cases where the husband is the transgressing partner and more in the case of exit affairs when either or both partners is just waiting for an opportunity to get out of the marriage.

Whatever the reason the affair took place, I would recommend that a decision on divorce be deferred until you've had an opportunity to work through your initial emotions and move on to survivor mode. Remember, you're right now still probably in shock and feeling victimised by your partner. You're also hurt and angry with your partner. And when emotions are running high, taking any long-term, life-changing decision is never a good idea. I'm not saying that you should never consider divorce. You certainly can. But preferably later. when you're calmer, more rational and have entered the survivor stage of recovery from the affair, at which time you can weigh everything in the balance and then take your decision on whether to be with the partner or not.

Constantly asking 'Why did you do this to me?'

There's no satisfactory answer to this one. It was a hurtful thing to do, but it was not done with the intention of hurting you, unless the affair in question was a revenge affair. In fact the affair didn't happen with you in mind at all. Had you been in mind, the affair may never have happened. An affair does represent a temporary cessation of rational thought, because nobody in their right minds would launch on one when they know its destructive potential and its capacity to hurt the partner, unless they believed that affairs are very legitimate and that they are therefore perfectly entitled to have one. Such a person is obviously not committed to the principle of monogamy, which is what marriage is all about, and you would likely have known this much earlier, in which case you may not be particularly surprised that an affair happened. But if your spouse has, in the past, expressed a commitment to monogamy, then chances are the affair was not something that was the product of rational thinking.

You might well ask, did at no point of time during the duration of the affair my partner engage in rational thought? My answer to that would be, probably yes. Every now and again fleeting thoughts would have passed through your partner's mind about the inappropriateness of the affair, but they would have been dismissed with felicity, since the emotional experience that your partner was going through probably took control, obviating any possibility of further thought in this direction. Every now and again, your partner and paramour would have decided to call off the affair because either or both felt it was the right thing to do. And every now and again, they may have even broken off the affair, only to resume later.

This is what emotional dependence does to people. It ultimately boils down to the question of: which emotional dependence is stronger? The one on you or the one on the paramour? It is emotional dependence that will determine whether, when push comes to shove, your spouse will want to reclaim the marriage or not. Of course, in the case of an emotional affair, there will be a period of feeling torn away from the paramour, but this disappears far sooner than you would think. Not because your spouse is callous, but because the emotional pull towards you is stronger than that to the paramour.

It can be concluded with reasonable certainty that when the transgressor wants the spouse and not the paramour, this represents a return to rationality, the notable exception being 'true-love' affairs, where it is likely that upon confrontation, your spouse may choose the paramour over you. But if this is what has happened, I'd imagine you're unlikely to be reading this, busy as you doubtless will be, with lawyers and in family courts.

Wanting to know all the lurid details of the affair

There are many aggrieved partners, more commonly women than men, who keep badgering the transgressing partner for all the lurid details about the affair. There are usually three reasons for this. One is that a clear picture of all the factors involved in the affair provides the aggrieved partner enough indicators as to what to be on the lookout for the next time round, in order never to be caught on the wrong foot again. The second is that aggrieved partners, particularly those to whom the discovery came as a surprise (through the grapevine or by confession) want to know everything about the affair, so that they are not surprised by new information emerging at a later date.

For instance, if the transgressing partner fails to mention that a vacation with the paramour was taken at a favourite holiday resort and the aggrieved partner finds out about this from some other source later, the degree of humiliation felt is intense and the healing process tends to get stuck. In other words, if provided with all the details, the aggrieved partner feels better equipped to deal with the consequences. The third reason is more personal. The aggrieved partner wants to know not merely information about the logistics of the affair, but the contents. Where they had sex, how the sex was, how many times they had sex, whose body was better, what sexual positions or variations were used, with whom was the sex better—spouse or paramour—what terms of endearment did they use to each other, whether marrying the paramour was ever contemplated, what gifts were exchanged and so forth. There is no rationale for these kinds of questions. It is a combination of curiosity and the intrinsic need to compare the marriage with the relationship, and the self with the paramour, that really makes the aggrieved partner seek out all the lurid details.

While there's really nothing wrong with seeking details for the first two reasons mentioned above, the lurid details are best avoidable. In fact, even to obtain the basic details about the affair, the aggrieved partner has to be in a state of preparedness to listen to and process them. Often, in the early stages of recovery, they are not quite ready to do so, despite which a compulsive need may exist to seek out the details and cause themselves more grief.

Obviously, when the transgressing partner shies away from providing the requested details, this leads to more anger and more fights and tends to put more pressure on the recovery process. My suggestion: spare yourself the pain and the transgressing partner the ignominy of sharing the gore. If indeed you need to know something, stick to the broad details and don't go any deeper at this point.

Talking to all and sundry about the affair

Since, as a nation, we are a very social people, and often function in large social networks, there is always a tendency, if we are the aggrieved partner, to talk to our loved ones—family members and friends—about the affair. For obvious reasons, the transgressing partner rarely talks about the affair. But if one lives in a joint family, there is every likelihood that the other members at home may know or may have realised what's happening. In such a situation, it's hard not to talk to them about the affair. Also, if family members or friends participated in the discovery process or were roped in to persuade the transgressing partner to let go of the paramour, they are hardly likely to not ask for more details or regular updates of the state of your mental health and the marriage. While I agree that their need to be part of the process comes from a good place—concern for you and your partner— their continued engagement in the process is actually detrimental.

Each person is likely to provide advice based on his or her own understanding or world view. Some are likely to commiserate with you and add to your pain by running down the transgressing partner. Some are likely to offer you strategies to deal with the partner that may or may not be counterproductive. Or worse still, some, by virtue of being very close to the aggrieved partner, may not respond positively to your need for comforting and thereby queer your pitch. Sometimes, affairs have not only deeply dented marriages, but have also torn families asunder, since family members tend to polarise around their own 'blood', as it were, and deeply buried family conflicts are aired out again and further worsen the situation. While family panchayats can be supportive and therapeutic in resolving family conflicts, they actually make marital issues worse, particularly when the marital conflict is related to an affair.

Sometimes, aggrieved partners tend to discuss the affair with mutual friends of the couple. This too can compound the situation, because when it comes to affairs, friends too, invariably take judgemental positions in favour of one partner over the other, and this can become a big bone of contention between the partners. Also, friends do tend to talk to each other and somehow word gets around, vitiating the recovery process even further. Also, the more one talks about the affair, the more one tends to keep it alive. I do appreciate that to deal with an affair one needs to talk about it, express one's pain and obtain comfort from someone who cares. I'm not suggesting that you shouldn't talk to anyone at all, although I know several couples who contain the affair by talking to, shouting at, crying to, fighting with only each other. If that doesn't work for you, I would suggest that each of you identify one close family member or friend whom you can trust and whom you can speak with and seek solace from. I would further recommend that if you're the aggrieved partner, and the identified confidant is a friend, it's preferable that the friend be of the same gender as yourself, for at this time you are very vulnerable, and the last thing you want is some further emotional entanglement to complicate matters.

Of course, it's highly unlikely that the aggrieved partner will ever permit the transgressing partner to talk to an opposite-gender friend, so that takes care of itself. If, for some reason, even this is unworkable (if say, you are new to the city and don't yet have a supportive network or are living far away from family and friends), find a counsellor or therapist to talk to. But don't ever talk to your children about the affair, or your emotions surrounding it. You may think they are old enough or mature enough, but in truth, they rarely are. Certainly not to handle something like this.

Crying on an opposite-gender friend's shoulders

There is no hard data on how many people, trying to recover from infidelity by crying on the shoulders of an opposite-gender friend or the transgressor's best friend, have ended up having an affair with the latter and making life even more difficult for everyone concerned. Of course, it all starts off harmlessly enough. The opposite-gender friend is as anxious to console as the aggrieved partner is desperate to be consoled. Sometimes it feels good to be talking to someone of the same gender as the transgressing partner for it's somehow not the same as speaking to a same-gender friend however close one may be to the latter. Also, sometimes it may appear to the aggrieved partner that a greater possibility exists to understanding the transgressor's mindset by connecting with someone who is of the same gender. However, inevitably, dependence develops. When the aggrieved partner reaches the stage of *'If only my husband / wife were like you'*, then believe me, trouble is brewing. Big trouble, in fact. And soon, before one knows what's happening, there is a holding of each other in an effort to comfort, for seeing the pain of an aggrieved person can be heart-wrenching for even the strongest of friends. Then the rationalisations begin (*We are only comforting each other; this is not infidelity; even if we get physical with each other, it's not the same as what my spouse did to me*) and so on. Take my advice. Stay away from a person of the opposite gender during the stage of recovery even if the person in question is a very dear platonic friend, for under these circumstances the risks are too high to run, and platonic friendships have known to have crossed boundaries.

Temporary separation from partner

Some aggrieved partners believe that the only way to deal with the affair is to get out of the family home and go somewhere else, either to a relative's home or to a retreat somewhere. Usually this happens when the aggrieved partner's experiencing a high degree of emotional pain, humiliation and disgust, and can't bear to be around the transgressing partner. Many people in the environment also tend to recommend temporary separation to heal. Doing this for a few days or a week is fine, for a change of emotional environment may help a bit. But there are two problems with temporary separations of a longer duration. The first of these is that aggrieved partners, instead of focussing on their own recovery, invariably tend to be thinking about whether, in their absence, the transgressor continues to be in touch with the paramour, and generally enter such a suspicious frame of mind that the purpose of the temporary separation is completely lost. The second problem is that healing from an affair is best done with the partner and long periods away from each other don't help each of you to re-connect with the other and share the process of surviving the affair. While I do agree that surviving an affair is essentially an individual process for each of you, it is necessary that proximity be maintained. Otherwise, you'll find that while both of you have independently survived the affair, the marriage gets left behind. So, if you want a few days to be by yourself or with your loved ones, by all means have them. But not more than just a few days.

Confronting or taking revenge on the paramour

Some aggrieved partners simply cannot get the paramour out of their minds. This happens often when the paramour was well known to the aggrieved partner before the affair happened, either as a friend or as a relative. The typical method of taking revenge is to 'out the paramour' by informing the paramour's spouse, family members and other friends about the affair, and waiting for natural justice to take its course. Other ways this is done is by posting something derogatory about the affair on the paramour's Facebook page, hacking into the paramour's email (it's quite extraordinary how many paramours use a combination of their name and their lover's name as passwords), changing the password and sending nasty emails to everyone on the paramour's address book, or by listing the paramour's name and contact details as hookers or gigolos on sex websites. Even co-workers and bosses of the paramour may be informed about the affair. The basic idea is to disgrace the paramour and ensure that the consequent humiliation and emotional pain caused, at least in some way, compensates for the aggrieved partner's pain.

Sometimes, some extraordinarily complicated measures are adopted. The most convoluted and over-the-top story I've ever heard is the method adopted by a man, let's call him Vikas, who was generally considered a 'loser' by everyone because he could never hold down a job or provide adequately for his family. He was very dependent on his wife Shobha who had a good job and kept the home fires burning, educated the children and even gave Vikas some spending money for good measure. She had every reason to divorce him, and was often persuaded to do so by her family and friends, but didn't, because she strongly believed that marriage was a sacrament and for life.

The sacrament theory went out of the window when she had an affair with a colleague, who was Vikas's childhood friend. Vikas found out about the affair soon enough, made a big scene and threatened to go public about the affair, as a result of which she had to terminate her relationship with her paramour, for above everything else, she valued her reputation. But Vikas wanted to teach the paramour a lesson. He didn't want to rat about the affair to the paramour's wife, for this would demean him and his wife as well. So he went back to the detective whom he had hired, with Shobha's money, to keep a tab on Shobha, to ensure that she didn't have any further trysts with the paramour. The detective and Vikas hatched a plan. One of the detective's female operatives made overtures to the paramour and using all her guile, made him fall in love with her. Then one day, at a pre-appointed hour, Vikas took Shobha as well as the paramour's wife to a nearby park on some pretext, where they came across the man and the female detective in an amorous clinch. That did it. Vikas killed two birds that day. The paramour's life was made miserable. And Shobha saw the 'kind of man' she had chosen to have an affair with.

Obviously, Vikas was an ingenious person with a twisted intelligence and lots of time on his hands to plan such an elaborate counter-deception. However, if you're planning to do something like this to get even with your spouse's ex-paramour, I would advise you strongly not to do so. Not only is nothing gained by doing so, for you keep your anger alive instead of dealing with it and moving on, but you run the risk of being found out and adopting the position of a transgressor instead of being the aggrieved. For the record, Shobha, on seeing an unusually high debit in her bank balance, investigated and found out that a cheque had been made out to a detective agency. When she went to the agency, she met her paramour's 'girlfriend' who hadn't recognised Shobha, and who introduced herself as a senior detective, asking her how she could help. She'd already been a big help to Shobha, who was smart enough to realise what had happened. Vikas and Shobha are now divorced. She's still single, not wanting to have anything to do with a paramour who didn't have the rectitude to avoid a 'honey trap'.

Suspicious mind

It's certainly understandable that when one is recovering from a spouse's affair, one is inclined to wonder whether the affair is really over or whether the transgressing partner is still in touch with the paramour. In the case of sex-seeking affairs, there's always the concern that the transgressing partner may still be attempting to seek out other sexual partners, particularly if any business travel has to be engaged in. It's not unusual, therefore, for aggrieved partners to periodically check the transgressing partner's mobile phones for text messages and call logs, or insist on seeing all the emails that are sent and received. If the transgressing partner behaves in an even remotely cagey manner, accusations are bound to be made and all the details of the affair brought to the surface again and thrashed out all over again. In case an unavoidable social event ensues, the transgressing partner's every movement is bound to be followed with gimlet eyes and any attempt at conversation with an opposite-gender person is going to be viewed with great suspicion. If the transgressing partner's phone line is busy when called, a phone call may be made to the paramour's phone, if the number is known, just to check whether both are in conversation with each other. If by chance both phones are engaged at the same time, it will most certainly not be put down to coincidence.

For a while, all this is inevitable. But at some point of time, the aggrieved partner will have to realise that it is impossible to monitor each and every move of the transgressing spouse. Moreover, living with suspicion 24x7 is next to impossible. But, if the aggrieved partner refuses to let go of the suspicion, we have a problem on our hands, for it sets the tone for the future of the marriage. Some aggrieved partners insist on a minute-by-minute description of the transgressor's whereabouts and all statements are met with hostile suspicion and cross-questioning. Any protest from the latter is met with a volley of accusations and a diatribe about the affair, so many transgressing partners just grit their teeth and bear it, hoping the third-degree treatment will stop some time.

Usually, this sort of suspicion is higher in affairs that were detected through third-party information and not based on the intuition of the aggrieved partner. The latter's principal fear is that unless additional caution is exercised, the deception could happen again unnoticed. In fact it works the other way—the more the suspicion and harassment by the aggrieved partner, the higher the possibility that the affair will be rekindled on the basis that *'Since I'm being anyway accused of something I'm not doing, let me go and do it.'*

This happens largely because being at the receiving end of spousal suspicion does not give transgressing partners the opportunity or the time to focus on their own emotions, shame and guilt. So, they start perceiving themselves as victims of harassment and may end up, in a moment of irrationality, doing something that both of them are bound to regret. My suggestion is that while some vigilance is inevitable—even if it's not really necessary since the affair is unlikely to happen again, at least not so soon—let it not end up making your spouse feel suffocated, for this then becomes a fresh recipe for disaster.

Punishing the transgressing partner

As we've discussed, anger is a widely prevalent emotion during recovery from an affair. So, it's not unusual for the transgressing partner to be, from time to time, at the receiving end of angry glares, tongue-lashings and bitter recriminations. While these can be handled by the transgressor who, if remorseful, might feel they're well-deserved, sometimes, aggrieved partners give the transgressors an overly hard time. This they do by either freezing the partner out, by ignoring the partner's presence, constantly focussing on and highlighting the partner's negatives, and very sadly, using this opportunity to even physically abuse the partner. Although it's more likely that aggrieved men may engage in physical abuse of their deceiving wives, wives assaulting their deceiving husbands is not as uncommon as you may think. I feel that whatever the offence, and however strong the provocation, physical abuse has absolutely no role in a marriage and should be handled with a zero-tolerance policy.

There are three possible reasons why aggrieved partners carry punishment for the transgression into perpetuity. One is that the aggrieved partner feels that the transgressor has 'got away' with the affair and that this is unfair. The basis of their complaint is that the transgressing partner is the one who's had the 'fun' and the aggrieved partner is the one who's had to pay for it. As a result, the need to make the transgressing partner pay is very strongly felt and acted upon.

The second reason is the fear that if the transgressor is not given a hard time, there is every likelihood that another affair will be repeated, based on the belief that it is the spouse's anger that's keeping the transgressor in check. As a result, even if the aggrieved spouse's anger is not all that intense, an attempt is made to communicate that it is.

The third reason to give the spouse a hard time, is perhaps more complex. If the marriage was a toxic one even before the affair took place, or if the transgressing partner was a controlling person in the marriage, the aggrieved partner now has a legitimate and unfettered opportunity to turn the tables and get on to a one-up position and call a few shots. Sadly, whatever the reason for doling out punishment, if it is continued, it will, after a point, start being counter-productive, for no transgressor, however remorseful, will take being put down for long.

I think it needs to be remembered that your partner having had an affair doesn't mean you have the right to pass sentence. Yes, something did go wrong. Something did happen that never should have. But you cannot play the role of the judge and jury and decide what punishment should be meted out to the transgressor. If indeed the transgressor needs to be punished, the only person who can decide on this is the transgressor. Although, as the aggrieved one, you are suffering the consequences of your spouse's transgression, you do need to remember that one misdeed does not make a person a bad one. And anyway, you cannot assume the role of the punishing authority, however much you may want to. All transgressors who experience remorse usually punish themselves in some form or other. And believe me, it's only when you punish yourself that you learn the most from your own delinquencies.

Controlling or manipulating the transgressor

Since control is a major factor in many marriages, it is entirely possible that some aggrieved partners will use the affair to take up the reins of the marriage. Since the transgressor is in the doghouse, or reeling under guilt, or is perhaps under pressure from family and friends not to react adversely to what the aggrieved partner is handing out, the reins of control are there for the aggrieved partner's taking, and only either a very resolute or a very irresolute person can resist the temptation to do so. If they resist it, there is the perceived risk that after a 'decent interval', the transgressor will get back into the driver's seat again. And if they don't resist it, after the same 'decent interval', both partners are going to start playing control games again. And things are only going to get messy.

Sometimes, if the aggrieved partner is the one who is in control of the marriage, it is quite likely that the affair will be used to completely crush the spirit of the transgressor and ensure that the controls for the rest of their married life rest in the hands of the aggrieved partner.

And sometimes, aggrieved partners manipulate their transgressing partners by playing on the guilt and make the latter commit to courses of action that might never have otherwise been taken. This too can give rise to messy situations, for once transgressors find out that the 'tears on demand' or the constant subtle references to the affair are all machinations just to put them on the defensive, so that aggrieved partners may have their way, fresh strains are bound to be placed on the marriage.

Often a lot of the manipulative and controlling behaviour is based on the advice given by friends and family of the aggrieved partner. Remember, the latter are also upset by the infidelity and the way the transgressor has treated the aggrieved. They are therefore likely to find ways and means, not always with the best of intentions, of getting the aggrieved partner to take charge of the transgressor in order that the issue of who controls the marriage is settled once and for all.

The way I see it, there is no alternative to transparency and sincerity if an affair is to be survived. And if the marriage is to continue after the affair, there should be no question of one partner trying to control the marriage. Marriages can never be controlled by a single partner. They have to be structured as companionable partnerships where each partner has too much respect for the other to exercise control. For as long as one partner insists on remaining in charge, the ground is fertile for more marital infractions including, though not limited to, infidelity.

Bending over backwards to please

Although on the face of it, this reaction might seem an unusual response to an affair, it does happen from time to time, particularly in those relationships where the aggrieved partner is at the receiving end of a revenge affair, or is overly economically or emotionally dependent on the transgressing partner, or has been thoroughly emotionally abused and controlled by the transgressing partner prior to the affair. In such situations, the need to restore normalcy is so high, that the aggrieved partner is anxious to do whatever it takes to get the transgressing spouse back on track. What happens in this kind of situation is that the emotions of the aggrieved partner are thoroughly repressed and the transgressing partner is forgiven too soon as long as a promise of sorts is extracted that it won't happen again. The aggrieved partner wants to restore their sex life at the earliest and does whatever the partner wants so that the affair may be quickly forgotten and the need for another affair never arises.

The transgressor is only too happy to accept this situation for, somewhere inside, there is a sense of humiliation at being caught having an affair accompanied by a fear that the aggrieved partner may use this opportunity to turn the tables and take the driver's seat in the marriage. Unfortunately, if this happens, one can almost guarantee that another affair is going to take place, since now the transgressor is emboldened and feels that getting away with another one will not be too much of a problem.

It's quite evident that the aggrieved partner's response is dictated more by insecurity than by pain and anger. Typically, this response is seen more commonly in women than in men, largely owing to the lopsidedness in the power structure in many marriages that are still governed by the mores of patriarchy. On the other hand, economically independent urban women are very unlikely to respond in this manner unless, of course, it is a revenge affair they are responding to and are anxious to set it aside on the principle, '*Now, we're quits*'. Of course, some men too might respond to their wives' revenge affair in this manner. However, whatever the type of affair, this kind of response takes away from the opportunity to rebuild the marriage along safer lines, and is certainly to be avoided.

Some things that aggrieved partners should perhaps do more of

Get into a routine

After the initial confrontation has taken place and the initial emotions have been expended, it is not uncommon for aggrieved partners to find that their day-to-day life has been thrown completely out of whack. And this makes them feel even more frustrated and empty. Of course, if you're working, then your workplace may force you to establish a routine, and if you have children, their requirements may also force a semblance of routine on you, but in your other spaces, things are very disorganised. You used to go to the gym for a workout, but now you don't. You used to watch television but you've stopped doing that. You used to meet a friend for coffee at least once a week, now you can't bear the thought of the coffee place. You used to cook fresh food or at least cut a salad every day, but now you're doing only takeouts or worse, hardly eating. You used to insist on doing the grocery shopping yourself, but now you don't care whether the home delivery chap is giving you date-expired goods. I'm really talking about the mundane day-to-day things that you used to do, which seem like unmanageable chores now.

For the first few days, this is perfectly understandable, but if you continue this way, you're likely to feel even worse than you already do, simply because since all of us function with certain rhythms to our days and nights, the first sign of comfort comes when we get ourselves into a basic rhythm. Even if you don't have the heart to do all the things you used to, getting into a basic routine will help your recovery. If you used to go to the gym every day, try going at least three or four times a week. If you did yoga for at least thirty minutes a day, shoot for twenty minutes four times a week. If you shopped twice a week, try doing it once a week and so on.

Why I'm harping on re-establishing your routine to near-normal levels is that this helps tremendously in making you feel purposeful, even though inside you may feel devastated. There is great comfort in doing familiar actions and it helps the body relax, as well as the mind.

Also, the distraction of doing some chores will make sure that you don't obsess about the affair.

Create enough space for themselves

Just as there are aggrieved spouses who abandon all routine, there are an equal number who bury themselves either in their work or other activities, just to keep their minds off whatever has happened. Honestly, this doesn't help either. If you don't think about what happened or listen to your feelings, it doesn't mean that they'll go away. In fact, if you don't give yourself enough space and time, your grieving over the affair is certainly going to be incomplete. So, rather than see the same movie again on television for the fourteenth time, or take your children to the neighbouring park to play with the other kids when they'd much rather be at home, or open up your laptop and plunge into next week's work, I'd recommend you try and make some time for yourself. If you demand not to be disturbed during this time, I'm sure nobody at home will dare to intrude, except, perhaps, your toddler, if you have one.

When you're by yourself, focus on your thoughts and feelings. Cry if you want to. Think nasty thoughts of your partner—or the paramour—if that's what comes to mind. Keep a journal of your thoughts and feelings if you're used to that. Write a vituperative personal blog that nobody will ever see (remember not to post it, you don't want everybody to know what you're thinking). Meditate if you like, if your thoughts permit you to. During your personal time, don't try and connect with anybody else, except in case of emergency. At the end of your hour, or whatever, just tell yourself that you're not going to think about the affair any more till the next day, and get on with the rest of your routine. In other words, when you give yourself a fixed time and place to focus on the affair, what you're doing is creating a situation where you think enough, but not too much about it.

Of course, it's not as if you're not going to think at all about it at other times. But when you do, take a few minutes off from whatever you're doing to give your thoughts and your feelings your full attention. What'll happen is that over the next few days, you'll find yourself becoming progressively less angry, hurt, humiliated and disgusted. It won't go away so easily, but it will at least reach manageable proportions and you won't feel overwhelmed by your emotions.

Contain discussion of the affair

I referred to this earlier when we spoke about things to avoid, but I'll say it again. When I say that the affair should be contained, I mean that nobody else should be part of the process of dealing with it, except for the one trusted family member or friend you have chosen to discuss it with, and your counsellor or therapist if you've decided to see one. It's certainly quite likely that other family members and friends are already aware of the affair, and have maybe helped you during the phase of discovery or the initial confrontation. You don't want to seem ungrateful to them by cutting them off your phase of recovery.

But marriage is a private entity and recovery from the affair has to be a relatively private process, and you can't have too many opinions, judgements and suggestions, all well intended I'm sure, interfering with what you and partner deem best to do. Usually, if you do it gently, most of your loved ones would be happy to respond to your request to contain the process, as long as they believe that you are confident of working things through. If you feel you're not ready, by all means talk to them about it, but do remember that the more you talk to your loved ones, the more emotions you are arousing in them that they themselves may not be in a position to process. Eventually, instead of you being the only person to forgive and re-engage with your spouse, you'll find half-a-dozen others also in the same predicament. I've also found that those around you who are anxious to help and support you through this, are quite relieved when you exempt them from doing so, because it tells them that you're beginning to believe more in yourself.

Allow themselves to experience positive emotions

Whatever trauma one experiences, it is self-defeating to be negative, hurt, angry or depressed all the time. There will be times when we feel like smiling at the antics of the children, laughing at something that the transgressing partner said or enjoying a brilliant sunrise or sunset. This doesn't mean we've stopped being hurt, angry or depressed. It's just the mind's way of balancing out the negatives with some patches of positivity so we don't cave in completely.

Unfortunately, many aggrieved partners do not permit themselves the luxury of enjoying the little patches of positivity in their lives, for fear that this would keep away whatever real emotion they 'ought to' be feeling under the circumstances. They almost feel they shouldn't experience good moments in the face of such terrible calamity. Also, there's the worry that if the transgressing partner catches one experiencing something positive, a certain relaxed attitude would set in and gum up the works, or worse still, the transgressor would feel let off the hook.

Some aggrieved partners tend to create positive spaces for themselves in their other relationships, so as not to let the transgressing partner find out that they are experiencing any positivity. So they may laugh and joke with their family and friends, but maintain an angry or hurt silence with their partner. This can, unfortunately, be counter-productive. I cannot say this enough: as much as you are hurt, so too is the marriage. As much as you must recover from your pain, so too must the marriage.

I'm not for a moment suggesting that you fake positivity with your partner in order to keep the marriage intact. Far from it. What I'm saying is that if you're experiencing a positive emotion even when your partner's around you, don't hesitate to express it. It would certainly have long-term benefits if you did.

I think we must remember that we need to listen to whatever emotions we are feeling, and experience and express them fully, whether it's anger or pain or joy or even love. Yes, love. There will be periods when you see how much the transgressing partner is also suffering the consequences of the affair and you may feel some love stirring in you. If you do, there's no sense in switching this off just because you think it's inappropriate to feel love when you've been so badly treated. The truth is that, hurt though you are, you still do have positive emotions for your partner for whatever you've shared over the years. This is not going to go away. If you exhibit love one day and anger the next, it doesn't mean that you're throwing mixed signals at your partner. It just means you're confused. And under the circumstances who's going to hold that against you?

Engage in calming activities

Given that the aggrieved partner is experiencing a maelstrom of negative emotions, some rest and calm are very necessary. Each of us has our ways of calming ourselves down, and we must seek and engage ourselves in such activities. Some people like reading, some like playing or listening to music. Others like to play golf or bridge or computer games. Some meditate or do yoga. Others pray and visit the temple, church, mosque or gurdwara. Some undertake pilgrimages. Others attend spiritual discourses. Some may like to watch children play in a park. Others may want to go for a walk on the beach. Some may like to take long drives. Others may like to window-shop. Whatever it is that calms you is the right thing to do, except those you may likely get addicted to, like the use of chemicals (alcohol, prescription or non-prescription drugs), retail therapy and the like. In other words, the object is to calm yourself down, not create a new problem for yourself that you'll have to deal with later.

By doing this, you actually give yourself a better chance at a more substantial recovery, as long as whatever activity you choose is engaged within moderation. There's hardly any point in spending your whole day reading or playing music, or spending weeks together with your guru, priest or at a spiritual retreat. If you do this, you're actually delaying your recovery, since you're using calming activities as you would take a tranquilliser, and keeping yourself further and further away from the legitimate emotions you are bound to experience. If you can squeeze in a few hours a week of your chosen calming activity, you will give yourself enough of a recharge to face whatever else your mind throws at you at other times during the week.

Think of themselves as attractive & sexy

I have seen far too many people, overwhelmed by feelings of rejection and undesirability, just letting themselves go, because they feel there's little point in looking after or grooming themselves. They feel that because the transgressing partner has chosen to be with someone else, emotionally, sexually or both, there's absolutely no point in their seeing themselves as attractive or desirable any more.

Some aggrieved partners, on the other hand, in a desperate attempt to look and feel desirable and attractive, tend to go the other way. They focus overly on their sexuality and try and come across as attractive, flirtatious and vivacious, not only to their partners, but also to other opposite-gender persons in their social and work environment. The underlying message seems to be '*See, this is what you gave up for your paramour.*' Sometimes they overdo it to the extent that they cut pathetic figures and unfortunately make themselves vulnerable to sexual predators in their environment who are only too eager to flatter and respond to their sexual signals.

As always, the middle path is the best one to choose. Don't let yourself go, but don't flaunt yourself either. Whatever you do needs to come from who you are. If you've always considered yourself a desirable person, then continue to feel that way, regardless of the affair. What I've said earlier bears repetition: the affair happened not because of your lack of desirability or attractiveness but for other reasons. If the same partner found you attractive and desirable until before the affair, then you can't all of a sudden have become unattractive and undesirable even if you've put on weight and your stomach's jutting out a bit or your breasts are sagging slightly.

What you need to remember is that the most attractive people are not the most physically perfect people. They're the ones who feel attractive in their hearts and minds. Their bodies will follow naturally. You would be sadly mistaken if you thought you'd be more attractive to your partner and to others if you concentrated on shaping your body or doing up your face better. In other words, your attractiveness is not defined by your partner or other people in your environment. It's defined by you.

By the same token, you need to feel attractive not for the sake of your partner, your marriage, or for other people in your environment. You need to feel attractive for your own sake. It's a fallacy to think that you need to return to being attractive to save your marriage. You need to return to feeling attractive to save yourself. Once you realise this, you will become naturally attractive again, simply because you're not trying too hard to be, nor are you completely ignoring yourself.

When you feel good about yourself, your natural sensuality and sexuality will return. You don't have to learn any new moves or techniques to hold on to your partner's interest. So, please don't try to be somebody you aren't. Even if your partner was seeking sex in the affair, perhaps because of a need to experiment with variety, please remember that by now it would have become clear to the transgressing partner that variety and experimentation do not necessarily make for better sex or for a better life. What your partner will be hankering for is a return to your normal sexual rhythm, perhaps a little more frequently than before, and perhaps with fewer inhibitions than before.

So, how soon after the discovery of the affair, should you return to marital sex?

Actually, there is no fixed answer to that question. All I'd say is do it only when you're ready. If you're still uncomfortable, don't do it. Some people may advise you that you should have sex at the earliest possible time, otherwise you might never overcome the discomfort. I'm terribly sorry, but these people are wrong. Once you've worked through your emotions, resuming your sex life will happen easily.

These same people may advise you, particularly if your partner had a sex-seeking affair, that if you don't sleep together soon, another affair is likely. They're wrong about this, too. If you have sex too soon with your partner, when you've still not recovered from your negative emotions, the sex is bound to be lousy and may put both of you off it for a long time. If you can't do it, don't fake it. If you'd like to keep your distance from your partner and perhaps, even sleep in a separate bedroom for the time being, go ahead and do just that.

Many couples believe that sleeping in separate bedrooms sounds the death-knell of the marriage. There is absolutely no basis to this. There are times in many couples' lives that sleeping in separate bedrooms may be desirable. If you feel that you'd do better to sleep separately, with occasional conjugal visits to keep the marriage alive, there's nothing wrong with this thinking, as long as it doesn't become the pattern for the rest of your marriage. Don't do it for too long, though. I'd say that the outside limit shouldn't be longer than a month. Preferably less.

Also, when you do resume your sex life, don't worry about a few hits and misses initially. This is normal. Your sexual rhythm will return sooner or later. Try and keep your partner's ex-paramour(s) out of 'your bed'. Also, don't encourage thoughts like '*Did they also do the same thing?*' or '*Did my spouse feel more satisfied with the paramour?*' Push them out of your mind and, whatever happens, don't ask them of your spouse. There's nothing more unsexy and off-putting for both of you, than taking the paramour 'to bed' with you.

Engage in neutral activities with the partner

You're living with your partner, but your emotions are still all over the place. And you, perhaps, want to have as little as possible to do with the transgressing partner. Unfortunately, the 'doghouse' approach to dealing with an affair doesn't really work, for you still have to maintain, if nothing else, at least a semblance of an equation with your partner. Not for appearance's sake, but in the interests of your own recovery. I know many couples who put up a front when it comes to interacting in the presence of others, but the minute they get home, they go to their separate corners and don't communicate with each other at all. This is not a healthy way of dealing with the situation, for a lot of energy gets expended in putting up a front, and you're left with very little energy when it comes to dealing with each other.

I fully appreciate that you're not quite ready to 'normalise' your communications with the transgressing partner, for you're still hurting too much. However, you need to provide at least some space for future normalisation to happen. When any part of the body suffers from trauma, the arteries around send out collateral vessels—new little arteries—that can supply blood to the affected part, so that the latter can get nutrients from the blood, and heal. Likewise, when the marriage bond has been traumatised, it too needs some little collaterals to at least initiate the healing process, so that in the future, the bond can regain its strength and connectivity. To facilitate this, at least some minimal activities between husband and wife need to take place.

Obviously, you're not quite ready for full-scale intimate contact yet, nor do you want to have conversations about the affair and rehash it all over again, but you can still engage in some neutral activities which don't require any intimate contact or any fake positivity, but are still activities that, as husband and wife, you used to do. Like taking the children to school together if you have children, or doing the grocery shopping together, or browsing in a bookstore together, or driving to work together if this is feasible, or going to an occasional movie or play together, or going to the gym together, or whatever together.

Basically, the focus should be on doing stuff together, but not the kind of stuff that you feel is too intimate given your present state of mind. Soon, you'll find yourselves doing some of the more intimate activities that you used to without discomfort. Just as, after a long layoff from working out, you need to pace yourself by doing a less strenuous workout and slowly getting yourself up to speed again, so is it with marriage. You just need to ease into it and pace things out until you decide about where you want to take your marriage.

Hopefully, you have, by now, an understanding of what all happens in the aftermath of the discovery of the affair. Hopefully, the transgressor has also read this and understood what the aggrieved partner is going through. And just as hopefully, the aggrieved partner will read the next chapter on what goes on in the mind of transgressing partner as well. It's not as long as this one, but it will certainly give the aggrieved a slightly larger perspective on the situation. Once this is done, you'll be quite ready to move from being the victim to becoming a survivor.

13

The Trauma
of the Transgressor

*I*nconceivable though it may sound to the aggrieved partner, the transgressor too has been traumatised by the affair. That the transgressor is the 'perpetrator' of the affair is indubitable. That the transgressor's actions are what have caused the aggrieved partner's pain is unarguable. That the transgressor had the choice not to have an affair, but went ahead and did anyway, is undeniable. But that the transgressor too suffers the consequence of the affair is unquestionable, even if it's hard to give the transgressor the status of the victim in such a situation. For, how can the perpetrator of the situation be a victim? Be that as it may, given the dexterity with which each of us makes our life difficult for ourselves, I suppose we are all, in a sense, perpetrators as well as victims of our choices.

Shock and denial

No matter how apprehensive transgressors are about their deception being found out, most people nurse a hope, rather than an expectation, that they never will be. Typically, when confronted with either intuitive 'evidence' or even hard evidence about the affair, the first response with most transgressors is denial. Usually, some bland explanation is offered, which even they may not be convinced by. The hope is that by underplaying the situation, they can somehow make it go away.

It's not as if all transgressors want to lie their way out of the situation. Some do, of course, but for the most part, your typical first-time transgressor just wants to have one last chance to terminate the affair, so the aggrieved partner need never know that an affair actually happened. The transgressor is also in a state of shock because, except for the consummate transgressors, very few have ever prepared a strategy to deal with such a situation. They may have tried to imagine what it would be like if their transgression was uncovered, but more often than that, they would have dismissed the thought, too afraid to even contemplate it.

Many affairs are discovered when the affair is actually on the wane, for that's when the transgressor is off guard and may actually not take as many precautions as were being taken earlier. The transgressor may have already decided to call it off with the paramour, without really knowing how to go about this. And when discovered before taking any action on this, the transgressor is even more desperate for just one chance to terminate the affair and pretend that it never happened. Which is usually why they come up with some facile lie when first confronted.

But when they realise that the writing is pretty much on the wall, particularly when the evidence is absolutely incriminating or the aggrieved partner's threats of going public are credible, many transgressors crumble and experience a sense of devastation. Most aggrieved partners think that this is only a reaction to being caught. That they are not really upset about having had an affair, but are devastated that they have been found out.

This is not always the case. Most transgressors who crumble when questioned do so because they were already experiencing guilt about having the affair or having had the affair (if the affair in question was something that happened in the past and has only now been discovered) and have been actively suppressing this feeling while in the throes of the affair. Now that they are cornered and have nowhere to go or no one to turn to, their defences fail and they crumble completely. How they express this depends on their personality and the kind of people they are, but most astute spouses know whether the transgressing partner is putting on a show or is genuinely distraught.

Of course, as discussed earlier, there are many transgressing spouses who persist in stout denial, even in the face of irrefutable evidence, either by claiming that the relationship in question is a good friendship and not an affair since there was no violation of sexual boundaries, or by coming up with some extraordinary explanations that are so wild that they may actually sound credible (*'Those are not my condoms. I was carrying them for my colleague because he didn't want his wife to see them.'* Or *'We were not having sex. He was raping me'*).

I have heard some pretty weird explanations in my professional career, which I'm not going to present here, for I don't want to give anyone ideas for innovative lies. My recommendation to the transgressing spouse is to know when the game is up and not dig an even deeper hole which is going to make the process even more difficult for all concerned. You're going to have to face the music anyway.

Some transgressors, particularly those in exit affairs or true-love affairs, may react differently. They may calmly accept the spouse's accusations and start talking in terms of divorce. In this situation transgressing partners actually don't want to stay on in the marriage. Hence, the affair and the discovery of the affair has actually brought the matter out into the open and they therefore try and push for an immediate conclusion of the marriage, with scarce regard for the aggrieved partner's emotions. The transgressor who has confessed the affair has already gone through an emotional wrench, and although is usually distraught at the time of confession, is much more composed and sensitive to the aggrieved partner's initial emotional reaction.

In all other modes of discovery of the affair, the initial emotional response of the transgressor is shock and denial. Even a normally controlling partner, when caught out in a transgression, loses composure and for at least the period of the confrontation, the aggrieved partner has the upper hand. It may not last, but the initial shock and confusion puts even the most confident partner on the defensive.

Relief

Perhaps not at the time of confrontation, but soon thereafter, most transgressors are awash with a sense of relief that everything is now out in the open and that they don't have to keep up the deception any more. An affair is a very draining process because it is so energy-intensive. It's not just about investing energy in the paramour, energy is also consumed in making elaborate plans to meet the paramour, dreaming up creative excuses to make the meetings happen, ensuring that the spouse doesn't know anything about this, working additionally hard to make up for the time lost in the romantic tryst, anticipating detection, and taking additional measures to leave no trail to the affair. It's no wonder that many people who have affairs, except those who have casual one-night stands, are highly stressed by the whole process, even if they convince themselves that the few stolen moments with the paramour are worth the effort. They're obviously not, if you go by the sense of relief that is experienced once the truth is out.

Most aggrieved spouses mistake this sense of relief as either smugness or as a couldn't-care-less sort of response. For it's not uncommon for transgressors, worn out after the confrontation and the months of juggling their lives around the affair, to actually have a few good nights' sleep, at least initially. This tends to infuriate the aggrieved spouse even more and provides the basis for the release of more anger and condemnation.

But, as I see it, relief is a good sign, for it tells one that the transgressor is not as unfeeling as the aggrieved spouse thinks. Obviously, there is a lot of pent-up disquiet about the affair in the transgressor's mind and the experienced relief is akin to the relief from pain when a painful abscess has been lanced. There is healing to be done, of course, but at least the toxic pus is out of the system.

Anger

Anger is a commonly experienced emotion by the transgressor. This may surprise the aggrieved partner who feels that the emotion of anger is the exclusive preserve of the latter. But the transgressor too is angry about several things. First off, there is anger that the transgression was discovered before the transgressor could either consummate the affair or terminate it, depending on what stage the affair was at. Then there is anger at the lengths the spouse has gone to in discovering the affair, particularly if the spouse had involved other family members and friends in this process. Then there is the feeling of anger that the transgressor has to now occupy a one-down position in the power hierarchy of the relationship, particularly if the transgressor is the husband or the hitherto controlling partner in the marriage. If the transgressor still feels that the affair was not an affair because there was no sex involved and that the paramour is not a paramour but a soulmate, but is being forced by other members in the family or the friends circle to accept that it still was an unacceptable extramarital liaison, there is a deep simmering anger directed against the spouse, the family members and the world at large. If the affair was discovered by a child or by the children, or if the aggrieved spouse has taken the children into confidence about the transgressor's affair, this too generates a lot of anger against the spouse.

Given that the transgressor is seen by the world to be the perpetrator and not the victim of the situation, it's often very hard for this anger to be expressed, for there is apparently no legitimacy in the emotion and therefore nobody is going to stand for it. Therefore, it tends to get displaced on to some hapless victims in the transgressor's environment, like staff, pets, subordinates at work, less sane users of the city's roads and so forth. Sometimes, the anger stays within and gives rise to a whole lot of health problems, such as blood pressure. Some transgressors couldn't particularly care even if the environment believes that they don't have the right to be angry. They just lash out at all and sundry, including the aggrieved spouse, family members and friends, holding everyone else responsible for the situation. Naturally, this vitiates an already fragile atmosphere even further.

Shame & remorse

Angry or not, controlling or not, most transgressors—even those in exit-affairs and true-love affairs—do experience shame and remorse at what they have done, for they are acutely aware of how they would have felt had the shoe been on the other foot. Despite the bravado on display, they do realise, even if they want to terminate their marriage, that this was not the way to have gone about it. Everyone has an intrinsic sense of honour and of right and wrong, and they are certainly aware that creating so much pain in the partner's mind and negativity in the home, is certainly not what constitutes honourable behaviour. Even if they justify the affair as being a result of an unsatisfying or toxic marriage, they don't feel particularly proud of the way they went about it.

Remorse, as I have said earlier, is a positive emotion and one that's important to surviving the affair. However, if you're not feeling remorse, don't try and fake it, for there's nothing as infuriating to the aggrieved partner as faux remorse. Even if you're not feeling remorse initially, you soon will. When you see the pain the affair has caused to people around you, unless you are singularly hard-hearted, you cannot fail to be moved. This usually happens once the transgressor stops rationalising the affair and starts taking progressively more ownership for it.

And in my experience, it happens in the majority of all affairs. Some people who have what is referred to as a narcissistic personality—those who are completely self-absorbed and love only themselves and nobody else—may find it hard to experience remorse, but then such a person is very hard to live with anyway, and the aggrieved partner may have to either learn to accept it or make some hard decisions.

Once transgressing partners get out of the shock, denial and anger stage, the focus shifts away from their own emotion to that of the aggrieved partner's. It is at this time that remorse usually sets in and the transgressor may either gruffly—or more gently—try to make amends for having had the affair. Unfortunately, this happens at a time when the aggrieved partner may be experiencing even more pain from having to deal with not just the affair, but also the transgressor's shock, denial and anger, and may not be so accepting of the transgressor's overtures. It's extremely important that, despite being rebuffed, the transgressor should persist in reaching out to the aggrieved partner, for this will go a long way in facilitating recovery from the affair. Remorse is an excellent balm to assuage, at least to some extent, the pain of infidelity. But only if it is genuinely felt and sincerely expressed.

Humiliation and guilt

Being caught with your hand in the cookie jar is a humiliating experience for most adults, and the transgressor, too, is not exempt from this. The humiliation of aggrieved partners comes from the fact that they, who thought their marriages would never be exposed to infidelity, have been aggrieved by their spouse's sordidness. But the humiliation experienced by transgressors is on account of the feeling that they, who thought they would never engage in something as sordid as infidelity, not only did so, but ended up getting caught in the act. As a result, their self-image comes crashing down and they feel they have completely lost the moral authority to take any position in the future.

Even in relation to their children. How do you teach your kids to be honest when you yourself have 'cheated'? This is the position that many transgressors feel they have put themselves in. That they cannot, in all honesty, blame anyone but themselves for this, even if they believe they had had mitigating circumstances, makes it a lot harder to deal with the feeling of humiliation.

Also, they are probably haunted with thoughts and images of the confrontation and the expression on everybody's faces if the confrontation was a crowded and messy one. And they wonder whether they can ever live this down. They can, and usually do. Not because they become brazen about it—although unfortunately some people do—but because, over time, they view their avoidable error of judgement as being a result of their human fallibility. They will learn never to be judgemental of others' fallibility, but will try and deal with it with compassion and sensitivity.

Nonetheless, there's a murky side to this as well. If this understanding is not wholesome and sincere, and is indeed only passing off the affair as just another consequence of human frailty, then their behaviour is basically not going to change.

Guilt is an emotion that is controlled by that part of our mind that Freud called the superego, which roughly translates into our conscience. Each of us has one, with the possible exception of people who can be diagnosed as having an antisocial personality disorder. In such people the conscience is either under-developed or perhaps even completely absent. But since they function very poorly in interpersonal relationships, they are less likely to be married anyway. Even if they are, they are hardly likely to stay married. For some people, superegos are perhaps overdeveloped and they end up leading very sanctimonious lives. But such people aren't likely to have affairs, anyway.

The rest of us fall somewhere between these two extremes. As a result, we are all prone to experience guilt when we do anything that displeases our superegos. And it is the rare transgressor whose superego will actually condone infidelity. The intensity of the guilt experienced by the transgressor will depend on how strong the superego is. In contemporary life, many people do tend to engage in less than appropriate behaviours in a wide variety of spheres, not just marriage. Such people may be able to take their own transgression in their stride even if they do experience some guilt.

But the majority, even if they condone or engage in less than honest ways in other spheres, do experience the guilt of infidelity. They may try and excuse their behaviour or try and 'expiate their sin' in the same way that they do in other situations, by, say, engaging in pilgrimages or reading the scriptures or making large charitable donations, or whatever. But they still feel the guilt. And this is largely because in our country we still think of marriage as a sacrament and any violation of a sacrament can result in terrible consequences befalling us.

This form of guilt is not really beneficial for the transgressor who wants to regain the partner's trust. If the guilt is experienced on account of displeasing some higher authority and not because one has aggrieved one's partner, then no aggrieved spouse is going to feel hopeful about the future of the marriage, for a marriage is, more than anything else, a commitment made by two people to each other. Thankfully, since the large majority of transgressors feel guilty only because they have let down their spouses, a large number of marriages are able to survive infidelity.

Although guilt is an emotion that can benefit us by teaching us to live within our value systems, it can also be a crippling one if we allow ourselves to be overwhelmed by it. The more guilty we feel, the more we will allow ourselves to accept whatever punishment our spouse lays out for us, and as discussed before, the only person who has the right to punish you is yourself. If however, you punish yourself too hard, you might well end up bending over backwards to please your aggrieved spouse to make amends for your 'errant' behaviour, and rather than survive the affair, all you'll end up having is a new pattern for the power structure in your marriage, which eventually will be to the detriment of all concerned.

Depression and anxiety

Transgressors, too, experience clinical depression and anxiety after their affair has been discovered, particularly if they are predisposed towards either of these conditions. The depression and anxiety may be severe enough to warrant psychiatric intervention with medication and psychotherapy. The condition rarely lasts long, though, unless the transgressing partner has a history of depressive or anxiety episodes in the past.

Unfortunately, they rarely tend to receive the support and understanding of the aggrieved partners at this time, since the latter, too, are grappling with their own emotions. Since I've already written in detail about the depression and anxiety that the aggrieved partner goes through, I am not going to repeat what I've said. The symptoms and the treatment of depression and anxiety are the same for both transgressor and aggrieved.

Self-disgust and self-loathing

As much as the aggrieved partner is disgusted by the transgressor's behaviour, transgressors, too, may end up experiencing feelings of self-loathing. These feelings are not brought upon as a result of what the aggrieved partner says but represents the distress on account of the transgressor's self-image taking a beating.

All of us have a self-image, which is an internalised representation of who we think we are. It is with this self-image that we relate to the world around us. This view of ourselves is carefully built up over the years and may or may not correspond with the way other people in our environment view us. This could be because we project different aspects of our self-image to different groups of people, or, because we are so out of touch with our real selves that we assume that the way we want to be is who we really are. Whatever it is, the large majority of people do believe they know themselves, and live within that framework.

The self-image does take a bit of beating even when the affair is going on, but since a lot of positive emotions are also experienced at the time, some sort of a balancing act takes place. Every now and again, during an affair, transgressors experience thoughts like '*What am I doing? This is not me!*', but they are only fleeting and easy to quell.

Every time the aggrieved spouse asks the transgressor, particularly one who's had a longish affair, '*Didn't you even stop to think about what you were doing? What were you thinking, every time you met your paramour?*', the transgressor is hard pressed to answer. In truth, some thoughts had passed through the mind, but they'd been quickly pushed aside. Had the transgressor encouraged such a thought process, maybe the affair would have either not happened at all, or been quickly terminated.

But that's what happens in affairs. For whatever reason the affair takes place, the experience of positivity, even if momentary or occasional, somehow seems to make it all worthwhile. Those who feel disgusted by themselves for having an affair, usually find that they experience some gain, too, from it, which seems to make up for the feeling of disgust.

People in sex-seeking affairs, where emotional investment is not very high and particularly those who engage in paid sex or sex with a domestic employee or a person who is of a distinctly different social class, may find it difficult to align what they are doing with their self-image. But if the sex is good, it does seem to compensate for the dent to their notions of self. But once the sex is over, the feeling of disgust does come into their minds, and they are quite anxious to get away as far as possible from their 'love nests'.

People in emotional affairs, too—particularly cyber-affairs—experience momentary flashes of self-disgust, but are drawn inexorably towards their paramours again. To come to terms with this, they often demonise their spouses and also idealise the paramour, often vesting the paramour with attributes and characteristics the latter may not actually possess. Often, in any kind of affair, when they are away from their paramours, transgressors are filled with conflicting thoughts. On the one hand they want to be with their paramours again, but on the other also experience a faint sense of disgust at feeling so—especially when they're with their spouses, families and friends.

The only exception to this is when one belongs to a sub-culture, or a group of peers, in which having an affair actually enhances one's status, and therefore self-image. In such groups, self-disgust and self-loathing are rarely experienced.

Once the affair is discovered, the self-loathing, that has been hitherto suppressed or rationalised, often crashes into the conscious mind of the transgressor. Even at this time, some transgressors try and suppress their reactions a while, in order to save their energies to deal with the crisis. But once this is past, they are left to face their thoughts in unexpurgated and unsuppressed intensity. And let me tell you, this is not an easy thing to do, even when one knows that one has brought it on oneself.

Sadness

Those transgressors who do not experience disappointment in themselves may find themselves feeling sad after the affair is over. When I talk of sadness, I am not talking of depression, which is quite different. The sadness that some transgressors experience is akin to pining for the paramour and the relationship they shared with each other. This doesn't mean that they all want to jump back into the affair, although some may well want to. But in their minds they romanticise the affair and therefore experience the consequences of its loss.

Needless to say, this can't and doesn't please the aggrieved spouse. Even if the transgressor does not share this thought with the aggrieved partner, the latter, whose antennae are by now sharp and finely tuned, is usually able to very easily catch on to what's happening in the transgressor's mind. Every time that faraway, wistful look appears in the transgressor's eyes, the aggrieved partner is likely to pounce and bring the former crashing down to earth.

From the aggrieved partner's point of view, *'It's bad enough that my spouse had an affair, but pining for the paramour? I ask you! How unfair is that?'* Or worse, *'My God! Don't tell me they are still in love with each other!'* This is understandable, of course, since the aggrieved spouse feels that what happened between the transgressor and paramour was a dirty thing that has sullied the marriage. So the expectation is that the transgressor should feel remorse—and only remorse—every minute of the day for tarnishing the marriage.

But, it is equally understandable that the transgressor wants some time and space to mourn the loss of the paramour. For, the affair, particularly if it included an emotional component, was not viewed as a sordid event. There were positivity, warmth and many good things in it. In fact, at times, the affair had even made the transgressor feel exalted, as falling in love often makes one feel. So, dismissing it as cheap and dirty raises the transgressor's hackles. Whether this results in an outburst or not, depends on the nature of the marriage and the level of guilt the transgressor feels. But, as a rule of thumb, every time aggrieved partners try to cheapen the emotional affair in an attempt to wean the spouse away from thinking of the paramour, they actually inadvertently make the transgressor romanticise the affair even more.

The transgressor *needs* time and space to mourn the loss of the paramour, for there were emotions invested in the affair. But my advice to the transgressor would be to do it on your own time, not when your spouse is around, and don't expect your spouse, certainly at this stage, to understand why you're mourning the loss of someone or something you had no business to be involved with in the first place.

Some things that transgressors tend to do that are best avoided

Overcompensation & overpromising

Genuinely ashamed of themselves and upset to have caused so much pain to the partner, it is perfectly understandable that some transgressing partners feel the need to make it up to the aggrieved partner. Expensive material gestures—like a vacation abroad or a brand new iPad—are pretty much par for the course, but obviously don't serve to reduce the pain of the affair.

Also, doing things that the aggrieved partner always wanted the transgressor to do, like giving up smoking, or joining a gym, or trying to reach out more to the aggrieved partner's family members, or coming home earlier from work, or hugging and holding more often, are also common making-up gestures. Except that, when transgressors realise that this is not producing the desired results (desired results = being completely forgiven by the aggrieved partner), they may tend to get a bit desperate and start overcompensating by doing things that they cannot sustain and making promises that they may not be able to keep. Like, '*I swear on our children, I will never again in my life, say or do anything to hurt you.*' Or, '*Henceforth, I will always take you whenever I go on a business trip.*' Or, '*I will do everything you ask me to without complaining or even making a face.*' Or, '*I will quit my job. In fact this industry. In fact this city itself.*' And stuff like that.

It is not unusual for aggrieved partners to insist their transgressing partners tell their bosses they will not undertake business trips any more. Or to ask to go on business trips with the transgressors until some comfort and trust re-enters the marriage. Or to ask their transgressing partners to quit their lucrative jobs because that's where the affair happened, and even though the paramour's not there anymore, there are a number of other attractive people of the opposite gender with whom another affair may happen. Or to leave the city where the affair happened, because the paramour continues to live in the same city, and move to a place of the aggrieved partner's choosing, and start afresh.

If the transgressing partner is in an over-compensatory frame of mind, there is every likelihood that, in an effort to please the aggrieved partner, major decisions may get taken that may actually have a negative impact on the quality of their lives. I have known people to leave lucrative jobs because their partners wanted to relocate from the city, as a result of which their careers subsequently went downhill. I have known transgressing partners to spend all their savings on taking their spouses along on their business trips because the company would obviously not pay for the latter's travel, accommodation and other expenses. I have also known one transgressor, a fashion model, to tonsure herself as her aggrieved husband wanted her to, and regularly tonsure for a period of two years, for that was the vow that she had taken in the presence of their family deity. She was too mortified to go back to work, even with a wig, so there ended her career.

Because you have aggrieved your spouse, and want to do something to make up, doesn't mean you have to go along with every irrational request that comes your way. Obviously, your aggrieved partner is angry and hurt, and perhaps wants to punish you a bit, as a result of which many of the expectations of you at this time may be coming from an irrational place. And if, in your haste and desperation to win your spouse back, you agree to comply with every demand however illogical, believe me, this doesn't make your spouse's pain go away. It just establishes a pattern whereby every time your arm needs to be twisted, your partner knows exactly what to do.

And what's more, you're probably going to end up making major life decisions that may actually take you on a downhill course. Even if you feel that your partner's demand that you leave your job, or that both of you leave the city, is a good thing to do, or that your partner is making staying on in the marriage conditional upon your acceding to the demand, or your entire family is holding a gun to your head to comply with your partner's demand, I'd recommend you don't do it just yet. Try and negotiate for a few more months' time before you take that decision, for this is simply not a good time to make major life choices. And who knows, after a month or two, both of you may think differently.

Peace at any cost is always too costly.

Trying to keep in touch with the paramour

All right, you're feeling sad and missing your paramour. Perhaps even thinking warm thoughts of him or her every now and again. I can understand this, for when you fall in love with someone, you invest your emotions in that person, and you can't just switch off your feelings overnight. Equally understandable is your spouse's requirement that you have nothing more to do with your paramour in thought, word and deed. It's also natural for your spouse to anxiously scan your face, your general demeanour, as well your mobile phone, for any signs of connectivity with your paramour. I also realise that this can put you off, but do try and appreciate that this will decrease over time, provided you learn to disinvest your emotions from your paramour and the affair, and concomitantly increase your investment in your spouse and your marriage.

There's always the risk that you may want to, in some way, reconnect with your paramour, if only to satisfy yourself that everything is fine at that end. My suggestion: don't even try it. I can't tell you how many people have done this, never with the intention of resuming the affair, and have paid a huge price for it. The operating dynamic is the guilt that, after engaging in an emotionally intimate relationship with the paramour, you've ended up abandoning that person. In truth, this is exactly what you have done. But you have done this because you had to make a choice—spouse or paramour—and have, for a variety of reasons, chosen the former over the latter.

Since you can choose only one of the two, you have to let go of the other. Whoever you abandon, there's going to be a lot of pain involved, and there's nothing you can do to take it away. You might think to yourself: '*But by getting into the affair, didn't I make a commitment to my paramour?*' Yes, you did. And you are going back on that commitment. But you're doing so because you decided that your commitment to your spouse is stronger than the one to your paramour. And when you've made a choice, this time, you're better off sticking to it, otherwise you'll be yo-yoing your life away between the two.

If you do succumb to the temptation of reaching out to your paramour 'just once', and you get away with it, you're going to do it 'just once more'. Given the fact that your home environment is pretty unpleasant right now, there is an extremely high probability that, before you even realise it, your affair is back in full swing. Needless to say, you can then kiss your marriage goodbye.

So, do try and find some time and space for thinking about your paramour. Or talk to a friend about it. Or to a therapist. But don't do it in your spouse's presence.

So, as much as the aggrieved partner needs space and time to deal with the aftermath of the affair, so too does the transgressor, who would certainly benefit from some slack being cut. And this needs to be done in the interest of both partners surviving the affair. Not as a favour to the transgressor.

Not taking help in dealing with a sticky paramour

Some paramours can be extremely adhesive, and unwilling to accept being abandoned. This could be because the paramour's dependence on the transgressor is very high, perhaps both financially as well as emotionally, or because the paramour is single and has been promised marriage by the transgressor and therefore now demands that the promise be made good. Or because after the discovery of the affair the paramour's marriage has broken up, and therefore an exploration is being made to speculate whether the transgressor's marriage could also be made to suffer the same fate, so the lovers can get back together. Or, perhaps, the paramour is just doing a bit of old-fashioned gold-digging and using the transgressor's current vulnerability to negotiate a settlement. Whatever the reason for the paramour's stickiness, for as long as the transgressor tries to deal with this without anyone's knowledge or help, there's going to be hell to pay.

No spouse will accept the excuse that all the calls on the transgressor's mobile, to or from the paramour, represent the transgressor's attempts at saving the marriage, and the family, and their collective future. Nor will the spouse find it acceptable if the transgressor says something like *'This is my mess. I created it. And I'm going to sort it out.'* Even if this is what the transgressor genuinely believes. *'It may be your mess. But you've dragged me into it and made it my mess too,'* is going to be the inevitable response. Any contact, of whatever nature, or for whatever reason, with the paramour, is completely unacceptable and the transgressor would be well advised to treat this as axiomatic when trying to survive an affair.

In such a situation, the most prudent thing to do would be to take the aggrieved partner into confidence, first about what the paramour is trying to do, even if this means having to listen to more recriminations. You could also take a friend into confidence and try and get the message across to the paramour that the affair is over, and that no contact between the two can ever be possible.

If the paramour is a vindictive person, it is quite possible that you will have to deal with, not only the aggrieved spouse's anger, but also that of the paramour. It is not unknown for jilted paramours to try and destroy the reputation of the transgressing partner and the aggrieved partner as well, by spreading canards through the grapevine or social networking sites, making scenes at workplaces, hiring goons to threaten and cause physical injury, and even causing further dissonance between the transgressor and aggrieved by anonymously making it known to the latter that the former is still seeing the paramour.

Sometimes, the nuisance value, or the threat to physical safety, may also be so high, both transgressor and aggrieved may well be forced to relocate. This has been known to happen, but only very seldom. Whatever you do, don't deal with this alone. You may be well in over your head on this and could use all the help you can get.

I've also observed that, often, when the paramour gets sticky, the couple seems to come closer together, in order to deal with a common adversary. Of course, it can go the other way as well: the disgusted spouse walks away, not wanting to be dragged through the muck.

Withdrawing from spouse and family

Some transgressors tend to isolate themselves from the aggrieved spouse as well as other members of the family. This they do because they're still angry at the traumatic process of discovery, or maybe they want to punish those around them for separating them from the paramour, or they could feel so ashamed and humiliated that they go into their shells, or because they are still so benumbed by the process that they can't react normally to those around them. Basically, they are communicating that they just want to be left alone to process and deal with whatever's happened. Some space to do this is not a bad thing at all, because anybody who's in this situation, even a self-created one, is entitled to lick whatever wounds have accumulated in privacy. However the question is always, how much space?

If the transgressor withdraws so much that there is little or no engagement with the aggrieved partner or with anybody else, that can't be a good thing. For, to recover from a trauma, one does need support and interaction with people in the environment. If the withdrawn behaviour continues for more than a few days, that can't be a good thing either, since staying in one's cave can't inspire confidence in the aggrieved spouse that the transgressor actually wants to recover from the trauma of discovery of the affair and make a go of the marriage.

In essence, we all live in a context, an environment, with people whom we love and who love us. And unless we engage with our environment, we are not going to be able to return our lives to normalcy. Put differently, I wouldn't encourage any form of disengagement from the environment, simply because no purpose is served by doing so. Asking for some space is fine, but expecting more space than your environment is prepared to give is perhaps a bit too much.

Wanting to restore normalcy too early

In the case of sex-seeking affairs and emotional affairs of shorter duration, transgressors may be in a desperate hurry to restore normalcy, so they can put the affair and everything that went along with it completely behind them and move on to a fresh lease of life. What they're looking for is almost instant forgiveness from the partner, to whom they have expressed a lot of remorse, and have taken complete responsibility for the affair. They're constantly scanning the aggrieved partner's face, expressions and behaviour to see if things are back to normal. And if they don't see signs of this, they may harass the aggrieved partner to forgive them. '*I've done something terrible and foolish. I have apologised sincerely for it. How long are you going to take to forgive and forget?*' is the sentiment that drives them.

They may keep plying the aggrieved partner with books or articles from the Internet that extol the virtues of forgiveness; they may ask family and friends to intervene on their behalf and persuade the aggrieved partner to let things go, and some of these may ill-advisedly intervene on the transgressor's behalf, telling the aggrieved partner how much the transgressor has changed and how it's time to let 'bygones be bygones', to 'forgive and forget', to 'wipe the slate clean' to 'forget the past and make a fresh start', and well-worn homilies along these lines, until the aggrieved partner either lashes out at them or caves into the pressure.

Some transgressors also pester the aggrieved partners to restore their sex lives at the earliest. The usual analogy quoted is (and I can't tell you how often I've heard this one), *'If you have an accident in your car, you must resume driving at the soonest, otherwise you'll always be afraid to ever drive again.'* An affair is like a car accident?

Or a veiled threat, *'If you don't have sex soon, it will encourage your spouse to stray again.'* Do these lines work? Sometimes, they actually do, but often they don't. I would recommend that the aggrieved partner be given enough time to establish enough comfort to restore normalcy. I do understand the transgressor's need. You want to be forgiven by the spouse because you find it hard to forgive yourself and can do so only when the spouse finally accepts your penitence

Remember, though, learning to tolerate frustration is absolutely necessary in this situation, since early or forced forgiveness is never complete. Your marriage could continue, in the future, to experience a lot of issues related to the affair, unless your spouse goes through the process at a comfortable pace. For, only then will forgiveness be complete, and real normalcy be restored.

Defending the paramour

Transgressors who've been in an emotional affair find it hard to let the aggrieved spouse get away with bad-mouthing the paramour. Often, one of the strategies that aggrieved partners, friends and other family members use to get the paramour out of the transgressor's mind is to paint a terrible picture of the paramour's character and general behaviour. The transgressor may listen for a while, but is unlikely to accept these statements unless (or sometimes even if) they are supported by convincing evidence. And then the transgressor may do something that makes things worse—actually mount a defence of the paramour.

Sometimes, even when nobody is doing any bad-mouthing, some transgressors may still defend the paramour in an effort to prevent any ill-will being generated against the paramour, thereby taking on the entire responsibility for the affair, as in *'Say what you will about me, but leave the paramour out of this. It's all my fault'*. When this happens, the spouse is convinced that the transgressor continues to carry a torch for the paramour, and will dismiss the transgressor's argument that whatever was said was with the intention of shifting the focus back to the marriage.

The transgressor is right, of course. There is no point in displacing all the anger and blame on to the paramour, for this is not really the most effective way of dealing with the affair, but many aggrieved spouses fail to appreciate this point.

Keep in mind the fact that nothing causes greater consternation to the aggrieved spouse than when the paramour is portrayed as a good person, however true this may be. The aggrieved spouse wants to—and will— believe that the paramour is an evil tempter or seductress who lured the transgressor into an affair. This is largely because aggrieved spouses want to believe that their partners were victims of someone else's machinations, because that way, they can hang on to at least some shred of respect for their spouses.

This is an irrational belief on the part of aggrieved spouses, for the transgressors are as responsible for the affair as the paramours. But, there is no point in making things worse by issuing character certificates for the paramour. At a later stage, perhaps, but not just yet.

Bad-mouthing the spouse

By the same token, it is extremely counterproductive for the transgressor to bad-mouth the aggrieved spouse in an attempt to justify the affair. This usually happens when the transgressor is in conversation with friends or other family members, and usually when the spouse is not present. Some transgressors, particularly those who are controlling or bullying in their marriages, do it even in the spouse's presence, in an attempt at preventing themselves being forced into a one-down position. The basic message here is that *'I did what I did because you provoked me into doing it'*—the same argument that the spouse-abuser uses to justify spousal abuse.

Sometimes, there is another dynamic in operation. By bad-mouthing the aggrieved spouse, the transgressor may hope to get off with a lighter sentence, as it were. By establishing that there were extenuating circumstances, the magnitude of the offence is somewhat diminished in the transgressor's own mind, thereby creating a platform on which the transgressor can regain some of the self-respect that seemed to have been irretrievably lost.

My way of looking at it is this. Perhaps, the reasons being cited by the transgressor are genuine reasons. Perhaps these unresolved issues did cause marital toxicity. And perhaps, the aggrieved spouse is not as much of a saint as is being made out. But the solution to all of these is not having an affair. If indeed these were compelling issues, they should have been addressed at the appropriate time and place. But by having an affair, the transgressor has shifted the focus from the real issues of the marriage to the act of deception that is now affecting everybody's life. Just like, even if the abuser was genuinely provoked by the spouse, the focus has shifted from the issues between husband and wife to the act of abuse. So, too, is it when one has an affair. Even if there were substantial issues in the marriage prior to the affair, nothing can really justify the affair. The accused cannot get away with counter-accusations, however legitimate these may be.

Strategising their dealings with the partner

Some transgressors begin to devise strategies by which they can win the aggrieved partner back, particularly in those situations where the aggrieved partner has taken a temporary break and gone away to a 'safe house', or is surrounded by a closed wall erected by family and friends. Strategies such as, *'Maybe if I stand outside her mother's house and just look up at her window for several hours at a stretch and, just when she sees me, l pretend not to notice her, but walk away in apparent tears.'* Or *'I'll invite his boss to dinner, then he'll have to come home and, maybe, if the dinner goes well, he might stay back at home instead of going back to his brother's house.'* You know the sort of thing I mean.

We are a melodramatic people. So, most of our strategies are based on tugging at our partners' heartstrings and forcing the affection back into their hearts. Since this is the result of our diet of films and soaps, we're actually convinced that the way we have scripted the whole thing so well that it will play out. And we're crestfallen when we find that the aggrieved partner changes the ending of the script entirely.

What we forget is that being at the receiving end of a deception makes one very sensitive to anything that even remotely suggests a return to transgression. And the minute we start strategising and implementing a plan, it is, in all fairness, an attempt at deception, isn't it?

You might argue that it comes from a good place, that the idea is to create a rapprochement, and all of that. Remember that from where your partner's standing, it can only come across as '*one more attempt at pulling the wool over my eyes*'. The need of the hour is spontaneity, not strategy. When you're trying to get out of the doghouse, let sincerity and spontaneity be your touchstones.

I'm not saying you shouldn't stand below your partner's apartment and gaze up at it wistfully. By all means, do so if you want. But if melodrama is what you're shooting for, you might, at best, end up with cervical spondylosis from too much window-gazing. At worst, your spouse could throw something at you.

Some things that transgressors should perhaps do more of

Aside of doing whatever the aggrieved partner should do more of to deal with the trauma of the affair (Chapter 12), there are two additional things that the transgressor should also consider doing.

Make the aggrieved partner feel secure

I'm sure you realise that for a while your spouse is going to be suspicious, anxious and uncomfortable about the possibility of your resuming your affair, or having another one. And you have probably decided that you'll, therefore, be patient for a while, until things blow over. Let me tell you, things aren't going to 'blow over' by themselves. You need to make this happen by doing whatever you can to make your partner feel a little more secure.

Your partner will feel reassured only when you become transparent, open and honest. More so, if you do all of this without being asked to. You could instal an app on your phone that helps your partner track you or check even those calls and SMS logs you've deleted—yes, such apps exist, or give your partner the password of your email id (and try not to create a separate email id unknown to your partner), or you could keep in regular touch regarding your whereabouts, or reduce your business trips for a while, or take time off from work and ask your partner to accompany you wherever you go.

Basically, the idea is to respect the fact that your partner doesn't have much faith in you at the present moment, and communicate that you'd like to do whatever it takes to be completely transparent.

Many transgressors are reluctant to do this, for fear that they might be called into account to explain away several other murky transactions that they may have engaged in. If this is your concern, now is a good time to come clean, for given the state of suspicion in your marriage, anything dodgy that's happened or is happening will be picked up. So, if you clean up your act a bit, it might actually be a good thing for both of you in the foreseeable future.

You might think you're setting yourself up for violation of your privacy for the rest of your life. Not true at all. Believe me, once your partner feels reassured, the need for such transparency will become redundant. What's more, once you establish transparency and openness in your marriage, and these bring you closer to your partner, you might not feel overly protective of your privacy after all. And more than anything else, transparency will certainly increase the closeness between the two of you. If you do this spontaneously and voluntarily, you can really show that you have nothing to hide. For everybody's sake, I sincerely hope you don't.

Disinvest from the paramour

We have discussed how the paramour can continue to be a factor during the aftermath of an affair. We have also discussed how, in emotional affairs, it is not at all easy for the transgressor to 'forget' the paramour, even if a clean break has been made. Difficult, though this may be, this has to be something that the transgressor needs to focus on to get things back on track. Typically, transgressors may feel a moral obligation towards their paramours, or a continuing emotional bond. Ties we are wrenched away from do cause us a lot of pain, but since the bond is neither as long-established or as strong as the one with the spouse (unless you've had an affair within months of getting married, or you're continuing an old affair that precedes your relationship with your spouse), it is still easier to recover from the pain that this break causes.

A conscious effort must be made to minimise, and possibly eliminate, all thoughts about the paramour. Thoughts like '*Wonder what she's doing now*', '*Is he eating properly*', '*I can never forget the way she looked at me*' or '*Will I ever see him again*' or things along these lines are bound to enter your mind. Normal though these may be, they unfortunately tend to romanticise the affair. Avoiding visiting places which both of you used to frequent will help, but merely forcing yourself not to think of your paramour is not going to help you. Think of your spouse instead. Research has demonstrated that when one feels attracted to someone other than one's spouse, one is more successful in preventing oneself doing anything about it by trying to think of the good things about your spouse, rather than just telling yourself not to think about the attractive person.

Even if you may not, at this time, have too many good things to think about your spouse, who's probably really angry with you, try and focus on the good times you've shared in the past. And don't tell me you haven't shared any good times (this is a pretty standard response from many people). If you search hard, you'll find the good times with your spouse buried deep below your recent memories of good times with the paramour. Try and substitute thoughts of the paramour with thoughts of your children or thoughts of the home you and your spouse have built together.

It's easy to think negative thoughts of the spouse, but as you try and list your spouse's attributes, and if you do this honestly, you'll probably surprise yourself by how long the list can actually turn out to be. Don't just spend a few minutes making this list. Do it over a few days. Then, list the good times you've had with each other and the good things you've done for each other. Slowly, over a period of time, you'll begin to understand that even though a lot of negativity has entered the scene, there is a reason that you've been with your spouse for as long as you have. You've actually shared a lot of good stuff in the course of your marriage. And your spouse is not as bad as you thought. In fact, not bad at all.

14

Getting on the Survivor Bandwagon

*P*robably the most difficult part of surviving an affair is to deal with its immediate aftermath, which is why I have spent so much time exploring this. If you've gone through the initial trauma without taking any impulsive decisions or without accepting impulsive decisions taken on your behalf, I would say that more than two-thirds of the battle has been won. Your healing is well under way. Over the last few weeks, you've probably used whatever resources were available to you in your environment to be able to get through the immediate pain and negativity that you felt. You probably clung to each other, to your respective families, your friends and perhaps even a therapist, if you chose to see one. And you're feeling a little better for doing all of this. Not completely okay, but things don't seem so miserably painful any more. You therefore think, you're now ready to tackle the marriage in an effort to strengthen it.

Not so fast. You still need some more healing before you're quite ready to do that. Both of you need to move from feeling like victim and perpetrator to feeling like survivors.

From victim to survivor mode

Overwhelmed by emotions caused by any traumatic situation, all of us feel victimised. One has hardly any time to think. One can only feel. And one responds to one's inner feelings by taking instinctive, intuitive and often impulsive actions. Sometimes, the emotions are so overwhelming that one feels paralysed in a state of inaction. To move from this state to a thinking or more rational state is not easy, for it doesn't happen at a flick of a switch. Which is why a transitory state—known as the survivor state—helps us in returning to complete normalcy. The survivor state—or survivor mode—as it is interchangeably referred to, doesn't represent a phase where you have already survived a crisis. It represents a situation where you're preparing yourself to completely overcome the crisis in a substantive manner.

After an affair, as we have read in the preceding chapters, both the transgressor and the aggrieved go through a traumatic emotional reaction, during which time, although they go through a welter of emotions, both feel sorry for themselves and for the state of their lives. When one feels sorry for oneself, one thinks of oneself as a victim. Here, the aggrieved partner feels victimised by the transgressor, and the latter feels victimised by the situation. Typically, most aggrieved partners refuse to accept that the transgressors also feel victimised since they feel that the whole situation was brought upon by the transgression. There is, of course, some truth to this.

But the point is, whoever caused the situation to happen, both partners have had to plumb emotional depths that they hitherto have perhaps never had to. So, even if the emotional pain and suffering resulted from slightly different dynamics in the respective cases of transgressor and aggrieved, the intensity of emotional pain experienced is not very dissimilar, whether this pain has been expressed or not.

But if both continue to feel like victims, their 'victim' mindsets will ensure that, in the months and years to come, they can easily lose whatever composure they may have so far recovered. And instead of rebuilding a trusting equation, the marriage may become one where each dutifully plays out the roles of the husband and wife, without much emotional connectedness. This is when the marriage becomes what's called a marriage of convenience. The couple stays in the marriage because it appears more convenient than going through a divorce, but the engagement with each other is either absent or low. And the bond between the two can be described as tenuous at best.

If you're looking for a more complete recovery, this is the time both partners need to think of themselves as survivors. There are certain things that survivors of affairs do—and these are discussed below—but even before this happens the first thing that needs to be done is to start thinking in terms of survival. '*Yes, a terrible thing has happened, but I'm going to get through this. And what's more, I'm going to come out of this a better person*' is the sort of thought process that needs to set in. The key to doing this is to remember that the longer you play the victim role, the more will be the emotional pain you're going to experience. So, if both partners make this commitment to their respective selves—that they're going to survive this crisis, individually or together—they have taken the all-important first step.

You may observe that I said, *individually or together*. I did so for a reason. Many people feel that getting into survivor mode may mean that they are saying that they've forgiven the partner and have decided to work on the marriage. In their hearts, they know they're not yet ready to do this, and indeed are not even sure whether they ever will be. And they feel uncomfortable telling themselves that they are survivors, not victims, until they feel ready to take that decision. As I see it, at this time, no permanent decision has been made. At best you're living with your partner under a temporary truce. Both of you are living under the same roof, licking your respective wounds in your respective corners, merely because it's more expedient to do so, since neither of you is really in a position to make up your respective minds about what decision to take about the future.

But to get to a stage where both are in a position to take that decision, you need find your inner strength and stability. To do this, you need to think like a survivor. Otherwise, whatever decision you take will be taken from a position of vulnerability, fear and uncertainty. So, start thinking like a survivor and not like a victim any more. No more '*Why me?*'. Only, '*I can deal with this*'. No more '*It's all my spouse's fault*'. Only, '*I don't care who caused this, but I can't be like this for ever*'. No more '*You've destroyed me*'. Only '*I won't allow myself to be destroyed*'.

Shifting the focus on to yourself

People who survive personal crises do so because they realise that the only way to deal with things effectively is to start looking after themselves. If you've ever taken the time to listen to the airline safety procedures that the cabin crew announce before your flight takes off, you might remember that they all advise you to fasten a mask (oxygen masks that drop from the panel above you in case of a fall in cabin pressure), around your nose first, before you help others, including children. The same principle is in operation when you're dealing with an emotional crisis. Yes, people around you are there to help. Sometimes what they say and do *might* help. Sometimes, they may end up annoying you. But you can't depend on others to bail you out of this one. You are the one that's suffering. And the best person who can help you is yourself. So, like you would reach out for the oxygen mask for yourself first, reach out for your crisis survival kit yourself, instead of asking others to do this for you. Since you are your own crisis survival kit, reach out to yourself first.

What do I mean by this? Should you become self-absorbed and ignore the needs of everyone in your environment—your children, family, friends, spouse? No, far from it. For a self-absorbed person can only be a victim. If you remember, when you were feeling a victim, you were thinking mostly of yourself and were almost completely absorbed in your misery and pain. That's not where you want to go again. You want to get to a place where you are conscious of what needs to be done in your environment—your duties, as it were—but you're equally conscious of your emotional commitment to yourself. You are aware that unless you obtain adequate nourishment, it's going to be hard for you to play your roles with comfort.

So, what do you do to shift the focus on to yourself? For the next few weeks, just stop thinking of the calamity that happened in your marriage. You've thought enough about it already. Stop thinking of what you need to do to fix things, because honestly, at this time, most of the answers that you're likely to come up with will result either in an overcompensated marriage or a divorce, for after the initial pain is overcome, the residual emotions are usually guilt or anger. I'm not suggesting you pretend that the affair never happened. You can't. Every now and again, some cue or the other will remind you of the affair and you might brood a bit over it a bit, but just try and make sure that it's only a bit. What you would be well advised to do is to shift the focus to understanding yourself better. To understanding your own emotions, fears and anxieties. To understanding where your strengths lie. To understanding and valuing the kind of person you are. And through this, making yourself a better person so that you can, whatever decision you take for the future, make your quality of life just that little better. This way, the affair can, despite giving you the pain it already has, also result in a more positive by-product: a more complete person who will have acquired some valuable tools to self-awareness and who will learn to value the inner self much more than before. And all this can be done through introspection, perhaps with the assistance of a therapist.

Introspection and self discovery

An important purpose of marriage, that most of us lose sight of, is to help us work through our own personal fears, anxieties and concerns that have grown in our minds since childhood and made us what we are. Once you've recovered from the immediate trauma of the affair, it is a good time to try and understand yourself a little better. You might consider doing this with the assistance and support of a therapist who may be able to nudge you in the direction of some insights you might otherwise never have obtained. If you've already been seeing a therapist during the immediate aftermath of an affair, you might consider exploring the possibility of moving the therapy in the direction of yourself. Let me make myself clear. I'm not asking aggrieved partners to explore whether they contributed to the genesis of the affair and whether they could have done something to prevent it. Nor am I asking transgressing partners to explore all the possible reasons that caused them to have an affair. That would be too limiting.

But when you shift the focus on to yourself, you focus on becoming a better person, not just a person who won't have affairs or won't allow the partner to have affairs in the future. This is not about the affair. It's about you. The person you are, the influences that have made you what you are, the things that you might need to do to iron out your flaws (unrelated to the affair). The things you might need to do to deal with your fears. The things you might need to do with some of the demons in your past, if indeed such exist.

The reason I'm suggesting you do this now is because you have been emotionally churned up, and when that happens, a lot of buried memories excavate themselves. Memories you may not have had access to in earlier times. Memories that may easily get buried again if you let them. Memories that, if 'exorcised', can make your life calmer and better. I have known many survivors of affairs who have realised that they have a deep-seated fear of rejection or abandonment. Some who've been able to get in touch with incidents of child sexual abuse, that have helped them understand their present attitude to sex and sexuality. Some have understood how over-dependent they were on their partners, as an extension of over-dependent behavioural patterns during childhood. Others have realised that their controlling behaviour patterns have come from experiencing severe unpredictability and uncertainties while they were growing up, and so on.

Of course, many of us may not have had such difficult childhood experiences and may have pretty much breezed our ways through happy childhoods, but somewhere along the way, we might have acquired some maladaptive traits that have made us the imperfect people we are today. Perhaps in the manner we handle conflicts or confrontations, or in the way we tend to downplay our positives, or in the diffidence we have when we interact with bosses, or in the discomfiture we experience when we are in social situations, or whatever aspects of ourselves that we have reason to be dissatisfied with.

If, for whatever reason, you are uncomfortable seeing a therapist, you might consider reading something about personal growth, preferably some good self-help books written by experienced professionals or survivors of great personal crises. However, I do need to caution you that even the best books can, at most, only stimulate a process of self-discovery. They can't and will not provide the answers to the specific questions you are seeking. So try and complement this with introspection too. And remember that the introspection is not to do with the affair or with the state of your marriage. It has to do who you are and what you can do to make your world better for yourself.

Seeking postive experiences

Having come out of an intense negative experience, it would be prudent if you sought some positive experiences, whether or not you've gone through a process of introspection. The objective of doing this is to create some sort of balance in your mind, so you can heal better and at the end of it, feel better about yourself. If you dwell on the negative, you're only going to make yourself toxic and this, as I'm sure you realise, is not going to help in the long run.

Many people feel that if they seek positive experiences at this time, they may forget about the affair and the marriage would just stay the way it always was. This isn't quite true. For I'm not suggesting that you do this in lieu of working through the affair. In fact, I'm recommending that this be a part of the *process* of dealing with the affair. It's just important that you get yourself to a more neutral space before you and your partner get into making future plans. So, for the next few weeks or so, try and do some of things that make you feel good.

What are the things you could do? Honestly, I haven't a clue. I don't have a list of things that are the best things to do under the circumstances, for each of us is different and as far as likes and dislikes are concerned, it's not a one-size-fits-all sort of thing. However, if you sit back and think hard enough, you'll realise that there are many things that you would have perhaps liked to have done, but never got down to doing, because you got bogged down with day-to-day life. You should perhaps take some time in choosing what sort of thing you'd like to do. It's important that whatever you choose has the potential to make you feel a little better about yourself, something that resonates with who you are.

Ask yourself what makes you feel inadequate, what makes you wish, 'I'd love to be better at this'. Public speaking? Expressing yourself through art or music? Being a more lively person? Being closer to nature? Being able to make a difference to the lives of underprivileged kids? Managing your anger? Being able to stand up for yourself?

Once you've identified what you'd like to do, look for ways and means of doing it. It may not be easy, for there aren't too many places where you can learn how to be a more lively person or how to stand up for yourself. You might consider hiring the services of a life coach. Don't worry. A life coach is not a counsellor or a psychologist or a psychiatrist who's going to probe your mind and help you obtain insights. They're people who are trained in how to help you make a life plan for yourself and will also assist in achieving your objectives. Rather like a personal trainer in a gym helps you make and achieve a fitness plan. Except that life coaches focus on your personality strengths and assist you in optimising them.

But don't get bogged down in discussing the affair with the life coach, for then the purpose of hiring one may not really be served. What you want out of your coach is an understanding of how to make your life better, not whether you should stay on in your marriage or not.

Designing a marriage template

Now that you have a better understanding of yourself, you could turn your attention to what you would consider a good marriage for yourself. The kind of marriage that would make you happy and comfortable for the rest of your life, whether with your present spouse or with someone else. When you start designing yourself a good marriage, don't be constrained by your present marriage or whether your spouse will be in a position to accept your revised design or not. What we're shooting for is your design for 'a good marriage', not how to make your present marriage better. You might begin with thinking about, what I refer to as the 'primary marriage template'— the set of expectations that you brought into your marriage when you first got married.

When we get married, many of us have little idea of what our marriage should be. Our expectations are generally based on the 'model marriages' we have seen, say those of our parents, our older siblings, our friends, whoever. Since we're rarely conscious of what we expect from our partners, we start defining our expectations based on what our partner's not giving us, than what we really want out of marriage. If you look back at your primary marriage template, you'll realise how close it is to that of your 'model' marriages. So, now that you're more in touch with your needs, it's time to design a revised marriage template, so you can have a more conscious idea of what you'd like your marriage to be.

The best way to do this is to prepare three lists of expectations you have from your marriage. The first is your *'Non-negotiable'* list. Whatever's on this list is simply not open for negotiation. It's mandatory and unless this is accepted, there can be no movement forward in the marriage. Don't put down *'No Infidelity'* on this list. That's a given, almost a factory-set default. The next list is your *'Necessary'* list. Items on this list should represent what you think are necessary for your marriage, but you're prepared to talk about them and refine them if required. Don't put down something as vague as *'Love'* on the list. Yes, love is critical, but the requirements on the lists should be something observable and tangible. For instance: *'To be loved for what I am and not for what I'm expected to do.'* The final list is your *'desirable'* list, in which you write down expectations that you feel would be desirable in your marriage, but you're prepared to wait a bit for them to make their appearance.

When many people try and make such lists, they are generally very long ones. For an optimal marriage template design, the Non-negotiable list should not be more than one, or at the very most two, items long. The Necessary list should optimally have not more than five items, and the Desirable list not more than three. So this means a lot of thinking needs to go into it, so you can shave your multi-page list down to these manageable proportions.

Keep refining the lists until you're satisfied that you have the recipe for a marriage that will work for you. There's no such thing as an ideal template for all, since each of us, depending upon our life experiences and personalities, have unique needs. So don't go shopping around for the best recipe. What *you* are pleased with, is the best recipe. Having made the lists, there is no compelling necessity to discuss them with your partner, since you haven't yet quite made up your mind whether you're still going to stay in the marriage. If you have and want to discuss your revised marriage template with your partner, nothing or nobody's going to stop you. Certainly not I.

Increasing contact with partner

Even as you are shifting the focus to yourself and concentrating on your personal growth and revising your marriage templates, it would be very useful to increase your contact with your spouse. You have, I imagine, been engaging in some neutral activities with each other until now. If you've not, now is the time to start engaging in these as discussed in Chapter 12. If you've already been doing this, now would be a good time to step things up a bit, so both of you can reconnect with each other a little more, so you can then work yourselves up to a more rational equation with each other. This will enable you to move to the next stage of surviving the affair, where both of you will have to make rational choices.

I'm not going to recommend any specific activity, as long as whatever you do enables both of you to engage in conversations that involve some joint decision-making. Like, say, about the children or finances. Try and choose activities that, in the past, came easily to both of you and which did not result in any major differences of opinion. The idea is for both of you to get back into the groove of joint decision-making. Because, soon, you'll have to take one of the biggest decisions you've made since you decided to get married to each other.

15

The Return to Reason

I know the way I have titled this chapter sounds dramatic. I must confess I did so just for a bit of effect. It's not as if, in the immediate aftermath of the discovery of the affair, you had abandoned reason or reason had abandoned you. It's not as if you or your partner were completely irrational wrecks or anything of the sort. I'm sure that a lot of rational thoughts passed through both your minds, some of which were perhaps, even too rational. However, your emotions were still raw at that stage and you were not really ready to process everything that had happened, and were probably so filled with conflicting thoughts that you were not quite sure how to move forward.

Which is why I'd suggested that you were not best placed to try and understand what hit you or to make considered choices. Now, both of you probably are in a better place, are in a better position to process the recent events in your marriage, and are able to think through your options a little more clearly.

How do you know if you're ready? I'd say, if both of you don't feel overwhelmed anymore by whatever emotions you were filled with immediately after the discovery of the affair, you're probably good and ready to move forward. I'm not suggesting that you're completely unemotional about the affair or you've put it out of your mind completely. Some residual emotions are bound to remain. But if you find you have more good days than bad days, and you can stand to be around each other, you're probably ready to apply your minds to deciding how you want to move forward.

There are probably two things you'd be ready to do at this time: Talk about the affair in an effort to understand it, and decide on whether you want to make the marriage work or call it quits.

Talking about and understanding the affair

There are many couples who, if they've gotten this far, decide that there's no point talking about the affair. They just treat it as a 'mistake' that one partner committed and the other partner forgave, because both partners believe in second chances. One situation where this approach may work is when the affair is of the 'revenge' variety or where today's aggrieved partner has also had an affair in the past. In this situation, the operating dynamic is *'We're quits now, so let's move on'*.

'Second chances' may also work just fine when it comes to a one-off predominantly sexual, one-night-stand sort of affair, where the transgressing partner is a man. Typical examples would be sex-seeking affairs, the variety-seeking affair, peer-pressure affairs, cyber-sexual affairs and thunderbolt affairs.

Another situation where the 'second-chance' approach may work is when it comes to predominantly emotional affairs where the transgressor is a woman, like cyber-emotional affairs and some soulmate affairs. The basic requirements here are that the affair was a brief one, the affair is now over, the transgressor is genuinely remorseful about the affair and there was no real toxicity or negativity in the marriage before the affair happened.

To a large extent, the second-chance approach to resolution is based on the sub-cultural beliefs that it's not uncommon for men to 'stray' and for women to go through periods of vulnerability when they may become emotionally dependent on a man other than their husbands. And while both partners do experience hurt and pain, they are not really devastated by the affair and are prepared to start afresh and make a go of it.

I have seen couples giving each other a second chance and getting by without any further extramarital mishaps. Whether they become closer to each other is hard to tell, but they seem to be chugging along quite comfortably.

However, not all couples in one-off sexual or emotional affairs, nor in other types of affairs, respond this way. Many of them are devastated and go through many of the emotions described earlier. And certainly, couples who have gone through an affair where the paramour was a real or a regular figure in the transgressor's life (as opposed to casual sexual encounters where the paramour could be anyone available at the time, or cyber-sexual where the paramour is seen as more virtual than real), can't let go of the affair using the 'second-chance' paradigm. For them, they have to progress from the stage of victim-perpetrator to the state of survivor, and eventually get to the stage of reason where they are no longer as devastated about the affair and can actually talk about it in an effort to understand it.

As you start talking about the affair, there are perhaps three things you need to have some clarity on, if you're to arrive at a more reason-driven understanding of it: *how to be non-judgemental of and have positive regard for each other, how to 'decriminalise' the affair, and what aspects of the affair you need to discuss.*

Non-judgemental attitude and positive regard

You might well ask me, and many people usually do, how on earth one can be non-judgemental after being aggrieved, particularly when it's caused so much of trauma and pain that you actually need to read a book or visit a therapist to work through it.

To understand better what I mean, we need to explore the whole business of judgement in relationships. Judging one's partner usually exists in two forms: rational judgement, and emotive judgement. When one concludes that when the partner has had an affair, one's trust in that partner has been severely shaken, this is a rational judgement. When one feels that by having an affair one's partner has betrayed one, this too is a rational judgement. When one is convinced that an affair is bad for a marriage, this is still rational judgement.

But, when we conclude that our trust in our partner can *never* be regained, this is an emotive judgement. Or when we feel that by having an affair, our partner's 'true colours' have been revealed and that therefore the partner is a bad or an evil person, then we are again squarely in the realm of emotive judgement. Or when we are convinced that since despite knowing that it was bad for the marriage, our partner went ahead and had an affair, it then means that the partner was never committed to the marriage in the first place, this too is emotive judgement.

In effect, what I'm saying is that rational judgement is good and necessary, for this is how we define our values and the parameters with which we intend to conduct our lives. But emotive judgements only end up making us feel angry and alienated by the irrational acts of others. Good people also do bad things. And occasionally, bad people do good things too. So, we need to differentiate between the act and the person. A transgressor doesn't become a 'bad or evil' person by behaving irrationally in one situation, however long this irrational behaviour persists. For as long as the transgressor admits that the act in question—in this case, the affair—was an inappropriate one, and one that caused immeasurable pain to everyone concerned, then the transgressor can be seen a good person who engaged in an inappropriate act.

If both of you are still at loggerheads about the inappropriateness of the act, we have a problem. But I am assuming that if you've come this far, both of you are in agreement that the affair was inappropriate to the marriage, that deception in a marriage is unacceptable and that infidelity certainly does detract from the marriage.

In order to be emotively *non*-judgemental of the partner, what we need to do is to stop playing the blame-game. Yes, the transgressor has accepted full responsibility for the affair, and it's clear that the aggrieved person cannot be blamed for this. But the aggrieved partner can be blamed for other things that may have preceded the affair. Certainly not for having caused the transgressor to go out and have an affair. But possibly for having been party to carrying forward unresolved conflicts in the marriage. So, once you start trying to ascribe blame, there's no end to it. Both of you can and will find enough things in the marriage that each can hold the other responsible for.

When we stop trying to blame each other, but just accept that the transgressor, who's not really a bad person, did something that shouldn't have been done, we can get on with the task of understanding why it happened. Try and talk about the affair, not dispassionately—for you can't ever be dispassionate about something like an affair—but without being emotively judgemental of each other. Without peppering the discussion with emotive statements and accusations.

Expressing one's hurt is certainly fair and acceptable, but hurling barbs at each other is going to be detrimental. The best way to start is with the understanding that both of you are imperfect people living in an imperfect world, struggling to come to terms with an imperfect marriage. If each approaches the other in the spirit of understanding, rather than looking for more ammunition to fight each other with, then I'd say, half the battle is won.

One of the first things that a rookie counsellor learns is to approach the client with unconditional positive regard. This does not mean that one has to suspend one's rational judgement and accept all irrationalities in the other. It merely means that, despite the other's imperfections, counsellors regard their clients as overall positive people whose negative side has been more on display during recent events.

Similarly, in a marriage, if a couple have learned to distance themselves from emotive judgements, and have been able to balance their negative emotions by reflecting on the positives of the partner and the marriage, they are probably already approaching their partners with positive regard.

It's still conceivable, though, that as the couple get down to talking about the affair, they will start, even without being aware of it, *criminalising* the infidelity.

'Decriminalising' the affair

When I use the term '*criminalisation*', I refer to a mental process in which, based on the dictates of our conscience, we tend to remain emotively judgemental of the affair itself, even if we have got our heads around thinking of the transgressing partner in non-judgemental terms. Many aggrieved spouses, while they arrive at the understanding that the transgressing partner is not really a bad person, but a 'good person who did a bad thing', do tend to shift their emotive judgement from the 'bad' person to the 'bad' thing. From the transgressor to the transgression. From the betrayer to the betrayal. So the affair still remains a 'crime' and if a person feels strongly against 'sins' and criminal acts in general, these feelings are also experienced in regard to the affair. So, they may approach the whole process by trying to understand how a 'good' person could have perpetrated such a 'terrible' act.

And this can be a major stumbling block to the process. For, if you continue to emotively judge the act as a crime or a sin, you cannot really understand it using a rational process. Emotive judgements can only be dealt with emotionally, by suppressing your feelings or compartmentalising them. So, it's important to move to a rational judgement of the affair. Such as: *an affair is certainly an inappropriate act because it is a transgression that causes so much pain all around, and one that's incompatible with monogamy and marriage, but it's always something that happens in a context and there are usually explanations for the affair, and the only way we can survive the affair is by understanding the context and circumstances that led to it.*

I'm not suggesting that you shift from thinking of an affair as a 'bad thing' to thinking of it as a 'good thing'. It's just a 'thing' that sometimes happens, and when it does, has to be dealt with. It's not either black or white. It's grey. Just as you've learned to deal with the transgressing partner with positive regard, you need to learn to regard the affair neutrally.

This is obviously easier for transgressing partners to do, not because they are the perpetrators and therefore are eager to get out of the doghouse by thinking about it neutrally, but because, having got themselves embroiled in one, they realise that different contexts make people respond in unexpected ways. As they themselves did. And therefore, they develop a better understanding of others who've had affairs as well as of others who've been aggrieved by their spouses.

But, aggrieved partners don't find it so easy, for they still fear that being neutral about the affair may mean that they actually give legitimacy to it. And strangely enough, some transgressing partners too feel this way. It's almost like they fear that if they became less emotively judgemental about the affair, they may feel encouraged to 'stray' again. This is not true at all, although the fear is certainly understandable.

'Legitimising' an affair would imply accepting it as not just inevitable, but even as desirable. This is not what I'm suggesting the couple do. What I'm recommending they do is to appreciate that *'although affairs are inappropriate and unacceptable, an affair has happened in my marriage and, instead of condemning it, I am going to try and understand why it happened, so both of us can ensure it doesn't repeat itself'*.

If you remember, in Chapter 1, we had discussed whether an affair is an immoral act or not, and I had argued that it's not immoral because marriage is not a sacrament, but a relationship between two people. Those who view it as a sacrament will find it harder to regard the affair neutrally, because they believe it violates a fundamental life principle. But marital fidelity is not a fundamental principle of life. It is a discipline practised by people who believe in the concept of monogamy, for exclusivity is an integral part of monogamy.

If somebody, for whatever reason, breaches the practice of this discipline, yes, what they've done is certainly a violation of the principles of monogamy. If they, however, see their behaviour as a violation, experience remorse for having caused emotional pain by their actions, and believe that they would like to re-commit themselves to the practice of the discipline, then obviously, they still believe in the institution of monogamy. As a result, their act is not one of moral turpitude, but one of failure to respect the basic requirements of the institution. For this, they punish themselves in their own ways.

What to discuss about the affair

If you've been able to begin viewing the affair with more rational and less emotive judgement, you have probably realised that what you need to do further is to discuss the context of the affair and the reasons why it happened, not what the transgressing spouse and the paramour did with and to each other. Obviously when two people are emotionally and/or sexually involved, they're going to be doing pretty much the same things as any other couple who are emotionally and/or sexually involved would do. There's little point in making an assessment of whether whatever the transgressing partner did with the paramour felt better than what both spouses do together, for it adds no value at all to your life.

If indeed the sex was so terrific, or if the transgressing partner experienced such high levels of joy or comfort with the paramour, the marriage would be over by now. The fact that it isn't and the fact that the transgressor too is experiencing remorse and wants to set things right, mean something, surely? So, rather than waste time and emotional energy on exploring who did what to whom, when and how, it's important to explore the background and context of the affair.

First off, it's important to understand the state of the marriage when the affair happened. Were the two partners close to each other when the affair happened, as it sometimes does in the 'thunderbolt' sort of affairs? Or were both spouses, while not really being distant, not really close either, because their respective lives had just taken them over? This is more likely to be the case, for most affairs happen in marriages which are not really bad or toxic, but in which a bit of boredom or predictability has set in, as a result of which the partners have drifted away a bit from each other. You might consider going through the different types of affairs described earlier (Chapters 5 to 8) again, to see what sort of affair the transgressing partner's dalliance was.

You might find that your affair happened in more unique circumstances than what you read in this book (which really explores the generic type of affairs that seem to take place in contemporary urban India). In this case, you might want to discuss in greater detail the specifics of your own individual situation to be able to get a fix on why the affair happened. There's no point concluding that the affair happened because the aggrieved partner was not responsive enough to the transgressing partner's emotional or sexual needs, for this places the onus of the affair entirely on the aggrieved partner, which is not fair at all.

What needs to be explored is all the different ways and means that the transgressor adopted to bring to the aggrieved partner's notice or attention that legitimate needs were not being met, as well as what was happening in the mind of the transgressor when the decision was made to have an affair. In other words, even if the marriage was stagnating a bit, why have an affair? Why were other things not tried? Like counselling? Or a vacation? Or whatever?

It's also important to explore what or whether something was missing in the marriage when the affair happened. Sometimes, one is not really aware that something was missing from the marriage at the time, and one realises what was missing only when one goes out looking for something or finds something that gratifies a need. For instance, it might transpire that what the transgressing spouse found fulfilling in the affair was the ability of the paramour to listen without jumping in with a solution or that the paramour and the transgressing spouse were able to connect to each other spiritually. I'm not saying, of course, that these were the reasons why the affair happened, nor that they justify the affair, but they at least give both the spouses an idea of what the issues are that they have to deal with and find solutions for as a couple.

And finally, it's also important to understand that the relationship between the transgressing partner and the paramour was not a really smooth one, particularly when a combined emotional and sexual affair was taking place, because no relationship is free of issues if it goes on long enough, and that the transgressing partner was just substituting one set of issues (that existed in the marriage) with another (those that existed in the extramarital relationship). Often, in affairs, once the initial emotional comfort has died down, both the transgressing partner and paramour get in touch with the sort of issues they are likely to be dealing with if they became a committed couple, and it is this that most often ensures that the affair remains an affair and doesn't progress to a committed relationship. The fact that the affair did not result in the transgressor dumping the aggrieved spouse and rushing to marry the paramour is something that needs to be given due weightage to.

Talking about the affair is not an easy thing to do, and does require that both partners approach it with a certain maturity and detachment. If either or both partners find this difficult to accomplish, I would urge you to consider visiting a couples therapist or a counsellor, who can provide you a secure, comfortable, non-judgemental, professional environment in which both of you can discuss the affair and handle whatever emotional fallouts take place. Usually, when both partners approach this in the spirit of mutual understanding, the emotional fallouts are really very small and easy to deal with.

To divorce or not?

To make a considered decision about whether to work on your marriage, you need to take three parameters into consideration: the strength of your marriage, the support systems that are available to both of you, and the reasons you would stay in the marriage if you chose to do so.

How strong is your marriage?

This would be a good time to make an assessment of how strong your marriage was before the affair happened. There is no formula to determine whether yours is a strong or a weak marriage. There are rating scales, of course, and if you surf the Internet, or if you read a lot of glossies, you'll come across several self-assessment questionnaires that I would recommend you desist from filling out. This is because they will give you, at best, a very crude assessment of the state of your marriage, and very few of these are standardised tests for you to make an accurate evaluation. I would suggest that you use your own experience of your marriage before the affair began as an index of evaluation.

For as long as yours was not a toxic marriage (one where you spent most of your time together, fighting each other for anything or everything, and please remember not to view your marriage through the filter of your recent events, for you would have spent a lot of time fighting in the recent weeks or months), there was no physical, emotional or sexual abuse in your marriage and whatever unresolved issues exist are reasonably resolvable, then yours was a strong-enough marriage to survive an affair.

Every marriage has issues and many of them remain unresolved because we don't really devote too much time to resolving them. These by themselves should not be the determinant of whether yours is a strong or a weak marriage. If both of you are agreed on what issues remain unresolved in the marriage, that's a good enough place to start.

Many Indian marriages are generally a little low on intimacy. And since most of them are still arranged, romantic love may or may not have been present. These need not be a major factor either, even if the transgressor was involved in an emotional affair with a paramour. What is important is the level of understanding that existed between the spouses even if this was not explicitly stated or discussed. If both partners feel that, regardless of whatever else that happened or didn't, they still had a reasonable degree of compassionate understanding for each other, we're still doing okay.

Since the stability of many Indian marriages is determined by how well the partners have played their respective roles in the marriage, this is a factor that can be evaluated. If each partner feels that the other partner was reasonably satisfactory, even if not brilliant, in the roles of provider, homemaker, parent to the children, child to the parents and parents-in-law, this too is a good enough place to begin.

If, on the other hand, the transgressor or the aggrieved partner was overly controlling, aggressive, abusive, uninvolved in family life, disinterested in the spouse, and was actively responsible for maintaining high toxicity levels in the marriage, then the problem is a pretty big one. It is unlikely that such a person would feel remorse and would want to actively work on the marriage to rebuild it. In this case, the choice gets made pretty much by default: both of you stay on in the marriage without really working on building it up if you have nowhere else to go, or you call it quits. Of course, it's likely that such a couple may have already done this and would have little use for a book such as this. But for the rest of you who do find the process useful, assess the strength of your marriage only by the factors discussed earlier: the presence of major toxicity, the presence of abuse (physical, verbal, emotional or sexual), the presence of control, the level of love, closeness or intimacy, and the satisfactory playing of marital roles. If, on each of these parameters, both of you think your marriage is a sustainable one, even if there are gaps and lacunae that need to be worked on, I'd recommend you consider rebuilding your marriage rather than seek a divorce lawyer.

Some of you may, of course, find that your marriage has done excellently within these parameters. In this case, you might want to consider skipping the rest of this section and going on to the next chapter. But if any of you feels that your marriage has been pretty weak in these parameters, I'd suggest you don't yet call directory enquiry for a telephone number of a divorce lawyer, but read on, just a bit further.

What are your respective support systems?

Living in a family-centric social structure, most of us have fairly well-padded networks that define the way we see ourselves and the way we live our lives. Sadly, some of us may not have this luxury. Perhaps we come from small and scattered families whose members are not really in touch with each other, or maybe illnesses and deaths have depleted our safety nets, or our families live far away from us and we don't have enough friends to provide us the support we need when we go through crises. Generally, people who have grown up without the benefit of a large, or even largish, social networks have worked out defence mechanisms that helped them cope and may not, therefore, feel the absence of a supportive network to deal with life's crises.

As a rule of thumb, the more supportive the network, the easier it is to deal with the crisis of infidelity. I am not saying that we have to discuss the crisis with all of the members of our social network, but the presence of family or friends in our lives makes us feel accepted, anchored and centred, thereby giving us the courage to face whatever googlies life may throw at us.

Also, our support systems help us find things to do, gives us something to smile and laugh about and helps us find recreational activities as well that are so important to balance our life, particularly when we are dealing with its vagaries. When both partners have strong support networks, they generally find it easier to find the emotional resources with which to rebuild their lives after an affair.

However, strong social networks have a flipside too. They can sometimes be detrimental rather than supportive, especially if the members of the network have strong views or feelings on affairs and infidelity. Typically, since in our country we tend to use the family panchayat as one of the early mechanisms of intervention in any marital conflict, pretty much everyone in the family knows what's happened. And since they are fallible human beings, they tend to be judgemental of one or other partner. Usually, a lion's share of the sympathy goes to the aggrieved partner from the networks of both partners. Although, it must be said, that not all family networks are necessarily that rational, and it's not at all rare to see members of the transgressor's network turn against the aggrieved partner in the belief that, in some way, the latter's behaviour is responsible for the former's transgression. As a result, they may try and drum up support for the transgressor based on 'righteous indignation', which actually results in putting more pressure on the process.

Alternatively, social networks may pressure both partners to stay on in the marriage, even if the couple feels that the marriage has always been a toxic one and would much rather part ways.

In other words, the mere existence of a large network is no guarantee of emotional support. But a network that understands both partners, writes off neither and is willing to be supportive of both spouses regardless of what decision they take is a boon in such a situation. And this sort of network is not a rarity by any means. Most family and friends have built individual bonds over the years with both partners and, as long as they are not asked by either spouse to sit in judgement of the other or forced to choose sides in an acrimonious mud-slinging struggle, they can be very calming sources of support for both spouses. Also, it's important that the individual members of the support network are not at loggerheads with each other, for this too can make for a messy situation.

So, if both of you have a reasonably supportive social network that's willing to pull together to help you deal with the crisis, without coercing you into taking one decision over the other, maybe your marriage has not necessarily reached the end of the road. But if one partner's network is more supportive than the other's, or if the aggrieved partner is getting all the sympathy and support from even the transgressor's network, or if the aggrieved partner demands the lion's share of the sympathy in view of feeling the 'victim' in the situation, then the support available becomes lop-sided. And, as is well known, inequity in any situation causes more pain than gain. In this case, the 'unsupported' affair-survivor, whether transgressor or aggrieved, can't really be blamed for feeling that the end of the road is near.

If you want to stay in the marriage, what would your reasons be?

Even more important than wanting to stay married is the reason for doing so. I say this because I have seen far too many people stay on in the marriage after being devastated by infidelity (sometimes multiple times) for what, even the least rational observer would consider patently wrong reasons.

A part of the ugly underbelly of patriarchy is the forced economic dependence of women on their men. Sadly, in our country, many women are compelled to stay on in their marriages because they have nowhere else to go. Their families don't want them back, and they know they don't have the wherewithal to feed, clothe and educate themselves and their children, if they have any. So they stay in marriages despite repeated transgressions simply because they can't see any way out.

Happily, recent generations of urban Indian women are not always compelled to stay in their marriages for this reason. Although they realise two incomes are easier on the EMI than one, they are more economically empowered than their mothers were, and do have the luxury of choice.

It also helps that urban Indian men have become more progressive and liberal in their thinking. Also, families of women have become more encouraging of them and are more reluctant, certainly in urban India, to push their daughters or sisters back into abusive or controlling marriages. But overall, when it comes to the issue of economics as the reason to stay on in a marriage, there's precious little that anyone can say or do, other than offer heartfelt sympathy and gently suggest that this might be a good time to start thinking about ways to empower themselves economically, even if only to give the oppressing partners some food for thought.

It's not as if men have it all that easy on the economic front either. As principal providers for their families, they have had to shoulder the financial burden, even if the role of provider has given them access to untrammelled power in their marital and family lives. Besides, since everyone in the family aspires to a higher quality of life, there is a much higher expectation of them.

So, the modern man is quite happy to share the economic burden with his wife. As a result of this, a fair amount of planning for the family's future is dependent on the availability of two incomes. In such a situation if the woman is the transgressor, the cuckolded husband, struggling to cope with the feeling of being emasculated, feels even more so because he also has reached a level of economic dependence on his transgressing wife. Such a man may choose to stay on in the marriage, not because he loves his wife or wants to be with her, but because he has no other economic alternative than to do so.

The second reason why many people choose to remain in unfulfilling marriages, whether or not these marriages have to deal with infidelity is, 'for the sake of the children'. Believe me, this is the worst reason to stay on with your partner if you feel that either or both of you would gladly have divorced each other had not the children been part of the equation.

Of course, all children want their parents to stay married. But only if they can be reasonably happy together, not if they're miserable and are counting the days till their children grow up and leave home, so they can then go their separate ways. It is also true that many couples use children as an *excuse* to stay in the marriage. What I mean is, they need to give themselves an apparently 'rational' reason not to get divorced and 'for-the-sake-of-the-children' becomes a rationalisation, enabling them to postpone taking a decision that they are, in reality, afraid to take. Afraid, because they fear loneliness, because they fear the unknown, because they fear the unfamiliar.

The third reason that many unhappy couples fear divorce is because of social ostracism, particularly if they come from conservative backgrounds. This, too, cannot be the 'right reason' for people staying on in a marriage. Neither can 'convenience'. Many couples find it more convenient—for a variety of practical reasons—to stay together even if the marriage is not a happy one.

These 'marriages of convenience' are not at all uncommon, wherein both partners have a tacit under-standing that they are free to do whatever they respectively want to do, provided they do so discreetly. Of course, in such marriages, infidelity is really unlikely to produce any ripples, unless it becomes a scandal that everyone comes to know about.

After either one has had an affair, couples should stay in their marriages only if they really want to and if both partners are committed to making an effort to rebuild a relationship that's been thoroughly shaken and stirred. If each doesn't give completely of themselves to the process, the affair is going to remain an unforgotten entity in the marriage, even long after it is over. Ideally if you want to stay in your marriage after surviving the immediate aftermath of the affair, it should be *because you want to not because you have to or because you can't think of anything else to do.*

And you will want to stay on in the marriage if you believe that the affair was an aberration, not the norm; a wake-up call, not the death-knell; an act of indiscretion, not one of malice. At this stage, aggrieved spouses may not feel overly loving to their partners, and transgressors may feel a bit tentative on this score, for the general feeling is that when love doesn't seem to be in evidence, what can save the marriage? If you ask me, the only thing that can save the marriage is the understanding on the part of both partners that both choose to stay in the marriage and work on it. Then, the hurt and pain will go away, to be replaced by love and companionship, provided the marriage is configured for these.

At this time, about 20 per cent of couples might also conclude that the only way they can survive the infidelity is by parting ways. Typically, this happens with couples that were not very close even before the affair, in the case of 'true love' affairs where the transgressor wants to leave the spouse for the paramour, in affairs where the aggrieved partner believes that the affair violates the sanctity of the marriage to such an extent that continuing to live with the transgressor is demeaning or diminishing, and in affairs that were so brazen and thoughtless that families or friends of both partners have been sharply polarised around the issue and exert enough influence over the spouses to keep them apart.

As long as the decision is taken with as little rancour or acrimony as possible under the circumstances, it wouldn't be too difficult to implement. But if there's a lot of anger on either side, I would still recommend waiting a bit longer to make the decision. Otherwise, the divorce would becomean extremely messy exercise and would be bound to cause even more pain, hurt and considerable loss of dignity to both partners, both families, as well as the children, if any.

If, on the other hand, the couple has decided to stay together, it should be remembered that either or both partners may not yet be fully convinced about the wisdom of doing so. Several doubts may legitimately linger in their minds. At this time, the decision to stay on in the marriage should be seen as a conditional decision, the two principal conditions being:

1. No more affairs. If indeed another affair happens, regardless of which partner has an affair, divorce must be seen as a viable alternative. Few marriages can survive multiple transgressions, except marriages of convenience. Unlike many other things in life, where dealing with something is easier the second time than the first, when it comes to infidelity, it becomes even more difficult to survive it the next time around.

2. The marriage needs to be worked on and reconfigured in order that it becomes an open, transparent, companionable marriage based on a strong bond of intimacy.

If neither partner feels comfortable with the strength of the marriage or their social support systems, and don't want to stay in the marriage unless they have to, they might want to consider a period of separation as a prelude to divorce. Hopefully, if they have to do this, they can do so amicably and not make it any worse for each other than it already has been.

If one partner feels a strong need to get divorced and the other wants to try and make it work, this may be a good time to spend a few sessions with a good couples therapist or counsellor who's experienced in handling marital infidelity, so that both of them can arrive at a mutually beneficial and considered decision at the end of the process.

On the other hand, if both partners are agreed that the marriage is a reasonably strong one—even though it had some gaps that permitted the affair to take place—that their support systems are strong enough to provide a safety net for both of them without intruding into their rebuilding process, that they want to stay in the marriage because they want to and not because they have to, and that both the principal conditions to stay on in the marriage are mutually acceptable, they can now turn their attention to forgiveness, trust and rebuilding the marriage.

16

Forgiveness and Trust

*I*n the final analysis, an affair can be said to have been dealt with when forgiveness and trust re-enter the frame. In the few weeks or months after the discovery of the affair, the marriage had likely to have been filled with suspicion, mistrust, hostility and resentment. Towards the end of this period, these negative emotions would have abated in intensity, even if they didn't completely disappear. It's almost like people limping back from the ruins after being devastated by a natural disaster. The initial feelings of unreality and victimhood are beginning to be replaced by a strong urge to move on and get on to the survivor platform. In the case of a natural disaster, one can't really blame anyone for the havoc that was caused. In the case of an affair, of course one can, and often, one does. Which is why the process of moving on demands that forgiveness takes place.

Forgiveness

It may not have escaped your notice that I have not mentioned forgiveness right until now, even though, if you are the aggrieved partner, everyone in your environment, including the transgressing partner would have been exhorting you, beseeching you and pleading with you to forgive the transgression. I have done this for a reason. And the reason is a pretty simple one. When you're feeling emotionally desolate and hurt and angry, the last thing you can do is to forgive the transgressor. If you try to forgive too soon, you'll end up suppressing or repressing your feelings and will not have the opportunity to go through the normal period of mourning that every aggrieved partner needs to. In her well-written book, *How Can I Forgive You?*, American psychologist Janis A. Spring describes this type of forgiveness as '*cheap forgiveness*' because forgiveness takes place for reasons other than acceptance of the affair; reasons like fear that the partner would leave us, or the fear of being alone. And when this sort of forgiveness takes place, the transgressor would not have had enough time or opportunity to reflect, introspect and understand the affair and the context in which it happened.

Needless to say, had you forgiven the transgression earlier, both you and your partner would have been extremely relieved and may have engaged in a process of 'forced normalisation' that may or may not have helped in the long run. If the affair was a one-off thing like, say, a sexual-variation affair, you may find it easier to forgive this as an error of judgement and move on. But if emotions were involved, it may not have been so easy to let it go.

However, now is a good time to work towards forgiveness. But do remember, that forgiveness has many layers and is not only a question of '*I forgive you for what you have done to me*' .

What is forgiveness?

In its simplest form, forgiveness means pardoning or absolving a person who did something bad to you. The aggrieved partner was deceived by the transgressor, who violated a boundary that exists implicitly and explicitly in a marriage, and in the process ended up betraying the trust of the former. If the aggrieved partner loves the transgressor enough, forgiving the latter for a boundary violation is not very hard to do.

Why, then, do people have such a hard time doing it? Is it because they believe that if they forgive the transgressor, they make themselves vulnerable to betrayal again? Or because the nature of the transgression is so severe as to make it unforgivable or, at least, difficult to forgive? Or because the remorse experienced by the transgressor appears inadequate? Or, perhaps, the transgressor is not doing enough to earn the aggrieved spouse's forgiveness? Or could it be that the transgression took place under such deceitful circumstances that forgiveness becomes harder? Or was it because the affair went undetected for such a long time and may have well continued if the discovery hadn't taken place? Or maybe because the aggrieved partner had no clue that an affair was taking place because the trust reposed on the transgressor was so high? Or was it the choice of the paramour that makes it so difficult to accept and let go of the transgression? Or because the transgressor refused to admit to the affair and the aggrieved partner had to go to extreme lengths to secure evidence convincing enough to 'nail' the transgressor? Maybe it had to do with the fact that the transgressor was continuing to have sex with and be loving to the aggrieved partner even while doing the same with the paramour, thereby making the whole thing so much more duplicitous? Or because having an affair makes the transgressor a morally depraved person?

All of these are some factors that come in the way of the aggrieved partner forgiving the transgressor for the affair. Infidelity research and clinical experience suggest that it's easier for the aggrieved partner to forgive the transgressor when:

a. the affair was of a short duration
b. the affair was a one-night stand
c. discovery of the affair happened on account of confession by the transgressor
d. emotional involvement with the paramour was minimal
e. the affair was conducted mainly online and through telephone calls with minimal face-to-face interactions
f. the transgressor's family is supportive of the aggrieved partner and denounces the transgression in no uncertain terms
g. the transgressor does not defend the transgression, but recognises it as inappropriate
h. the transgressor experiences remorse about the affair without being persuaded to
i. the transgressor does not blame the aggrieved partner for the affair, or attempt to negotiate the blame
j. the aggrieved partner intuited the affair that led to its discovery
k. the transgressor did not bad-mouth the aggrieved partner to the paramour or make out that the marriage was a bad one in order to pursue the affair
l. in the immediate post-discovery phase, the transgressor has taken a lot of effort to help the aggrieved partner deal with the pain
m. in general terms, before the affair happened, both partners did experience periods of connectedness, closeness and companionship
n. the duration of the marriage is more than five years, for in marriages of shorter duration, the bond between partners has not built up adequate strength
o. the partners are relatively mature or got married at a slightly older age (late twenties), so that some of this

maturity was taken advantage of in understanding and surviving the infidelity

You may have noticed from the foregoing that the most difficult thing to forgive is not the affair itself, but the deceit that surrounded the affair. In other words, it is extremely difficult to come to terms with the fact that a spouse who was loving and loved, could, regardless of the state of the marriage at the time, actually allow another person into a hitherto private and exclusive mind space and did so in secrecy. Of course, if the transgressor was generally known to be a secretive person, and has a track record of deceptions in other areas (such as financial or property matters), the aggrieved spouse may find it easier to accept, though not necessarily forgive, the transgression.

But, however close to or distant the spouses were to each other, however supportive or unsupportive the social environment, however short or long the duration of the marriage, forgiving infidelity is hard. This is something that the transgressor would do well to remember, for expecting quick forgiveness is something that many transgressors do, particularly when they experience high degrees of remorse and guilt.

Who forgives whom?

On the face of it, this may appear to be a no-brainer. The transgressor is the perpetrator and the aggrieved partner the victim. So, it is the victim that forgives the perpetrator. *Duh!* As with most things in this book, it's not quite simple and straightforward as that. That the aggrieved partner has to forgive the transgressor is unquestionably a no-brainer, but it doesn't stop with that. Aggrieved partners also have to forgive themselves. Transgressors too need to forgive themselves. And—hold your breath—transgressors also need to forgive their aggrieved partners.

And on top of all this, both partners have to forgive and be forgiven by close members in their social networks who were willy-nilly drawn into the whole scene, although I'm not going to get into exploring what family members have to do, for this book is only about the married couple. But all said and done, there's a lot of forgiving that needs to take place.

Let's first begin with the need for both partners to forgive themselves. While it is readily apparent why precisely transgressors need to do this, it may not be so easy to understand why aggrieved partners need to forgive themselves. It might not have escaped your attention that this book has been written to be read by both aggrieved spouses and transgressors. Put differently, transgressors also need help in understanding and surviving their infidelity. Even though they were the architects of the situation, they are also, in a way, victims of the infidelity. Having allowed themselves to either initiate or get drawn into an affair, they too have experienced guilt and distress, even if they did experience some joy out of it. They are not particularly proud of what happened and about the pain and grief they have caused to their spouses and families. Once they come to terms with the magnitude of what they have done, and have understood why they did it, they have to actively forgive themselves for having done what they did. When they start doing this, many aggrieved spouses feel they are letting themselves off the hook. But this is far from true. Believe me, it's only when transgressors forgive themselves, that they will put themselves as well as the marriage on the road to recovery.

As much as they need to forgive the transgressing partner, aggrieved spouses need to forgive themselves. They have gone through a lot of emotional pain during the whole process and have perhaps behaved in ways that they may not be particularly proud of, particularly when they tried to track, monitor and control the transgressing partner's behaviour both before and after discovery of the affair. Perhaps they were overly suspicious of their partners; perhaps they were overly insecure; perhaps they were generally distrusting of their partners. Whatever it is, even though they were not the ones who had the affair, their behaviour would have been difficult to tolerate for the transgressor too.

Also, it's conceivable that they may have played a role in generating toxicity in the pre-affair marriage, even though there may be a variety of explanations for why they did what they did. The bottom line is that in most marriages, both partners have done things that, in hindsight, they should never have; things they may even be ashamed of or embarrassed about. Now is probably a good time to start forgiving themselves for their behavioural imperfections that caused difficulties not only for themselves, but for their partners as well.

Transgressors too need to forgive their aggrieved partners for the humiliation and hurt caused during the process of discovery as well as during the immediate aftermath of discovery. Most transgressors are able to recognise that their partners' behaviour during this period was largely on account of the trauma of discovery, but what they find hard to deal with is the emotional consequences of the escalation of the situation to others in the social network. The transgressor may feel humiliated because the aggrieved partner escalated the situation to the boss, parents, other family members or friends. Being at the receiving end of negative judgement from the social network is never easy, and many relationship dynamics undergo subtle, or often, dramatic shifts, when others come to know of one's shenanigans.

Be that as it may, even though the transgressor may understand the reason all this was done by the aggrieved partner, it's possible that the latter's anger was not merely at the affair, but also all the perceived 'injustices' that were endured through the marriage (when one's in the 'victim mode', one tends to remember only the negative events that transpired during the course of the marriage). As a result, the transgressor may have been tarred and feathered in everyone else's eyes and would have had to go through a lot to reclaim credibility.

For all of this, transgressors may blame their aggrieved spouses but may not really be in a position to express this, for since they are in the doghouse, they are expected to accept their 'punishment' without fuss. However, the resultant resentment may sometimes be substantial and play havoc with the marriage later. In order to prevent this, they too need to forgive the aggrieved spouse for the manner in which the discovery process and its aftermath were handled.

Why forgive, why not just forget?

This is a question I've often been asked by aggrieved partners. They usually tell me, 'Look. *In course of time, I will forget what happened, what my partner did to me. But why on earth should I waste precious energy in trying to forgive something I can never condone?*' The reason this question gets asked is on the assumption that forgiveness is very hard, and forgetting is easier.

But if you ask people who've survived affairs, they'll tell you that it takes really ages to forget, more so if you've not forgiven. It is, in fact, easier to forgive than to just try and delete it from your brain. For a while to come, both partners will, in response to cues in the course of their lives (such as bumping into the paramour somewhere, or seeing a movie where the story is too close to one's own), be reminded of the affair. And this can cause pain. Unless they've forgiven the partner and the self, in which case, even if the memory does come back, it's not likely to cause that much pain.

There's another very fundamental reason to forgive your partner. For as long as one remains unforgiving, one will continue to be in a state of victimhood. The victim state is never easy to stay in, for it constantly makes one feel vulnerable and unhappy. To make yourself less vulnerable and more happy, you need to forgive yourself and your partner for the affair and its aftermath. In other words, *you forgive, not because your partner has earned your forgiveness, but because it makes you feel better*. It helps you heal from your emotional pain and makes you feel less vulnerable to the vicissitudes of married life.

Of course, if your partner continues to be profligate or suspicious or controlling of you, it's hard to forgive, for you need a proper emotional ambience in which to do so. When you forgive your partner, the environment at home changes and the partner is also enabled to get onto the forgiveness platform.

Sometimes, partners recovering from infidelity remain locked in a war of attrition, to see who blinks first. This is unfortunately a war that nobody wins. Usually, couples in controlling marriages, where either or both spouses have been generally rigid and unyielding, do tend to get trapped in such a stalemate, and as a result, their recovery from the affair takes a fairly long and protracted course.

In my experience, when one partner forgives first, the other follows suit soon after.

When the transgressor is the one who initiates the forgiveness process, it creates a lighter atmosphere in the marriage, for the aggrieved partner realises that the former doesn't seem to react adversely to the monitoring and the mistrust and is generally comfortable maintaining openness and transparency. This, in turn, enables aggrieved partners to initiate their own process of forgiveness.

If the aggrieved partner forgives first, the transgressor too is more than ready to engage in the forgiveness process. The key element is that both partners should arrive at forgiveness only after accepting and understanding the infidelity and what it represented. Forgiving too early may not create comfort, and delayed forgiveness may be too little, too late.

How to forgive?

The short answer: just forgive yourself and your partner and get on with rebuilding your marriage and your life. But it's not that easy, is it? If you've read the section in Chapter 15 on the difference between rational and emotive judgement and have actually moved to judging the situation as well as your partner rationally rather than emotively, you would have already concluded that neither you, nor your partner, are really bad or sullied because of the infidelity.

We are all merely imperfect people, struggling to find a balance and anchor-points for ourselves in an imperfect world. While you will always feel that what your partner did was inappropriate and insensitive—and you should feel this way so that such an infraction doesn't take place again in your married life—you needn't do so with indignation or outrage. If you see survival from an affair as a learning process, even if a harsh one, that may actually end up benefitting both of you, you will find that you can refine your marriage and its boundaries for the future. When you realise that the affair has actually got both of you talking again about serious issues like fundamental values and the like, you'll feel that, even though this amount of pain was unnecessary, you can still get something out of it for the future.

In the final analysis, forgiveness comes from the understanding you obtain about the situation and your marriage, from the realisation that although your partner was the one who transgressed, it could well have been you doing the transgression had the situation been a little different, from the insight you obtain that forgiveness is done for your own sake and not for the partner or the marriage, and from the entry of rationality into the healing process. And when you find that after you've forgiven yourself and your partner, you feel so much better and are truly empowered to rebuild your marriage the way both of you want to, this will give you enough reason to stay in a state of forgiveness.

The inherent capacity to forgive

Some of us find it inherently easier to forgive than do others. And I'm not talking about those who do so in a careless or blasé manner. Some people can genuinely forgive infractions on the part of others because they realise that this helps them deal with their lives in a much better way. Such people, though they suffer as much as anyone else when being aggrieved by an affair, still heal faster and move on, for they are able to move from emotive to rational judgements much more quickly.

Transgressors with such spouses have truly 'lucked out', for they too are able to forgive and go through their own healing process more effectively. Although it must be said that some transgressors of such spouses also experience more guilt, for they realise that a person who forgives easily will usually have far less tolerance for further boundary violations. The underlying equation seems to be, '*Yes, you did a callous thing, but I'm not going to hold it against you, for I want both of us to be happy. But if this happens again, then consider the marriage over!'*

In other words, those who have a greater inherent capacity to forgive are not pushovers, as is mistakenly believed. Their capacity to forgive comes not from a desire to gloss over inappropriate behaviour or negative life events, but from an understanding that they have choices in their lives and they know how and when to exercise these. They are generally people who have a stronger sense of self-belief, and extend their forgiveness from a position of strength and not one of vulnerability. In fact, it is this very capacity to forgive that reduces their feeling of vulnerability and renders them stronger and more balanced when it comes to dealing with life's crises.

There are also some of us who, perhaps by virtue of a series of unresolved negative experiences, find it harder to forgive many things, for we feel that we have been, for no fault of ours, compelled to carry more than our fair share of crosses throughout our lives. As a result, we may, despite having an understanding of the affair, find it hard to move from emotive judgement to rational judgement. Not because we don't want to, but because we think we don't know how to.

Actually, we do know how to forgive. If we look at our lives dispassionately, we will realise that we have forgiven a lot of people for a lot of infractions without even being conscious of doing so. It's just that we're afraid to forgive, for we may fear that if we do, worse things may happen.

But if we work on strengthening our self-belief and understand that we always did, always do, and always will have choices that are available to us, in the unlikely event of such a thing ever happening again, we know precisely what we will do. If you don't already know, this is a good time to think about it and devise a strategy. And in the meantime, you can concentrate on making it feasible to expand your choices. This you can do by working towards having a more interdependent relationship with your partner; one where you find that neither is over-dependent on the other economically or emotionally.

Dependence is an important part of any good marriage, but being over-dependent on your partner can be depleting for both partners. So, working on your own self belief and working towards interdependence, rather than staying in a state of helpless dependence, actually makes your marriage stronger and both of you less vulnerable. To get to this state, you first need to forgive, and then to trust.

Trusting the partner

Most people do lie to their spouses sometime or the other during the course of their marriage. Small lies, big lies, white lies. And although, when the spouse finds about these lies, there's usually some hell that needs to be paid, the spouse generally forgives and both partners move on. Rarely is trust lost under these circumstances. Trust becomes an issue only in two situations: when one partner lies repeatedly and unabashedly to the other, or when infidelity takes place.

Where has the trust gone?

Infidelity, represents the violation of an extremely fundamental marital boundary. A lie here or there may be tolerated. Maybe even some financial profligacy. But, not infidelity. Inevitably, the aggrieved partner feels betrayed by the transgressor and trust immediately goes out the window.

Or does it?

When one looks closely at what happens during the aftermath of discovery of infidelity, even though suspicion levels are high, if the aggrieved partner has remained in the marriage to fight for it, trust has never completely disappeared. If it did, then the partners wouldn't be able to spend any time together. For when trust goes, there's only indifference to the partner. In other words, you can't love somebody and not trust them at the same time, even though you can trust someone and not love them.

When you invest your emotions in someone, the first thing you invest is trust, for this forms the basis of the bond between people. Everything else follows from this. By the same token, when you disinvest your emotions from someone, the last thing to be disinvested is trust. For as long as two partners are attempting to engage with each other, this means that trust, even if has been shaken on account of the transgression, is still present in the relationship. The thing to do is to get back in touch with it and enhance it.

If this is indeed the case, why the suspicion? Actually, suspicion enters the equation on account of the fear of repetition of the transgression. And at times, it's not merely the aggrieved person who's suspicious, some transgressors also become suspicious. This happens on account of the fear experienced by transgressors that since a door to infidelity has been opened in the marriage, even though they were the ones that opened the door, aggrieved partners may one day be tempted to find and open this door, and become transgressors in their own right. So, both partners feel a sense of fear and this is manifested in some suspicious and monitoring behaviour.

But this fear shouldn't be confused with lack of trust. As long as both of you are together, and can even tolerate each other's presence occasionally, then there is basic trust and basic comfort. But this trust is covered by layers of hurt, pain, anger and fear. It needs to be rescued and rehabilitated so that the marriage can get back to a mutually comfortable platform again.

The inherent capacity to trust

As in the case of forgiveness, some of us find it easier to trust than others. As a rule of thumb, those of us who've had fewer negative experiences in our relationships from childhood onwards are generally able to build more trusting relationships. All of us may not have been quite so lucky, though, and, on account of childhood or adolescent trauma, may have made some inappropriate choices during adulthood and burnt our fingers in relationships, thereby making us less prone to trust. Such of us are bound to deal with infidelity with greater difficulty.

If some amount of trust had been built into the marriage before the affair happened, it becomes slightly easier, for having learned the technology of trusting, we at least know that we are capable of relearning it.

But if the affair happened in the early stages of the marriage, the recovery is bound to be slower. It's a bit like Snakes and Ladders actually. One finds a tall ladder and builds trust, only to land on a snake and go down again. You may recall though, when you played Snakes and Ladders as a child, for every snake in the vicinity, there was a ladder somewhere within reach, and eventually everyone made it to the top.

It also needs to be remembered that even those with an inherently strong capacity to trust aren't going to do so forever, unless some amount of reciprocity is experienced in the marriage. So, if a transgressor, on the basis that the aggrieved partner is a trusting person, is tempted to repeat the indiscretion, please be warned, you do so at your own peril. For when a trusting person is pushed too much, there is a total and often irrecoverable, breakdown in trust. Unlike people who've been at the receiving end of several negative relationship experiences, the trusting individual has not, and has therefore not learned how to deal with serial deception or multiple negative experiences, and is therefore more likely to give the marriage the boot.

The basis for recovering trust

On what basis is the aggrieved partner expected to trust again? The fact that the transgressor is remorseful for having caused pain all around, will certainly help, but cannot in itself be the basis for recovering trust. The fact is, a boundary was violated and so how can the transgressor guarantee the aggrieved partner that it will never happen again?

Many aggrieved partners are looking for this guarantee. Of course, transgressors' words and assurances have little credibility, and their post-discovery behaviour comes under such close scrutiny that everything they say or do could end up appearing contrived and unnatural. But still, the aggrieved spouse looks to the transgressor for some basis on which trust can be restored in the marriage. What many people seek is *trustworthiness*. The questions in the aggrieved spouse's mind are, *Has my spouse earned my trust? Is my partner trustworthy enough?*

The way I see it, the easiest thing in the world to do is to trust a trustworthy person. Anyone can do it. There's little or no effort involved in this. The more challenging thing to do is to trust someone whose trustworthiness you're not completely sure of.

But is there really anyone in the world who's completely trustworthy? If you really look around, you'll see that nobody really can be, for everyone screws up in some form or other, especially in the area of human relationships. So, if you expect your partner to become completely trustworthy, that too after committing a boundary transgression, I'm afraid you're asking for the impossible. The question you'd be better off asking yourself is, *Can I trust my partner not to have another affair?* This is the question that you really need an answer to.

Where will your answer come from? The degree of remorse experienced by the transgressor? Yes, to some extent. The understanding and insights that both of you have obtained through the process? Yes, those will help. The support from family and friends that both of you have access to? Yes, a little. The fact that both of you were reasonably close in the earlier stages of the marriage? Yes, definitely. That both of you are committed to working on the marriage and restoring trust? Most certainly. This, if you ask me, is one of the most important elements of trust restoration.

But there is still one element that is even more important than this.

Trust in your partner gets restored only when you reach the point where you *trust yourself* enough and understand that trust comes from within you and is not based on your partner's behaviour. You trust your partner because you believe that you have it in you to trust another human being. Because you are capable of making the right choices for yourself. Because you know that if the trust that you have reposed in your partner is violated ever again, you will know exactly what to do. Also, because you realise that to live a life of suspicion is inordinately painful and unsustainable. And that trusting is actually easier than distrusting, and gives you a better sense of equanimity.

When you tell yourself that trusting is something you do because it makes you feel better, you'll find that your partner's post-discovery behaviour is actually not all that bad and the things that made you suspicious don't seem to produce the same response in you anymore. In the final analysis, trusting your partner is a leap of faith. But faith in yourself, not in your partner. Now, you're back in the driver's seat.

17

Rebuilding Your Marriage

*T*o survive an affair, a marriage needs to be rebuilt. Not because the affair has brought the marriage crashing down, but because a few chinks were present in the marriage before the affair and these created the basic fault line which permitted an affair to happen.

And believe me, the best of marriages have a few chinks in them. Please don't think your marriage was a terminal case merely because an affair happened. Also, at this stage, you need to make a distinction between the issues relating to the affair and those pertaining to the marriage. The affair happened and created grief that had to be dealt with, but it also threw some light on the issues in the marriage.

This doesn't mean that the affair has been justified on account of marital issues. It has not, for marital issues can be dealt with in many different ways, and having an affair is not one of them. However, now that you've dealt with the initial aftermath of the affair, this would be a good time to deal with the chinks in your marriage that predated the affair, but were never really paid much attention to.

And if we do this in a blame-free emotional environment, we can ensure that the marriage gets strengthened and reconfigured to deal with whatever issues come your way. This can be done by making yours a Fifty-50 Marriage.

Make yours a fifty-50 marriage

In the *Fifty-50 Marriage: A Return to Intimacy,* the second book of the 'New Indian Marriage' series, I had described in great detail how a marriage could be enhanced by reclaiming it and making it a more intimate one.

It's become increasingly clear that probably the best solution to marital issues lies in enhancing marital intimacy and connectedness, for it is these attributes more than anything else that pave the way for couples to find meanings in their marriages.

Solutions to issues are not really hard to find. It is the *will* to seek solutions that determines whether conflicts are resolved or not. Often, when two people are emotionally well connected to each other, they find their answers soon enough. The essence of the Fifty-50 marriage is that, regardless of who or what the sources of the problems in the marriage are, both partners have to take equal responsibility and ownership over the resolution of their issues. In other words, Seventy-30 or Sixty-40 don't work. It has to be an equal and reciprocal Fifty-50 responsibility.

This necessarily means that partners stop blaming each other for their woes and forge an alliance that seeks mutually beneficially solutions. The best way to do this is by being accepting of each other and not passing judgement on each other.

Dropping the blame game and being mutually non-judgemental of each other requires a certain ambience in the marriage. To get there, the couple needs to get six things right:

1. Make a second commitment (or re-commitment)
2. Debug the marriage
3. Balance your life-space investments
4. Redefine your 'We' and 'I' spaces
5. Enhance intimacy
6. Change the way you fight

All of these are described in detail in *The Fifty-50 Marriage: A Return to Intimacy*, and you might want to get hold of a copy of that book to help you understand the nuances of the process. For the moment, I will just provide brief overviews of what each of these stages involves, for it's quite conceivable that, during the process of surviving the affair, some of you may have already done some of the things described.

The second commitment

It is usually desirable for all married couples to make a second commitment sometime during the course of the marriage, particularly when they have drifted away from each other. But, when surviving an affair, a second commitment is not merely desirable, it's quite necessary.

Look at it this way. When you both got married, you made a commitment to each other to love, trust and respect each other in the process of building an intimate, connected relationship. Then, among other things, the affair happened, and the commitment flew out of the window. Now, having decided to work through your issues and stay on in the marriage, there is a definite requirement that both partners renew their commitment.

Let's try and understand this business of commitment. It's a term that tends to spook many people, for they find it hard to make a commitment to someone who has disturbed their sense of fair play. Sometimes, even when some form of forgiveness has happened, there is still a reluctance to make a re-commitment. The underlying question seems to be '*What if I make a commitment and find that things don't work out? How can I make a commitment to someone who's already let me down once?*

Here's the thing: When you make a commitment, you make it not to your partner or your marriage, but to *yourself*. You commit yourself to make as much of an effort as you are capable of to make the marriage work. You're not selling your soul to your partner!

If your partner does not make an equal and matching commitment, obviously the marriage is not going to work. So, both spouses have to make their respective commitments together and clearly articulate to each other what precisely they are committing themselves to.

Do remember that you cannot coerce your partner into making a commitment. You can only make your own commitment, and if you find that your partner's commitment is not going deep or far enough, you're at perfect liberty to reject it.

From my experience I'd say that couples who have got to this stage of surviving an affair generally do not either fear or negotiate the commitment they respectively make.

Debugging the marriage

This is slightly harder to do than making a re-commitment. Since both of you have been talking about the affair and what it meant to the marriage, you would probably have touched on some of the other chinks in the marriage that both of you were perhaps aware of, but had not really addressed in the past. Now is the time to take a more serious look at the marriage, again in a blame-free environment, and evaluate what needs to be done to re-invent the marriage.

Sometimes, couples get a bit stuck at this stage. The aggrieved partner may tend to feel that by shifting the focus to the marriage, the transgressor may feel let off the hook and shift the blame for the affair on the chinks in the marriage. Also, the latter, who has been in the doghouse these last few weeks (or months) and has been staying in a one-down position during this period may, now that the opportunity has been created, end up overplaying the aggrieved partner's flaws, just a bit.

Let's be clear about one thing. The chinks in the marriage did not cause the affair. It was the transgressor who chose to have the affair. But you can't get away from the fact that the unresolved chinks in the marriage did provide some footholds for the affair to have happened. And these need to be plugged, not just to prevent another affair, but also to enhance the quality of married life.

The best way to approach debugging the marriage is not to examine who was responsible for the bugs, but to arrive at a mutual understanding of what was missing in the marriage. Instead of dredging up past issues and debating them, you would probably be best advised to focus on what each partner wants the future marriage to look like. This can be done by looking at the needs that each partner has of the marriage and of each other—how each would like to be treated by the partner.

You might consider taking a relook at the three lists you'd made (described in Chapter 14)—the *non-negotiable list, the necessary list and the desirable list* and tweaking them a bit, if required. At the end of this process, you'd probably be clear what each expects of the other, as well as to what extent each will be in a position to meet the expectations of the partner.

Balancing your life space investments

All of us function in a variety of social domains or 'life spaces' in which we engage in relationships of varying degrees of intensity depending on the demands of the space. At the core is our personal space or 'I' space. This space relates with the marriage space, the primary family space (which includes those members of your family you live with or are very close to and engage with on a regular basis), the secondary family space (other members of your family), the friends space, the work space and the community space. The manner in which you make your investments in each of these spaces will determine how strong your marriage is and how connected you and your partner are to each other.

By 'investment', I refer to emotions as well as time. If you over-invest in your work space or, for that matter, in any of your other life spaces, obviously your marriage is going to have a hard time. So at the time you are rebuilding your marriage, prioritising this space may be a good thing to do. Perhaps, when both of you feel that the marriage space has become secured, you can slowly then increase your investments in your other spaces, but only by mutual consent. But as a rule of thumb, I'd recommend that the investment in your marriage space never be less than 30 per cent of the investment in all your life spaces put together.

Redefining 'I' and 'We' spaces

To facilitate the process of balancing your life space investments, the best place to begin would be with your respective personal spaces and the marriage space. Not so much in terms of only the time and energy commitment in these spaces, but also the content or the activities that both of you will undertake in these spaces. After the affair, the aggrieved partner will be wary of the transgressor's 'I' space, particularly if the latter is made inaccessible. Once the immediate aftermath of the affair has been dealt with, forgiveness has started on its course, and some modicum of trust has re-entered the marriage, the transgressor's 'I' space is usually not a source of major stress.

It is important to remember that every marriage should have two distinct 'I' spaces, otherwise individual identities are hard to preserve. Typically, what happens in your personal space is your business, but if your marriage is a comfortable one, you will probably not mind your partner stepping into it every now and again, although never unbidden. As much as you expect your partner to respect your personal space, you do need to reciprocate this expectation even if your partner is the transgressor.

Try not to make your spaces too large or too inaccessible, for then both of you will end up becoming like islands in the stream of your marriage, in touch with each other only during high tide. An 'I' space is meant to provide you some time and space to unwind, relax and do your own thing without being conscious of your partner's needs or expectations. Your personal stuff should be treated by your partner as inviolable and vice versa. Remember, though, that readiness to share your personal space during some phases in your married life does not mean that you're giving it up entirely. In fact, it will add to the closeness you feel as a couple, but only when both of you do this willingly and comfortably. If every time you want some personal space, your partner follows you in, then you've got to assert your boundaries a little more strongly.

As important your personal space is, so too is your marriage space or the 'We' space. During recovery from an affair, I would recommend paying a little more attention to the marriage space than your respective personal spaces which can be negotiated at a slightly later date. Aggrieved partners typically feel insecure and vulnerable at this time and if the transgressor is overly preoccupied with personal space activities, obviously, the process of re-bonding is going to be affected. So, try and do things together that you used to derive joy from before the affair. For those couples who didn't have a well-enough defined marriage space before the affair, perhaps owing to interference from the other social domains earlier, this is a good time to carve out a marriage space and populate it with 'togetherness activities' that will increase the bond. And please do remember, when I say 'marriage space activities', children and parents aren't included. It's just the two of you. Whether you go away for a weekend together every couple of months, or learn how to dance the salsa, or join a spiritual forum or a book club, just make sure you do things together that both of you can enjoy and benefit from. Also, make time to spend quiet time with each other every day, downloading each other's day's events, or even sitting together in companionable silence.

Enhancing intimacy

When you look back at your marriage, you might realise that one of the problems you had was expressing intimacy appropriately. Not that you didn't love each other. It's just that you stopped showing each other that you did. Even in arranged marriages, a lot of love does exist (which is why I hate using the term 'love marriage' since it seems to imply that this is the only form of mate selection that results in love), but since many people who choose to engage in an arranged marriage are a bit traditional at heart, the manner in which they express intimacy is also quite traditional.

In our country, non-sexual physical displays of affection between adult men and women, even in private, are frowned upon and when they happen in public (which they do largely because there're too many people at home), the cops get after you. We generally feel that physical displays of intimacy happen only in the movies or as part of foreplay. This is most unfortunate, for when we feel this way, we are shutting out the best form of closeness known to humankind—tactile communication. The sense of touch should not be reserved only for sexual communication. Have you noticed how much we touch and hug our children? Fortunately, urban Indians are getting better at expressing emotional intimacy to each other. And this augurs well, not just for recovery from affairs, but for marriages in general.

Couples who are emotionally well connected to each other generally experience high levels of intimacy in their marriage. Keeping in touch with each other through the day helps, since it establishes a basal degree of connectedness, as a result of which, when you meet each other at the end of the day, you don't have to start connecting with each other from scratch. (It's a bit like keeping your modem-router on throughout the day, so your computer or other device automatically connects to it when switched on.)

But more important than just staying connected is programming yourself to *signal* your needs effectively, as well as to *tune into* your partner's signals, something that even modem routers get right every time, once they are adequately programmed. There is no such thing as a one-size-fits-all algorithm to signal and tune in. Each couple needs to develop their personal algorithms for this, and in my experience, most couples, once they start the process, are generally very inventive and do very well. Otherwise, if we use our factory-set defaults to show our love, wives have to show love by cooking their husbands' favourite foods, and husbands will have to eat a lot of their wives' cooking to show they love each other. Which probably explains why urban India is slowly set to become the obesity capital of the world. Obviously, we are a very loving nation.

Changing the way you fight

Fights, as I've said before ad nauseam, and will continue to say again ad nauseam, are normal in all healthy relationships and are a sign that both partners are attempting to get closer to each other. Partners who are indifferent to each other rarely fight for they've pretty much given up on the hope of their spouses fulfilling their expectations. But fights can get repetitive and we tend to fight the same fights over and over again without understanding what they mean.

A fight in a marriage is like pain in any part of the body. It signals that something is wrong inside and unless we take adequate measures to address the cause of the pain, it's going to keep recurring. So paying attention to *why* we fight as well as the *way* we do it is not a bad idea. Otherwise, we'll find that we are communicating our needs to each other only when we fight. When we do this, obviously the partner is not going to recognise it as a legitimate need, since we present the need as an accusation to the partner or as a demand, rarely as a genuine need. We can do better than this.

If we learn to devise strategies by which we can reduce the intensity of our fights, try and understand their meaning, and learn to express our needs of each other proactively, rather than by suddenly springing it on the partner in the middle of a massive exchange of hostilities, we'll be able to stay connected without too much difficulty. Fights do represent temporary breakdowns in connectivity and communication. Also, as many fighting couples have realised, make-up sex is much better when you're younger, but not worth the effort of fighting as your marriage matures.

I have provided, in the foregoing passages, only a capsule of the process involved in rebuilding your marriage, to give you an idea of what areas you might have to address to completely move beyond the affair. More information on the finer points involved are available in my previous book, *The Fifty-50 Marriage: A Return to Intimacy*, and I would refer the interested reader to this.

Affair-proofing the marriage

For somebody who's never had an affair, like many aggrieved partners who are reading this book, this section may seem superfluous, for they might believe that the only way to affair-proof a marriage is to not have an affair. However, if we just assume that it's all about will power and morality, we run the risk of becoming sanctimonious about affairs, thereby making ourselves and our marriages more vulnerable to transgressions.

Accepting vulnerability

Many people I know are smug in the belief that they will never have an affair, because they are sure that they have the discipline to hold back and because they have a certain—there's no better word to describe it—contempt for those who actually 'stoop that low'. This attitude, believe me, is a most unfortunate one to have, if you want to affair-proof your marriage, for more often than not, it's the sanctimonious ones who are much more vulnerable to boundary transgressions. In truth, all marriages are vulnerable to affairs. The best of us can end up having an affair. In fact, it is very rare for a person to actually set out to have an affair, except in the case of revenge affairs or peer-pressure affairs. Most affairs happen unexpectedly and catch us off-guard when we are most vulnerable, when the marital attachment is at its weakest.

It is, therefore, of critical importance that we accept our vulnerability, and accept the reality that we are going to, at some point or other in our lives, find somebody, other than our spouse, very attractive. How we deal with this attraction will determine whether or not we have an affair. The more we fight the feeling of being attracted, the more vulnerable we become. But if we accept the attraction, we are better placed to institute strategies that will distract us from a potential paramour.

If we realise that a strong attraction to someone else—and I'm referring to an emotional pull, not the hormone-driven physical attraction—is an indicator that something's missing from our marriage, we might be able to turn our attention to whatever lacunae exist in the marriage, and try and find fixes for them.

Whether you discuss your attraction to someone else with your spouse depends on the kind of marriage you have, but unless you're very sure that your spouse's reaction to such a discussion will not be catastrophic, I would advise you to keep it to yourself, deal with it and spend as little time with the object of your attraction as possible. Sometimes, this may be difficult, for you may be attracted to a co-worker, a friend who's part of your social circle and whom you meet on a regular basis, or even a member of your or your spouse's family. Even so, it's imperative that you practise some avoidance of the person or, at least, minimise your exposure, in order that you don't find yourselves alone with each other some enchanted evening.

On other occasions, even if you're not the one primarily attracted, you may be flattered by the blatant signals an attractive person of the opposite gender is sending your way, and might get drawn into an affair. This, too, is something you should guard against, if you want to keep your head above water. If you're approaching middle age, you're more vulnerable to such flattery. If you can spend just a few minutes projecting into the future, and understand where this could take you, you'd probably know how fast you should run.

It's not unusual to fantasise about having an affair with the person whom you're attracted to or who's attracted to you. But many people tell me that often, the fantasy includes discovery by the spouse. While occasional fantasy is usually harmless, repetitive fantasy is the first red flag that your mind is raising. The more you allow yourself to fantasise or ruminate about the person, the more vulnerable you become. The minute you find yourself rationalising the possibility of having an affair with the object of your attraction, think of this as the last and biggest red flag your mind will send you. This is the pre-affair stage, where people feel they can pull off an affair without being discovered and if the spouse doesn't find out, it cannot be considered an affair. Please do remember that more than 90 per cent of affairs do end up in discovery at some time or the other. Even if you think you've covered all your tracks, your spouse will, more likely than not, find out what you were up to from completely unexpected sources, in completely unanticipated ways. In fact, it's very likely that pretty much everyone else at a party knows exactly who's having an affair with whom, without a single word being said. Such is the power of intuition and body language.

However, if both of you accept your vulnerability to an affair, then it's possible to develop strategies to guard against one. It's pretty much like buying life insurance. You buy it even if you have no intention of dying in the foreseeable future, because you realise that the unexpected can always happen. Likewise, prepare for the unexpected affair, by being aware that it could happen, by understanding how to recognise the early signs, and by having well-thought-through avoidance strategies.

Flirtation

It's only over the last couple of decades or so that our country is showing signs of liberating itself from its hitherto repressed sexuality. Men and women now have more opportunities to engage with each other socially and professionally. So new communication strategies are being learned, more equations are being forged, more boundaries are being blurred and more hormones are in circulation. Flirtatious behaviour too has become more common, both at work and at play. At work, of course, there's always the fear of sexual harassment that keeps overly flirtatious behaviour at bay, though not always. But at play, there are no real checks and balances. Which is why more people flirt with each other than before, and when alcohol's thrown liberally in, the situation becomes fraught with possibilities.

By and large, flirting is a relatively harmless activity, provided it's done openly and causes no discomfiture to the spouse. If your partner's uncomfortable with it, it's perhaps wiser to step back a bit, for your partner's intuition is probably the best index of where the boundary should be defined.

It's quite conceivable that your partner may disapprove of even the mildest flirtation. If such is the case, and you find you flirt only when your partner's not around, you increase your vulnerability to transgressing a boundary. Lack of transparency and comfort between partners can only mean a chink-in-progress.

If you're unable to convince your partner on the subject of flirtation, and you feel that in most other ways there are no major outstanding issues between the two of you, you're probably better off not flirting. Honestly, you can live with this. And it's simply not worth the effort to fight for the right to flirt.

It's of course a different matter if your partner is suspicious of every person of the opposite gender you have even non-flirtatious conversations with. Then an Othello situation could be incipient, and you might want to take some help in resolving it.

Platonic relationships

Another aspect of the liberalisation of relationships in recent times is the increased incidence of platonic relationships. Although this term rolls off many tongues very easily, I often suspect that participants in such relationships often have little clue as to who Plato was, except that he was not Indian and allegedly had several platonic relationships with women in his time.

A platonic relationship refers to any equation between people of opposite genders that does not include a sexual component, but does include a good degree of emotional investment. In other words, when a man says a woman is his platonic friend, what he's saying is that he cares for her, enjoys her company, is dependent on her for some things in his life and misses her when she is not around, but he cannot think of her as *the* woman in his life for she does not sweep him away, nor is there any sexual tension between them.

It's important to remember that the friendship a person has with someone of the opposite gender is qualitatively different from one with somebody of the same gender. In the latter, there is no underlying sexual tension between the two even when the most intimate of secrets are being shared. But, when a woman and a man engage in an intimate conversation, an underlying sexual tension is known to have made its unsolicited appearance. That neither may choose to act on this is what keeps the relationship 'platonic' or at least 'quasi-platonic'.

However, platonic friendships are not just about the absence of sexual chemistry. They are basically relationships that involve an emotional investment. Friends invest feelings in each other, help and support each other, spend time with each other and make a commitment to each other. In the absence of these, a 'friendship' or whatever else you choose to call it, remains a fair-weather equation. Like all other relationships, a friendship also grows and requires periodic emotional investment to grow. It is this emotional investment that platonic friends need to be cautious about. For, if it comes at the expense of the marriage, the fine balance in one's emotional life suddenly goes out of kilter. You might find that your spouse is not so understanding when it comes to your supporting your platonic friend through some life stress, when legitimate spousal needs are being compromised.

The upshot of what I am saying is this: We have to work as hard at our platonic relationships to keep them platonic as we do at our marriage and other relationships. If you find that you're unfavourably comparing your spouse's quirks with your platonic friend's calm, or every time you have a work-related problem you run to your platonic friend and 'forget' to share it with your partner, a crisis is simply waiting to happen.

On the other hand, if you do define your boundaries with your platonic friend and are able to keep the relationship within these, if you keep the intensity down to manageable proportions and do not have irrational expectations of each other, you could well have a long, productive and meaningful friendship that does not take away from your other relationships, and might well end up enriching you and the marriage as well. Also, if you keep your spouse in the loop of your platonic relationship, you will end up reducing your vulnerability to having an affair with your platonic friend.

I'm not suggesting that you share everything you and your friend discuss or do together with your spouse, but if your spouse is generally in the know, it increases the connectedness between you and your spouse, thereby making for a more easy-going friendship as well. And who knows, you may even end up with a blessing from the oft-quoted Plato himself, even if you neither know nor care who he was or what he did.

18

Just One Last Thing . . .

Now that you've come to the end of this book, you may have noticed that I haven't offered any prescription or formula to survive affairs. This is because there aren't any. I have only attempted to give you an understanding of affairs and the steps that many couples have taken to survive them. Hopefully you will learn from their experience and apply your new understanding to enhance the quality of your marriage and your life.

If you read this book because either you or your partner have had an affair, I am hoping both of you have reached a place where you feel you've understood infidelity and have survived the affair. Both of you, more than anyone else, know how hard it was to deal with the affair, which in itself, I expect, will ensure that there are no encores.

I hope you've been able to find it in yourselves to make a second commitment to each other and make yours a Fifty-50 Marriage. If, for whatever reasons (and I'm sure they must be good ones), you've decided to go your separate ways, I hope all the pain you've gone through and the understanding of infidelity that I have tried to provide you, have made you a more empowered person, not an embittered one.

If, on the other hand, you picked up this book, because you didn't find anything else to read and have actually managed to finish it because your flight's been interminably delayed, or it's been raining continuously outside, you've hopefully understood that having an affair is not worth the emotional devastation that thousands of others before you have endured, and also that, however much the pain they leave in their wake, affairs can be survived.

If you picked up this book with the expectation that you might find a few tips based on how other people have had affairs, I hope, even if you've not been quite cured of the intention of having an affair of your own, that you have read enough to realise that the majority of affairs, of whatever denomination, do get discovered, regardless of how well the protagonists think they've got things covered.

Marriage is an institution you may or may not subscribe to, and that's certainly your prerogative. But if you are married, it might be more sensible to try and get it right, keeping in mind that when it comes to marriage, three is always a crowd.

Recommended Reading

The following well-written books may be of interest

Not 'Just Friends': Rebuilding Trust and Recovering Your Sanity After Infidelity by Shirley P. Glass & Jean Coppock Staeheli. Free Press. ISBN: 9780743225502

After the Affair: Healing the pain and Rebuilding Trust When a Partner Has Been Unfaithful by Janis Abrahms Spring with Michael Spring. Harper Perrenial. ISBN: 9780060928179

How Can I Forgive You?: The Courage to Forgive, the Freedom Not To by Janis Abrahms Spring with Michael Spring. Harper Perennial. ISBN: 9780060009311

For Better: The Science of a Good Marriage by Tara Parker-Pope. Dutton Books. ISBN: 9780525951384 (*although this book is not just about infidelity, it does describe some research studies on infidelity and also provides an excellent bibliography*)